THY WILL BE DONE

Strategic Leadership, Planning, and Management for Christians

Thy Will Be Done

Strategic Leadership, Planning, and Management for Christians

PETER M. DANILCHICK

ST VLADIMIR'S SEMINARY PRESS
YONKERS, NEW YORK
2016

Library of Congress Cataloging-in-Publication Data

Names: Danilchick, Peter M., author.
Title: Thy will be done : strategic leadership, planning, and management for
    Christians / Peter M. Danilchick.
Description: Yonkers, New York : St Vladimir's Seminary Press, 2016. | Includes
    bibliographical references and index.
Identifiers: LCCN 2016046606 (print) | LCCN 2016047861 (ebook) | ISBN
    9780881415483 | ISBN 9780881415490
Subjects: LCSH: Christian leadership—Orthodox Eastern Church | Church
    management.
Classification: LCC BX340 .D365 2016 (print) | LCC BX340 (ebook) | DDC
    253/.319—ds23
LC record available at https://lccn.loc.gov/2016046606

COPYRIGHT © 2016

ST VLADIMIR'S SEMINARY PRESS
575 Scarsdale Road, Yonkers, NY 10707
1-800-204-2665
www.svspress.com

Biblical quotations are from the Revised Standard Version of the Bible,
copyright 1952 [2nd edition, 1971] by the Division of Christian Education of the
National Council of the Churches of Christ in the United States of America.
Used by permission. All rights reserved.

ISBN 978−088141−548−3 (paper)
ISBN 978−088141−549−0 (electronic)

PRINTED IN THE UNITED STATES OF AMERICA

This book is dedicated to my grandchildren,
Zoë, Alexandra, Oliver, Nicholas, Hanna, Henry, Beatrix,
and Jasper. May they become future leaders in their own ways,
so needed by the world and the Church!

The interactions I had over the years with many mentors in
the academic, corporate, and church worlds influenced and
inspired me. I would like to acknowledge four of these individuals
as examples of outstanding leadership. In the Church, Fathers
Alexander Warnecke and Alexander Schmemann were living
icons of action, outreach, and mission, encouraging me at a young
age to serve God and his people. In the corporate world, Dr Horst
Assmann and Mr David Kingston never failed to inspire me with
their energy, enthusiasm and courage.

I owe a significant debt to all those involved with St Vladimir's
Seminary Press, who took the gamble of publishing this book.
I would especially like to thank Juliana Allen, who edited the
early draft of the manuscript, and Victoria Sherry, who edited the
final copy. Their gift with words and thoughts was indispensable
in clarifying concepts and avoiding confusion.

I hope that the readers of this book find it helpful
in their formation. I ask for their good will,
patience, forbearance, and prayers.

Table of Contents

Preface

I began writing this book in order to talk about strategic planning and management from a Christian viewpoint. Now retired, I worked thirty-three years as an executive in one of the world's largest corporations and also served as a deacon in the Orthodox Church for most of that time. More recently, I became convinced that planning and management principles, however valuable in themselves, are not fully effective unless the basic and critical aspects of leadership, especially Christian leadership, which underpin those principles, are grasped, understood, and practiced.

In the Church, newly ordained clergy, including bishops, are often thrust into the job with little practical experience in dealing with others in a managerial or leadership sense, let alone in assuming responsibility for their spiritual development and care. Lay members of a parish council or another ministry group may have difficulty relating with one another, seeing new ways of performing their responsibilities, or working with others in determining and implementing desired change. In the wider Church, i.e., "the world," similar difficulties may arise when it comes time for one to undertake a leadership role at the office, factory, or home. And when one is a Christian, there can be confusion as to how to fulfill these leadership responsibilities *as* a Christian.

My hope is that this book will help leaders of churches and other organizations to address leadership issues appropriately in an effective, harmonious, and ultimately Christian way. It will also help individuals working outside the Church in secular occupations to exercise Christian leadership in what may be an agnostic or even anti-Christian environment. As in all spheres of human activity, any welcome change or positive development begins and ends with individual persons. Ultimately, Christian personhood and community is what this book is about.

There are scores of volumes on "leadership" that present varied and sometimes contradictory approaches for how to acquire and exercise leadership skills. Christians may wonder if there is any real Christian leadership model, or whether we just need to be content with secular offerings. This book presents such a Christian leadership model. It declares that the fundamental goal of Christian leadership is the simple statement in the Lord's Prayer: "Thy will be done." The questions that Christians need to ask are: What is the Lord's will for me, our family, our parish, and our organization, here and now? How do we discover and agree upon the Lord's will? In implementing his will, how should we best interact with each other as fellow leaders and parishioners, neighbors, and colleagues? Are we united in one purpose and, if not, how can we be? To answer these questions is the task of Christian leadership.

We might ask if such a Christian leadership model can be used in a secular setting, such as an office or factory floor. My answer to that is the same as the warning of our Lord: "No one can serve two masters; for either he will hate the one or love the other."[1] We do not have to invoke our Lord's name externally to others, but surely we should behave and act externally as though he is directing us inwardly, wherever we may be.

THIS BOOK

The title of this book refers not only to leadership, but also to *strategic* leadership, planning, and management. Why the emphasis on "strategic"? And why include "planning and management"?

The word strategic comes from the Greek *stratēgia*, which means "leading an army; the office of a general." It implies taking the resources that one has, improving them, and employing them to achieve a set objective. Strategic leadership means always taking into account the people with whom one works and the goal they wish to achieve together. It does not look at the leader alone, nor focus just on the leader's desired characteristics, but goes beyond that to the way the leader relates to others in order to attain the goal.

[1] Mt 6.24.

Often, the concepts of leadership, planning, and management are opposed to one another. For example, it is frequently assumed that leaders are the initiators, planners are the thinkers, and managers are the doers. In fact, however, effective leaders are required to be both good planners and good managers if they want to ensure that their ideas are properly thought through and can be implemented as planned. Planners need to ensure that plans are grounded in a broad leadership vision, yet specific enough to avoid stumbling blocks when put into action. Managers must be involved in both vision and planning, and can effectively lead the individuals whom they are managing. All these functions need to be integrated strategically to ensure that appropriate goals are set, resources are properly marshaled, and the goals are achieved.

This book intends to enable the reader to:

- Understand the fundamental goal of Christian strategic leadership as consciously doing the will of God, not only personally but also in community, rather than fulfilling one's own desires for influence and power.

- Obtain Christian insight into what a leader is and how leadership is exercised in specific Church ministries, as well as worldly responsibilities. The text provides specific Christian leadership guidance and principles synthesized from Scripture, the writings of the Church fathers, and Church tradition, as well as practical experience gained by the author over more than four decades.

- Learn and be ready to apply practical principles of strategic planning and management to properly carry out the responsibilities of Christian leadership. The book outlines a specific process for strategic planning that can be used in personal, Church, community, and corporate situations. It provides focused recommendations to address issues with working with other people and to effectively carry out management responsibilities. It draws heavily upon the author's personal experience in Church and corporate life.

Part One discusses the essential foundation for everything that follows: seeking the will of God and doing his will in practice. Part Two discusses the foundations and goals of Christian leadership, drawing heavily on the Scriptures and the writings of Church fathers. Part Three delves into the particular aspects of ministerial leadership, adding to the above sources the baptism and ordination services of the Church. Part Four outlines the basics of strategic planning, giving enough detail and guideposts to enable a Church organization or nonprofit to conduct strategic planning. Part Five discusses selected management topics of interest to both Church and general organizations.

ABOUT THE AUTHOR

I have been a deacon in the Orthodox Church for forty years, serving in six countries, several different Church jurisdictions, and across varied cultures. I have organized new missions and worked with established parishes. I have served on various governing boards and councils of parishes, dioceses, metropolitanates, and other church organizations, including a seminary. I have consulted on administrative and strategic planning issues for various Church organizations, including parishes, a seminary, a monastery, and a summer camp for children.

While I was educated as an engineer, my professional work has been in international business development, negotiations, and management. Most of my responsibilities involved supervision, management, planning, and leadership as an executive in one of the world's largest global corporations. At the same time, I was associated with various other organizations around the world, involving other industry advisory roles and educational governance responsibilities.

My corporate career development and continuing education followed a familiar pattern. First, I worked as a sole contributor, then supervised a few others. My role expanded to management of ongoing projects and organizations and, lastly, to leadership of new, creative, and breakthrough ventures. In business, this progression is known as career development and managed by committees within the corporate organization.

However, when it comes to Church organizations, this kind of organic yet intentional activity happens rarely, if at all. In fact, training in leadership, planning, and management skills is sorely lacking.

My hope is that this book will contribute to improved leadership development among Christians called to lead the Lord's flock, whether it be large or small, many or few, in Church as well as secular environments. May his will be done.

Introduction

Vince Lombardi once said that leaders are made, not born. As an ultra-successful former head coach who led the Green Bay Packers to five NFL championships, Lombardi ought to know. So if we agree that leaders are made, the question is, how are they made and who makes them?

Since this book is about *Christian* leadership, we will look at the lives of some of the Bible's great leaders for some answers. These leaders were very different from one another. But they all had one thing in common: they became leaders after a profound encounter with God.

LEADERS: DISCOVERED, FORMED, AND CHALLENGED

Let's begin with the Prophet Amos. There is no stronger, more powerful, or less likely preacher in the Old Testament. Amos was a simple shepherd and farmer who earned his living pricking the fruit of sycamore fig trees to hasten their ripening. Could one imagine in this day and age a more unlikely candidate for leadership? No Harvard Business School for him, no aristocratic childhood with education by tutors. Yet the Lord chose him to go and speak to his people Israel, in extraordinarily strong and forceful terms.

What about the Prophet Jeremiah? When the Lord asked him to go and preach, Jeremiah resisted. He complained that he was too young and could not speak in public. He had no gift of blarney, no training in homiletics or rhetoric. So how did he manage to become a great leader? The Lord put his own words in Jeremiah's mouth. And thus Jeremiah became a powerful preacher. The Lord *discovered* the prophets Amos and Jeremiah, and then gave them the tools and the words to lead.

Jesus' disciples were also discovered and called by him, one by one. They faced an even greater task than the prophets did. Jesus formed them during his three-year public ministry by means of his continuous teaching, healing, scolding, serving, suffering, and dying. It was not an easy job. They were difficult to deal with: they doubted, they deserted, and one betrayed. But in the end, except for one, they became true apostles. Later, the Apostle Paul was called and converted from the persecutor and zealous Pharisee Saul into Paul, the apostle to the Gentiles. Paul endured dangerous and weary voyages, imprisonments, and frequent disappointments in the newly formed Christian communities. At the same time, he experienced the joy of companionship with his fellow workers. All this *formed* their persons and apostleship.

After the resurrection and ascension, the Holy Spirit continued to inspire the first Christian leaders with the remembrance of all that Jesus taught them, not only by his words, but also by his life. The Lord *challenged* the disciples by the very facts of his life. The temptations of poor and inadequate leadership—exemplified by the betraying Judas, the denying Peter, and the doubting Thomas—were shown to be in direct opposition to the living example of the obedient-even-unto-death Son, the steadfast and loving Master, the faithful Servant of all. The challenge for Christian leaders today is to refer every idea, every action, and every feeling to the example of the one who said, "I came not to be served but to serve," and who commanded us to love one another as he has loved us—namely, to give our lives for one another.

WORKING WITH OTHERS TOWARD THE KINGDOM

According to the Scriptures and the teaching of the Orthodox Church, the goal of the Christian life is union with God and eternal life in his kingdom, as persons and as a community. Persons and community go together. Jesus Christ declared that love for others is central to discipleship: "By this all men will know that you are my disciples, if you have love for one another."[1] The early Church assumed that "one Christian is no Christian"

[1] Jn 13.35.

(*Unus Christianus—nullus Christianus*).[2] St Seraphim of Sarov, a Russian saint of the late eighteenth century, stressed the importance of the personal acquisition of the Holy Spirit and also saw the enormous impact this could have on the community: "Acquire a peaceful spirit, and then thousands of others around you will be saved."[3]

Leadership is not something done in isolation from others. It needs to be done within a community, with mutual activity on all sides. The glue that binds everyone together is the recognition that we are all subject to the ultimate leadership of God.

God is the real and ultimate leader, since he is our Lord and Master and King. We are his subjects, and we are guided by his commandments. We accepted those commandments when we entered the Church. We re-commit to them every time we participate in the sacramental life of the Church. Each time we pray the Lord's Prayer, we say: "Our Father who art in heaven. . . . Thy will be done, on earth as it is in heaven. . . ." This commitment reaffirms that we are subjects of his kingship and members of his kingdom.

However, kingship and leadership do not stop with God. In every age, the leadership of God in this world has been delegated to man, who is made in God's image and likeness. In the beginning Adam was given dominion over the animals. Whatever he called a beast of the field or bird of the air became its name. In fact, the Lord God patiently waited "to see what he would call them."[4] However, Adam decided to be a leader in his own right, with his own goals and ideas, not God's. That did not turn out well for him, or for us. The Old Testament leaders Abraham, Moses, Aaron, David, Samuel, and the prophets all acknowledged their dependence on God. But whenever any of them became "independent of God," calamity and tragedy inevitably ensued.

New Testament leaders similarly rose and fell depending upon their willingness and ability to follow God's commandments. The writings of

---

[2]Georges Florovsky, *Bible, Church, Tradition: An Eastern Orthodox View* (Belmont, MA: Nordland Publishing Company, 1972), 59.

[3]Metropolitan Kallistos Ware, *The Inner Kingdom* (Crestwood, NY: St Vladimir's Seminary Press, 2000), 133.

[4]Gen 2.19.

the Apostle Paul are full of observations of how the leaders of the early Christian communities either cleaved to or departed from doing the will of God. The Church fathers speak of both difficulties and victories within later Christian communities that sought to make their way to the kingdom while living within the confines of the empire. The Church has persevered to this day by seeking to do God's will. As Christians, we must work together as leaders to attain the promise of the kingdom.

Christian Leadership. It is loving one another. It is doing the will of God. It is striving together for union with God in his kingdom. We can put these concepts together into a definition of Christian leadership, as follows:

> Christian leadership is the conscious working together in faith and in love, in a community of fathers and mothers, brothers and sisters, to do God's will on earth as it is in heaven, and to attain to the kingdom of God, in the love of the God the Father, the grace of our Lord Jesus Christ, and the communion of the Holy Spirit.

This "working together" implies that each of us in the "community of brothers and sisters" contributes our own divinely given gifts and talents. We work according to our own specific responsibilities, with some as "apostles, some prophets, some evangelists, some pastors and teachers."[5] All will be mutual servants of God and of one another. All will be leaders.

PLANNING TOGETHER

The title of this book refers not just to leadership, but to *strategic* leadership. A leader may lead in many different directions, but it is important to note that not every possible direction is appropriate or even useful. Strategic *planning* is the subset of leadership that establishes proper direction, objectives, desired actions, and mileposts. It enables leaders to be disciplined stewards of the responsibility placed in them by others.

The very notion of strategic planning may strike some as bringing a foreign and not necessarily comfortable idea into the Church. Over the

[5]Eph 4.11.

years, I have heard many people say, "Planning is for business, not the Church." I have also heard the statement, "If we had complete trust in God, we would not need planning."

Our need—and indeed, our obligation—to do planning for the Church is not the result of a lack of trust in God. Rather, it is the recognition that the Lord has placed his trust in us, and he accordingly sets high standards of responsibility and stewardship. As he said, "You did not choose me, but I chose you and appointed you . . . [to] go and bear fruit."[6] The commandments of God start from the greatest ("love the Lord your God with all your mind and soul and strength") and the one like it: "Love your neighbor as yourself."[7] This commandment of love and action demands from us constant self-examination, repentance, and recollection if we are to do, with God's help, what he requires.

Strategic planning is an effort by the members of a community to undergo an examination of conscience—to measure themselves as a group, ordained by God to fulfill a particular purpose, as to whether they are in fact fulfilling that purpose. Having done this, they next determine God's will for them and what the Lord wants them to do. Then, they actually go forward and do the Lord's will seriously, with dedication and utmost honesty concerning their own weaknesses and their dependence upon the Lord in everything. They do all this in assembly, involving not only the members of the community but all whose lives are impacted by that community. Finally, the mutually agreed-upon, God-directed work is managed and performed carefully and properly, "decently and in good order."[8]

God did not leave us with a blank slate, without direction or purpose. He has plans for us that he wishes us to follow: "For I know the plans I have for you, says the Lord, plans for welfare and not for evil, to give you a future and a hope."[9] We know them also, especially from Scripture. St Peter, in his first sermon after the descent of the Holy Spirit at Pentecost, proclaims that Jesus was handed over to the Jews "according to the definite plan

[6]Jn 15.16.
[7]Mk 12.30–31.
[8]1 Cor 14.40.
[9]Jer 29.11.

[Greek, *boulē*] and foreknowledge of God."[10] The best known instance of the "plan of God" is contained in the first chapter of St Paul's Epistle to the Ephesians: "For he has made known to us in all wisdom and insight the mystery of his will, according to his purpose which he set forth in Christ, as a plan (*oikonomian*) for the fullness of time, to unite all things in him, things in heaven and things on earth."[11]

Our plan in the church, and our plan for our ministry in the world, must be consistent with God's purpose, counsel, and administration. We are to be united in him. Plans are foundational guideposts, lights, and compass bearings to direct us on the path to the kingdom. Those plans must be based upon God's word, for as Jesus said, "Every one then who hears these words of mine and does them will be like a wise man who built his house upon the rock."[12] Every plan of the Church must be based upon the gospel, then tested for consistency and alignment with it. It is not easy to fulfill this task. It requires commitment and discipline and working with others in openness, truth, and love.

MANAGERS AS LEADERS

In most organizations, leadership is considered to be a separate category from management. For example, some experts say that leaders inspire, while managers merely organize. According to this model, the leader is considered "superior" in the organizational chart to the manager, just as a CEO is "superior" to a regular shop floor employee. However, management is in fact a subset of leadership and completely contained within it. A leader needs to know how to manage, and a manager needs to know how to lead. Both are critical.

Take the chairing of a meeting, for example. We might think that a manager chairing a meeting need only know how to keep time, how to exercise the rules of procedure the organization uses (e.g., Robert's rules of

---

[10]Acts 2.23. The word *boulē*, translated in the RSV as "plan," is translated in other versions as "determinate counsel" (KJV) and "set purpose" (NIV).

[11]Eph 1.9–10 (RSV). The word *oikonomian*, translated in the RSV as "plan," means stewardship, administration, and management.

[12]Mt 7.24.

order), how to follow the pre-determined agenda, how to appoint someone to keep minutes, and how to keep the meeting running smoothly. Many meetings are deemed successful when these objectives are achieved.

But while these things are important and indeed necessary, the chair must also be a leader if he or she is to maximize the meeting's effectiveness. The chair must tap the creativity of the participants and encourage them to be more than mere attendees, but also fellow workers. The chair must empathize with the participants, sensing unspoken thoughts, ideas, and unexpressed emotions that may hinder or help the work of the meeting. The chair must be able to depart sharply from the appointed agenda when the need arises. Finally, the chair must be able to bring the meeting to a close with a sense of unity and a mutually decided path forward.

It is sometimes said that leaders see the long-term, big-picture vision, while managers see only the short-term, daily details of ordinary life. Managers certainly need to deal with the details of ordinary life, but there is no such thing in the Church as "ordinary life." All is to be filled with the presence of God, and all is to be done in his name. There are no "ordinary" interactions with people. Everyone is to be seen as an icon of Christ, made "in the image and likeness" of God. There are no "ordinary" actions of our bodies, for as St Paul says, "Glorify God in your body."[13] Every action of ours is under the oversight of, and in service to, God. This stewardship to God applies not only to what we do, but also to how we do it.

Managers are delegated with responsibilities, just as Adam was given dominion by God "over every living thing that moves upon the earth."[14] The kings of Israel were given covenant responsibilities by God. David said of this responsibility: "I have kept the ways of the Lord. . . . All his ordinances were before me, and from his statutes I did not turn aside. . . . For he has made with me an everlasting covenant."[15] In our time, managers need to know about financial matters, compliance with laws and regulations, and ethics and misconduct. They cannot escape these often disagreeable responsibilities.

[13] 1 Cor 6.20.
[14] Gen 1.28.
[15] 2 Sam 22.22–23; 23.5.

Managers must be skillful and encourage the skills of others. In the Exodus account of the building of the tabernacle, stress is placed upon the ability of those coming to help. Moses said: "Let every able man among you come and make all that the Lord has commanded. . . . and all women who had ability spun with their hands, and brought what they had spun. . . ."[16] In our time, managers need to know how to encourage others to bring their skills to the organization, while learning enough of those skills themselves to effectively oversee the work.

Managers need to have a generous and willing heart. The tabernacle story illustrates the enthusiasm and love that was in the hearts of those who built and decorated it.

> Then all the congregation of the people of Israel . . . came, every one whose heart stirred him, and every one whose spirit moved him, and brought the Lord's offering to be used for the tent of meeting, and for all its service, and for the holy garments. So they came, both men and women; all who were of a willing heart. . . .[17]

All work must be an offering of love to God. In our time, managers need to know how to transmit this love to the people, to counsel their subordinates, to resolve conflicts, to come to common agreement even with those who disagree with them, to encourage others to contribute resources to support the common effort.

ALL TOGETHER

Often, people make an artificial distinction between leadership, planning, and management. However, when considered strategically, these three fundamental tasks overlap considerably and one implies much of the other two. Although there are several separate parts to this book, each focusing on the tasks mentioned above, the best course is to read the entire text before applying any of the parts exclusively, and to avoid concentrating on one to the exclusion of the others.

[16]Ex 35.10, 25.
[17]Ex 35.20–22.

PART ONE

Leadership: To What End?

The critical question regarding leadership is "to what end?" As leaders, where are we leading our people? What is our motivation for leading our people? Is it to achieve an organizational mission? Or is it to advance our own career, standing, power, or privilege?

All leaders must know the ultimate goals towards which they lead others. Usually, these are external goals, such as organizational targets. But they also need to acknowledge the internal goals they have set for themselves, whether consciously or unconsciously. Sometimes these external and internal goals conflict with one another, as in this real life example.

In a financial reporting position I once held, I was ready to make a presentation to the board. When my manager saw my presentation, he said to me: "Wait a minute. You're going to report bad news. Don't do it. Let someone else be the first to tell the board about it." He feared becoming the target of the "shoot the messenger" game, and thus risking damage to his and my career prospects. In the Church, reports of misconduct are silenced sometimes for the same reasons. Laity and clergy are afraid of speaking to their bishop. In such situations, the leadership goals are confused. Truthful financial reporting in the corporate world and scrupulous insistence on proper behavior in the Church are both goals explicitly stated in the respective manuals of conduct. Yet they may be ignored because of conflicts with the hidden internal goals of the leaders.

Problems may arise even for leaders who have consistent internal and external goals. Leaders sometimes succumb to the temptation to set their own goals without reference to fundamental principles, or to the counsel of others. Such missteps are especially likely when the leader has been "successful," which increases his confidence that he is on the right track—and always will be. Leadership can then become driven by egotism, confidence in one's own perspectives and judgments to the exclusion of others, indifference, and even hostility to conflicting opinions.

When leaders get set in their ways, it becomes more and more difficult to change. Change requires strength of will, courage, and humility. In the corporate world, it is common for leaders to attend some form of organized leadership workshop, retreat, or seminar every few years in order to review their leadership styles and perhaps change them for the better. The best of these events are a bit like Marine boot camp, with recruits being broken down and built up again. Layers of acquired leadership traits are peeled away to reveal the fundamental core of one's own values. These traits are then built up again in a way which will improve the leader's effectiveness in that particular corporate environment. Unfortunately, such workshops are much less common in the Church, but are no less essential.

How might such a break-down-and-build-up-again approach work, especially for Christians? First and foremost, one questions one's own innate or acquired presuppositions, followed by a search in a focused and intense manner for those overarching principles which should—and hopefully will—guide one's actions, decisions, and behavior.

Let's take one of the common leadership traits: self-confidence. While this trait certainly makes sense as a quality which helps inspire the confidence of others, it can be dangerous if not managed appropriately. The dark side of self-confidence is self-deception. One of the famous spiritual works of the Orthodox Church has as the title of its second chapter, "One should never believe in oneself or trust oneself in anything."[1] Surely most of us would agree that we have never come across this statement in any of the usual leadership texts. Most of them emphasize the importance of self-confidence. However, what is likely to happen when one's self-confidence is challenged or shaken? Will one respond aggressively, dismissively, or

---

[1]*Unseen Warfare: Being the Spiritual Combat and Path to Paradise of Lorenzo Scupoli as edited by Nicodemus of the Holy Mountain and revised by Theophan the Recluse*, E. Kadloubovsky and G. E. H. Palmer trans. (London: Faber and Faber Limited, 1963), 81.

angrily? These are not mere psychological or behavioral issues. They are intensely spiritual, arising from the depths, from the heart and gut of the inner person.

For those of us who believe in God, our entire approach to leadership must be consistent with that belief. If not, then we have a basic problem right from the start—an inner conflict. Can we separate our existence into two spheres, one in which we are believers in mind and heart, and another, i.e., work and home, where we spend all our time? Many of us in fact do that. And that is a real problem for a Christian.

One of the assumptions of this book is that the reader is a believer, or perhaps seeking belief. As a result, the reader wishes to be consistent with that belief as a leader (or at least to see what that Christian belief implies as far as leadership). In order to do this, one must break down one's fundamental presuppositions about oneself and build them up again with a foundation in God and his word. One must first believe fervently in the goodness and validity of the end goal before one can inspire others to follow.

What is the overarching goal for Christian leaders? At the beginning of the Gospels, we hear of large numbers of people from Jerusalem and its surroundings who travel into the wilderness to hear the words of a strange preacher, clothed in camel's hair and eating locusts and wild honey. They were searching for something, perhaps for forgiveness and redemption, or perhaps merely for the "next new thing," as did the Pharisees and scribes. Then John the Baptist and Forerunner of the Lord proclaimed the goal of their pilgrimage by heralding the coming of the kingdom: "Repent, for the kingdom of heaven is at hand!"[2]

Jesus repeated these same words following his baptism at the hands of John and his forty-day sojourn in the desert.[3] Every Sunday and feast day, Orthodox Christians hear the destination and goal of our life's journey announced at the beginning of the Divine Liturgy: "Blessed is the kingdom of the Father, and of the Son, and of the Holy Spirit!" Simply put, then, our goal is the attainment of the kingdom of God. Addressing the question of

---

[2]Mt 3.2.
[3]Mt 4.17.

how to attain this kingdom in communion with others is the ultimate task of Christian leadership.

As defined in the introduction, *Christian leadership is the conscious working together in faith and in love, in a community of fathers and mothers, brothers and sisters, to do God's will on earth as it is in heaven, and to attain to the kingdom of God, in the love of the God the Father, the grace of our Lord Jesus Christ, and the communion of the Holy Spirit.*

1

Seeking the Will of God

Our first premise is that everything done in the Church, including the actions of our leaders, must be in accordance with God's will. However, we may rightly ask, "What is the will of God for me in my life?" Normally, this question arises around certain major life decisions, e.g., whom shall I marry, where should I live, what work should I do?

Striving to do the will of God (or not) impacts the very foundation of who a person is. It is reflected not only in how a person lives his or her own life internally, but also in how that person responds to others, particularly in times of challenges and difficulties. For a Christian, seeking and obeying the will of God is paramount. Fr Alexander Schmemann[1] underscores this point in his commentary on the Lord's Prayer:

> I would have to say that precisely this petition, "Thy will be done," is the ultimate yardstick of faith, the measure by which one can discern, in oneself first of all, profound from superficial faith, profound religiosity from a false one. Why? Well, because even the most ardent believer all too regularly, if not always, desires, expects, and asks for the God he claims to believe in that God would fulfill precisely his own will and not the will of God. The best proof of this is the gospel itself, the account of Christ's life.[2]

[1]Former dean of St Vladimir's Orthodox Theological Seminary, Crestwood, NY (1962–1983).

[2]Alexander Schmemann, *Our Father* (Crestwood, NY: St Vladimir's Seminary Press, 2002), 46.

While Jesus was healing the people, they were with him. When they thought he was going to free them from oppression by the Romans, they greeted him with cheers. When he was doing what they wanted him to do and saying what they wanted to hear, all was good. But when he allowed the demons to go into the swine, with the inevitable result of death, or when he preached about denying oneself, or when it became obvious that his kingdom was not of this world, the tables turned toward rejection and condemnation.

For Jesus, the will of God was the path to the cross: "It was the will of the Lord to bruise him; he has put him to grief; when he makes himself an offering for sin, he shall see his offspring, he shall prolong his days; the will of the Lord shall prosper in his hand."[3] And Jesus' response to the cup he saw before him was, "'Abba, Father, all things are possible to thee; remove this cup from me; yet not what I will, but what thou wilt.'"[4] Furthermore, Jesus says, "My food is to do the will of him who sent me, and to accomplish his work"[5] and "I can do nothing on my own authority; as I hear, I judge; and my judgment is just, because I seek not my own will but the will of him who sent me."[6]

Christians follow their Savior, Jesus Christ. As he did the will of God, so must we at all times, in all places, and in all things. But how can we be certain as to what his will is? The counsel of the Church fathers is never to assume that it is what we want it to be. A great fifth-century saint, St Nilus of Sinai,[7] who in his previous life was a high-ranking official in the court of Constantinople, advises:

> Do not pray for the fulfillment of your wishes, for they may not accord with the will of God. But pray as you have been taught, saying: Thy will be done in me (cf. Lk 22.42). Always entreat Him in this way—that His will be done. For He desires what is good and profitable for you, whereas you do not always ask for this.

[3]Is 53.10.
[4]Mk 14.36.
[5]Jn 4.34.
[6]Jn 5.30.
[7]Fifth-century ascetic writer and disciple of St John Chrysostom.

> Often when I have prayed I have asked for what I thought was good, and persisted in my petition, stupidly importuning the will of God, and not leaving it to Him to arrange things as He knows is best for me. But when I have obtained what I asked for, I have been very sorry that I did not ask for the will of God to be done; because the thing turned out not to be as I had thought.[8]

In this counsel, St Nilus addresses himself to the person who is actively seeking to do God's will, and who believes he knows what it is and asks God's strength to do what he wants to do. However, the saint warns us that this may not be God's will at all. What then can we do?

We need to step back a bit. We need to first recognize that we are human. We need to recognize that the only one who has done God's will perfectly is his Son, Jesus Christ. Everything that Jesus did was referred to and had its basis in the Father.

Christ's teaching is from the Father.[9] His authority is from the Father.[10] His actions are according to the will of the Father.[11] His very sustenance, his food is to do the will of the Father.[12] Yet—and this is the great hope—it is clear according to the testimony of the gospel that we can also do the will of the Father. But—and this is a big but—we need to do this completely and unreservedly. Jesus is very clear that if we are to be his true followers, we may not simply proclaim superficial allegiance: "Not everyone who says to me, 'Lord, Lord,' shall enter the kingdom of heaven, but he who does the will of my Father who is in heaven."[13] Moreover, Jesus declares that an intimate family relationship is possible, "for whoever does the will of my Father in heaven is my brother, and sister, and mother."[14]

---

[8]Evagrius Ponticus, *On Prayer: One Hundred and Fifty-Three Texts*, 31–32. In *The Philokalia: The Complete Text Compiled by St Nikodimos of the Holy Mountain and St Makarios of Corinth*, Vol. I, G. E. H. Palmer, Philip Sherrard, and Kallistos Ware, trans. and ed. (London & Boston: Faber and Faber, 1979), 60. [While the manuscript tradition ascribes this work to St Nilus, scholars identify Evagrius as the author.—*Ed.*]

[9]Jn 7.16.
[10]Jn 5.30.
[11]Jn 6.38.
[12]Jn 4.34.
[13]Mt 7.21.
[14]Mt 12.50.

How then do we discover the will of God for ourselves? Is it perhaps obtained through accepting the advice and counsel of others? As an abbreviated account, we cannot do better than the following statement of the third-century bishop of Carthage, St Cyprian. In the words of St John Chrysostom, Cyprian offers "a kind of summary of what the Divine Will demands from its followers." Please read this quotation slowly.

> The Will of God . . . is what Christ has done and taught. It is humility in conduct, steadfastness in faith, scrupulousness in our words, rectitude in our deeds, mercy in our works, governance in our habits; it is innocence of injuriousness, and patience under it, preserving peace with the brethren, loving God with all our heart, loving Him as our Father, and fearing Him as our God; accounting Christ before all things, because He accounted nothing before us, clinging inseparably to His love, being stationed with fortitude and faith at his cross, and when the battle comes for His name and honour, maintaining in words that constancy which makes confession, in torture that confidence which joins battle, and in death that patience which receives the crown. This it is to endeavor to be co-heir with Christ; this it is to perform the commandment of God, and to fulfill the will of the Father.[15]

Do we need anything more? This statement could be read again and again, each word pondered over and over, and we would never exhaust its power. However, although these words are amazing, most of us need something more organic, more experiential. We usually have a hard time just accepting a set of the best principles, even if eloquently stated, before they become our own. Is there another approach that would help us to instill these principles in our very being?

The advice of many of the Church fathers is to turn first to Scripture. Fr Theodore Stylianopoulos notes:

> One does not have to read very far in the theological and practical writings of the Church fathers, such as Basil and Chrysostom, to see

---

[15]Jeremias Drexelius, *Heliotropium: Conformity of the Human Will to the Divine* (Rockford, IL: Tan Books and Publishers, 1984 [1st Latin ed. 1627]), 54f.

the massive authority they attached to the letter and plain meaning of Scripture as secure instruction about God and his will for all. These fathers relied heavily on the clarity and stability of meaning resident in the biblical text . . . and assumed that any reader could follow without esoteric techniques.[16]

[handwritten: → intended for or likely to be understood by only a small number of people with a specialized knowledge or interest.]

While I was a graduate student at Syracuse University in the late 1960s, I often enjoyed talks with my pastor and mentor, Fr Alexander Warnecke. One of his "extra-curricular" jobs was as vice-president of the Syracuse Area Redevelopment Commission. One day he told me he had just returned from inspecting a renovated multi-family home in a run-down neighborhood. It was already occupied by a poor family. He happened to overhear two ladies speaking in the kitchen about the family problems one of them had. The other said, "Let's open the Good Book and see what it says about what you should do!" Fr Alexander was a good man and a great activist within the Church, a builder of a school, a camp, a seminary, and an old age home. In my experience, he was not a particularly sentimental person. But he was profoundly touched by the simple and fundamental faith of those ladies.

The Christian leader needs to know the Scriptures in an intimate sense, not simply in an academic or theoretical fashion but in a living and vital way. The Lord God is not simply Creator in the past tense, winding up the universe and then letting it go, as some believe. He is also Master and King in the present tense. If we believe that, then we are his servants and subjects. And to seriously accept those roles has significant consequences.

As leaders, much is required of us by God. The words of Scripture are effective reminders of what is practically required by the Lord for our life. Each of us needs, as the instruction to newly tonsured readers in the Orthodox Church states, "to peruse the Scriptures daily."[17] If we do this diligently, we may hear echoes of the words of Luke and Cleopas: "Did

---

[16]Theodore G. Stylianopoulos, *The New Testament: An Orthodox Perspective, Volume One: Scripture, Tradition, Hermeneutics* (Brookline, MA: Holy Cross Orthodox Press, 1977), 181.

[17]*Service Book of the Holy Orthodox-Catholic Apostolic Church*, Isabel Florence Hapgood, trans. (Brooklyn, NY: Syrian Antiochian Orthodox Archdiocese, 1965 [1st ed. 1906]), 308.

not our hearts burn within us while he talked to us on the road, while he opened to us the scriptures?"[18]

For the leader, the words of Scripture must be a constant reminder, or perhaps better said, a revelation of what is required by the Lord God for real life. In the remainder of Part One, our attention will be primarily focused on certain persons of the Old Testament and their relationship with God.[19] Why should we look at these persons? What is special about them? The Old Testament is filled with stories of the personal encounter between God and those whom he has called to himself. It portrays a dialogue between these persons and God, in very specific terms. Professor Dimitar Kirov explains that, in the Old Testament, "revelation has a personal character. It presupposes the relationship between at least two persons, an encounter between revealer and receiver. It is an intimate interpenetration of two personalities."[20]

---

[18]Lk 24.32.

[19]See David T. Gortner, "Retraining Ourselves in Thought and Action: A Thematic Exploration of Leadership Literature," *Anglican Theological Review* 92.1 (2010): 189–213, at 202ff. Gortner cautions against considering these persons (e.g., Moses, the apostles) as model leaders. He recognizes that trust must be placed in God, but then proceeds to imply that "over-application" of this trust precept leads to inadequate self-assessment, discipline, and intellectual strength. Our own review of these persons is not necessarily to offer them as full and complete images of outstanding leadership, but to point to the relationship they had with God and the ways in which that relationship unfolded. Our section on strategic planning will address the issue of self-assessment and discipline.

[20]Dimitar Popmarinov Kirov, "The Unity of Revelation and the Unity of Tradition," in *Orthodox and Wesleyan Ecclesiology* (Crestwood, NY: St Vladimir's Seminary Press, 2007), 105.

2

The Five Requirements

The encounter between God and Israel resulted in the covenant, the establishment of a special relationship that involved promises and responsibilities. In Deuteronomy, Moses assembles the people of Israel and preaches on the meaning of the covenant. He declares the people to be chosen, holy, and loved by God. In the midst of his long sermon, immediately following his account of the forty days and nights on Mount Sinai and the giving of the tablets by the Lord (i.e., his personal encounter with God), he exclaims:

> And now, Israel, what does the Lord your God require of you, but to fear the Lord your God, to walk in all his ways, to love him, to serve the Lord your God with all your heart and with all your soul, and to keep the commandments and statutes of the Lord, which I command to you this day for your good?[1]

As serious Christians, we need to ask ourselves each and every day, "What does God require of me?" Moses' declaration is a worthwhile foundation for our reflection on what God really wants from us. The five requirements are to fear, to walk, to love, to serve, and to keep.

FEAR THE LORD YOUR GOD

Normally, fear is not considered an attribute of leaders—rather, wisdom is emphasized. For the Christian leader, a prime source for practical godly

---

[1] Dt 10.12–13.

wisdom is the book of Proverbs. The preamble to this book declares Solomon's purpose in writing: "That men may know wisdom and instruction, understand words of insight, receive instruction in wise dealing, righteousness, justice, and equity."[2] However, the instruction is preceded with a warning that "the fear of the Lord is the beginning of wisdom."[3]

Wisdom and instruction are not connected with abstract or theoretical advice, but rather with a Person who is to be feared. It is one thing to read a book of advice and consider it, critique it, and then close it. We do this in private, free to accept or reject the advice as we please. It is something else entirely to encounter a person whom we respect, and whose words challenge us. Most of us have had a mentor in our lives—a parent, teacher, neighbor, or boss—who spoke with us in ways that were different from those of others. For some, we would do anything to avoid disappointing them. We would probably never have said that we feared them as people, but we were certainly afraid of offending them. Why would that be? Because we loved them, they meant the world to us, and we looked up to them. And, perhaps, because they cared about us as probably few others did.

The Lord God loves us and cares for us as our mentors did. But he is more than a mentor. He is our Creator, Master, and King. His face is always before us. We have pledged to obey him and do his will. On the other hand, we can always ignore him and his commandments, yet we do so at our peril. Israel provides an example. The nation was always in and out of trouble as it struggled to learn the way of the Lord. Old Testament law, the prophets, and wisdom literature provide lessons for us which, if taken seriously, can help us avoid Israel's painful experiences.

The first and most important lesson is that the Lord is to be obeyed—truly obeyed. That's just how it is. If we do not believe that, then we need to go back to the beginning and re-boot our understanding of what it means to be Christian. The second is that disobedience has negative consequences, no matter what our station in the Church (bishop, clergy, layperson) or society (executive, factory worker, and so on) may be. We cannot

[2]Prov 1.2–3.
[3]Prov 1.7.

escape the reality that our God, whom we worship with our lips, is a jealous God[4] who seeks justice and righteousness.[5] He has set standards for conduct. Granted, when we disobey, he may not strike us down with his own hand. But we may ourselves bring the consequences of which he warned us upon our own heads. To use an everyday analogy, we may dislike the traffic slowdowns caused by red lights. We may decide to disregard them. But the result may be that the car we are driving is t-boned at an intersection, with possible personal tragedy to our loved ones. Who caused that accident and its terrible consequences? We did it to ourselves.

The thundering warnings of the prophets provide ample evidence of those who honor the Lord God with their lips, but whose heart is far from him.[6] The book of Proverbs clearly states, in terrifying words, what will happen when God's wisdom is ignored:

> Wisdom cries aloud in the street. . . . "How long will scoffers delight in their scoffing and fools hate knowledge? . . . Because I have called and you refused to listen, have stretched out my hand and no one has heeded, and you have ignored all my counsel and would have none of my reproof, I also will laugh at your calamity; I will mock when panic strikes you, when panic strikes you like a storm, and your calamity comes like a whirlwind, when distress and anguish come upon you."[7]

This does not mean that our failure to fear the Lord always results in immediate tragedy. One can be exceedingly successful in the eyes of the world while ignoring the ultimate claim of the Lord God to be the Master of all. As the Lord says in the prophecy of Jeremiah: "They do not say in their hearts, 'Let us fear the Lord our God. . . .' They have become great and rich. . . . They judge not with justice the cause of the fatherless, to make it prosper, and they do not defend the rights of the needy."[8] Jeremiah laments, "To whom shall I speak and give warning, that they may hear? Behold, their ears are closed, they cannot listen; behold, the word of the

[4]Deut 5.9.
[5]Am 5.24.
[6]Is 29.13.
[7]Prov 1.20, 22, 24–27.
[8]Jer 5.24, 27–28.

Lord is to them an object of scorn, they take no pleasure in it."[9] Is this not the way our society operates today?

The people of Israel decidedly did not fear the Lord: "They have not given heed to my words; and as for my law, they have rejected it."[10] The hidden things of their hearts and minds testify to the fact that they have, in the words of Isaiah, turned things "upside down"; the potter was regarded as the clay, and the created said of the Creator: "He did not make me."[11] Some call it self-affirmation, a renaissance of thought and will, but it is still rebellion.

Does all this talk about dependence upon and fear of God seem harsh? For some people, there are no absolutes, no standards, or at least none applicable to themselves. They say, "Who are you to tell us what is right? We can determine it for ourselves. We have freedom to do what we want, and to listen to whomever we wish." Yes, that is certainly true, and everyone has the right to sit back and enjoy the consequences. Years ago, there was a TV commercial for a brand of automotive engine oil filters with a mechanic saying, "You can come to me to buy this now, or come back to me later with engine damage. Fine with me either way. But it will cost you a lot more later." Israel had to learn this lesson over and over again. Not for nothing did the Lord call them "a stiff-necked people."[12]

An authentic fear of the Lord does not lead to paralysis, psychological or otherwise. Rather, paradoxically, to fear the Lord means to have no fear. At its heart, this is the incredibly loving and spectacular message of the whole of the Old and New Testaments. The Lord and his prophets continually encourage the people of Israel "Fear not, stand firm";[13] "Do not fear or be dismayed";[14] "Fear not, for I am with you, be not dismayed, for I am your God."[15]

---

[9]Jer 6.10.
[10]Jer 6.19.
[11]Is 29.16.
[12]Ex 33.3.
[13]Ex 14.13.
[14]Josh 8.1.
[15]Is 41.10.

Unfortunately, this message can be twisted so as to transfer this fear of God to fear of man, especially those in power and authority. Certain eleventh-century Russian writings on the Christian life advise the reader to fear not only God, but also those of higher social standing. One Russian historian objected, "This conception of fear has nothing in common with the Old Testament idea of God's fear. In the prophetic religion of Israel, fear of God frees us from the fear of man."[16]

To fear the Lord is the first step in understanding his will, for it places us in the right relationship with God—that of servant and master, subject and king—and a relationship of ultimate seriousness. The foremost example is provided by St Paul: "In the days of his flesh, Jesus offered up prayers and supplications, with loud cries and tears, to him who was able to save him from death, and he was heard for his godly fear."[17]

The presence of the Lord brings comfort to those who have accepted him as their Master and King. The Lord Jesus Christ encourages the terrified disciples when he came to them walking upon the sea: "Take heart, it is I; have no fear."[18] Our confidence is focused on the person of the Lord, not on a set of abstract propositions or on ourselves. Ultimately, perfect fear leads to perfect love. As the Apostle and Evangelist John declared, when we abide in God and God abides in us, then we "have confidence in the day of judgment," for "perfect love casts out fear."[19]

The fathers of the Church even link the fear of God to love, sweetness, and joy. St Diadochos of Photiki[20] explains the relationship between love and fear: "No one can love God consciously in his heart unless he has first feared him with all his heart."[21] Likewise, we love little if we fear little. Fear of God purifies the soul, "bringing it to a love of God's great goodness."[22]

---

[16]George P. Fedotov, *The Russian Religious Mind* (New York, NY: Harper Torchbooks, Harper & Brothers, 1960), 208.

[17]Heb 5.7.

[18]Mk 6.50.

[19]1 Jn 4.17–18.

[20]Fifth-century bishop and ascetic writer in northern Greece.

[21]St Diadochos of Photiki, *On Spiritual Knowledge and Discrimination: One Hundred Texts* 16 (*Philokalia* I, 257).

[22]Ibid.

Indeed, St Diadochos sees the fear of God bringing us sweetness and urges us "to sweeten (our) soul continually with the fear of God."[23] St John of Karpathos[24] sees a similar connection between fear and joy. "Mary Magdalene and the women with her ran from Christ's tomb with both fear and great joy (cf. Mt 28.8); and perhaps we, too, shall one day come out from our spiritual tomb with fear and joy."[25]

How can someone be fearful and at the same time feel love, sweetness, and joy? It doesn't make sense, does it? When we think rationally, it certainly does not, and we need to admit that. But we are not in a rational environment when we encounter God. We are not calculating the pluses and minuses in arithmetic. We are in love with a person so infinitely above us in every way possible that we cannot understand why he loves us so much. That love shakes us to our very core, to the uttermost depth of our being.

We experience this inner trembling in the liturgy of the Orthodox Church. The great litany at the beginning of the Divine Liturgy acknowledges that those assembled in "this holy house . . . enter with faith, reverence, and the fear of God."[26] The concluding prayer of the litany declares:

> O Lord our God, thy power is incomparable. Thy glory is incomprehensible. Thy mercy is immeasurable. Thy love for man is inexpressible. Look down on us and on this holy house with pity, O Master, and impart the riches of thy mercy and thy compassion to us and to those who pray with us.[27]

Power, glory, mercy, love, and compassion are all brought together in one song of praise and awe. According to Nikitas Stithatos,[28] this feeling of awe brings us from the first level of fear—the fear of punishment from

---

[23]Ibid., 263.

[24]Seventh-century monastic writer.

[25]St John of Karpathos, *For the Encouragement of the Monks in India who had Written to Him: One Hundred Texts* 14 (*Philokalia* I, 301).

[26]*The Divine Liturgy According to St. John Chrysostom* (New York, NY: Russian Orthodox Greek Catholic Church of America, 1977 [1st ed. 1967]), 29.

[27]Ibid., 31.

[28]Eleventh-century theologian in Constantinople.

offending God—to the second level of contemplation of God's glory, which results in love of God.[29]

Later in the Orthodox liturgy, before the Gospel reading, we pray that the Lord himself will "implant in us the fear of His blessed commandments."[30] The consequence of this fear is that we listen and adhere to the word of God as proclaimed in the gospel. Fear and love are linked again at the great entrance ("Grant them to worship thee blamelessly with fear and love"[31]) and in the invitation to Holy Communion: "In the fear of God, and with faith and love, draw near!"[32] Following the partaking of the holy Eucharist, we offer the prayer of thanksgiving and ask, "O Master . . . strengthen us all in thy fear."[33]

In conclusion, the Christian leader must stand continually before his Master, Lord, and King, in perfect awe, in perfect fear, and in perfect love. Awe, fear, and love are awakened in him or her by the example of the one who gives life, creates all things, and is above all things, yet exercises boundless love, mercy, and compassion to the least of his creatures. The Christian leader knows that he or she can do nothing other than follow this example—to follow the one who made heaven and earth, who came in the form of a servant, and who died the death of a criminal for the least of his brethren. Fear within the true Christian leader results in constant self-examination and comparison with the Lord's commandments, taking nothing for granted, and calling continually upon the name of the Lord for strength, guidance, and mercy.

WALK IN ALL HIS WAYS

Leaders lead and others follow, but along what path? The Lord God promises the people of Israel good things if they will walk in his way.

---

[29]Nikitas Stithatos, *On the Practice of the Virtues: One Hundred Texts* 56 (*Philokalia* IV, 93).

[30]*Divine Liturgy*, 41.

[31]Ibid., 52.

[32]Ibid., 80.

[33]Ibid., 84.

> If you walk in my statutes and observe my commandments and do
> them, then I will give you your rains in their season, and the land shall
> yield its increase, and the trees of the field shall yield their fruit. . . .
> And I will walk among you, and will be your God, and you shall be my
> people.[34]

The first of the five requirements recognizes our complete dependence
upon God, which manifests itself in the fear of God. When we fear, we are
alert, listening, and ready to obey. But this obedience is not something
mechanical or far away. We are called to walk, to be active in God's ways.
We follow in his steps. Amazingly, he promises that he will be with us
every step of the way.

However, if Israel does not walk in God's way, he warns of considerable punishments in very explicit and drastic language: "terror, consump-
tion, and fever"; "plagues . . . wild beasts"; "a sword . . . pestilence."[35] Moses
speaks softer words following the giving of the Ten Commandments: "You
shall walk in the way which the Lord your God has commanded you, that
you may live, and that it may go well with you, and that you may live long
in the land which you shall possess."[36]

The more pleasant implications of walking in the ways of the Lord are
picked up by the first words of the Psalmist David:

> Blessed is the man who walks not in the counsel of the wicked, nor stands
> in the way of sinners, nor sits in the seat of scoffers; but his delight is in
> the law of the Lord, and on his law he meditates day and night. He is
> like a tree planted by streams of water, that yields its fruit in its season,
> and its leaf does not wither. In all that he does, he prospers.[37]

This psalm, which is chanted at the beginning of every Saturday great
vespers service, clearly shows the relationship between what a man does
(i.e., walks, stands, sits) and his relationship with God. The one who
delights in the law of the Lord and thinks about it continually will be like

[34]Lev 26.3–4, 12.
[35]Lev 26.16, 21–22, 25.
[36]Deut 5.33.
[37]Ps 1.1–3.

a tree, well-grounded and watered, which grows and gives shade and fruit to all who dwell near it. Zechariah and Elizabeth, the parents of John the Baptist, were guided by these words, and "they were both righteous before God, walking in all the commandments and ordinances of the Lord blameless."[38]

The theme of walking is transformed and raised to a new level with the coming of Christ, the one who walks on the water. Peter sought to imitate his Lord, requesting that Jesus bid him to walk on the water as he did. But Peter began to sink when he looked upon the wind instead of at Jesus. He lost his concentration, his focus on Jesus. All too often, we lose focus on the things that are really important in our lives. We become distracted and easily upset by obstacles in our daily activities. We lose our determination, and we stumble.

There are three themes which I would like to address here: walking in *good works,* walking in *light,* and walking in *love.* Each of these concepts, if we periodically call them to mind, can lead us to a greater sense of determination and focus.

St Paul speaks of walking as our *work*: "We are . . . created in Christ Jesus for good works, which God prepared beforehand, that we should walk in them."[39] The walking to which St Paul refers is neither a stroll nor a pleasant diversion from daily activity. According to St John Chrysostom, it is a purposeful and unending quest for the kingdom of God.

> We should walk in [good works], for we need a virtue which shall last throughout, and be extended on to our dying day. If we had to travel a road leading to a royal city, and then when we had passed over the greater part of it, were to flag and sit down near the very close, it were of no use to us.[40]

In other words, we must be attentive during the day to what we are doing if we wish to ensure that it is consistent with God's ways. Further, we must

---

[38]Lk 1.6.
[39]Eph 2.10.
[40]St John Chrysostom, Homily 4 on Ephesians (NPNF[1] 13:68).

not become disappointed at trials, for God is walking together with us on our path.

St Paul encourages us to "walk as children of *light* (for the fruit of light is found in all that is good and right and true)."[41] St John the Evangelist picks up this theme of walking in light: "If we walk in the light, as he is in the light, we have fellowship with one another, and the blood of Jesus his Son cleanses us from all sin."[42] That light is Jesus, who encapsulates in his person all the commandments and ways of God. "Again Jesus spoke to them, saying, 'I am the light of the world; he who follows me will not walk in darkness, but will have the light of life.'"[43]

The law is the light of Christ: "Thy word is a lamp unto my feet and a light to my path."[44] St Ignatius Brianchaninov[45] encourages us to "accomplish the course of our earthly pilgrimage with the greatest attention and watchfulness over ourselves, unceasingly calling upon God in prayer for help. Let the lamp for our journey be the gospel."[46] We must continually refresh our understanding of God's ways through prayer and contemplation. In prayer we also concentrate on being enlightened by God's light through the gospel. As the prayer says before the proclamation of the gospel in the Divine Liturgy, "Illumine our minds, O Master who lovest mankind, with the pure light of thy divine knowledge."[47]

St Paul also implores us to "walk in *love,* as Christ loved us."[48] The commandment of love now takes a higher turn: we are to love one another as Christ has loved us, that is, in the way that he gave himself up for us, having condescended to becoming one of us, suffering, and dying on the cross. "By this we may be sure that we know him, if we keep his commandments. . . . Whoever keeps his word, in him truly love for God is perfected. By this we may be sure that we are in him: he who says he abides in him

---

[41]Eph 5.8–9.

[42]1 Jn 1.7.

[43]Jn 8.12.

[44]Ps 119.105.

[45]Nineteenth-century Russian bishop and theologian.

[46]Bishop Ignatius Brianchaninov, *The Arena: An Offering to Contemporary Monasticism* (Jordanville, NY: Holy Trinity Publications, 1997), 133.

[47]*Divine Liturgy,* 41.

[48]Eph 5.2.

ought to walk in the same way in which he walked."[49] The greatest commandment is love, for God and one's neighbor.

"When walking in the way of righteousness," warns St Isaac the Syrian,[50]

> it is impossible not to meet with trouble. . . . But if anyone is walking in the way of justice and righteousness . . . and something of the kind happens to him, he should not turn away from the trial that has come to him, but should receive it with joy, without questioning, and should thank God for sending him this good gift.[51]

This walk is a spiritual struggle, a battlefield, a campaign, as St Jerome comments: "Who is it that truly walks in love? The one who, for the salvation of others, contends against sin to the point of shedding blood, so as even to give up his soul for them. That is the one who walks in love, imitating Christ."[52]

With the coming of the Holy Spirit, our steps are strengthened by his indwelling in us. There is still conflict occurring within us between the flesh and the spirit, however. St Paul encourages us to "walk by the Spirit, and do not gratify the desires of the flesh."[53] If we do this, the benefits are great, for "the fruit of the Spirit is love, joy, peace, patience, kindness, goodness, faithfulness, gentleness, self-control; against such there is no law. And those who belong to Christ Jesus have crucified the flesh with its passions and desires."[54]

In conclusion, to walk in the ways of God means to love to hear the voice of the Lord; to continually strive to know his ways; to shine Christ's light upon our path, so that we may see clearly and without delusion; and to walk with him on his path to Golgotha, trusting him to be with us and strengthen us by his presence. Despite the difficulty in seeking

---

[49] 1 Jn 2.3, 5–6.

[50] Sixth-century bishop and ascetic theologian.

[51] St Isaac the Syrian, quoted in Brianchaninov, *The Arena*, 107f.

[52] St Jerome, *Epistle to the Ephesians* 3.5.2 (PL 26, 519A; *Ancient Christian Commentary* VIII, 182).

[53] Gal 5.16.

[54] Gal 5.22–24.

the mind of God, as recognized by St Paul ("how inscrutable [are] his ways!"),[55] we have received the gift of knowing God's ways through Jesus Christ, who is himself "the way."[56] In taking upon ourselves his cross, we become faithful servants of the Lord, open to the workings of the Holy Spirit within us, and able to say honestly and without guile, "Thy will be done in me."

LOVE GOD

The earliest Old Testament reference to "love of God" is in Ex 20.6 (see also Deut 5.10), which relates the giving of the Ten Commandments. In this passage, the Lord God declares that he shows "steadfast love to thousands of those who love me and keep my commandments." Later in the Deuteronomy account, we hear the Shema Yisrael: "Hear, O Israel: The Lord our God is one Lord; and you shall love the Lord your God with all your heart, and with all your soul, and with all your might."[57]

Jewish children are taught this critical scriptural passage very early on. Practicing Jews recite this verse at least twice daily, as well as upon retiring to bed, in keeping with the following verses: "And these words which I command you this day shall be upon your heart; and you shall teach them diligently to your children, and shall talk of them when you sit in your house, and when you walk by the way, and when you lie down, and when you rise."[58] St Peter of Damaskos,[59] commenting on Deuteronomy 6.5 ("and you shall love the Lord your God with all your heart, and with all your soul, and with all your might"), says, "How much have the fathers said and written—and still say and write—without equaling what is contained in that single phrase?"[60]

The Lord God makes the requirement of love in a forceful manner, indicating that it is something necessary, not optional. Further, the connection

[55]Rom 11.33.
[56]Jn 14.6.
[57]Deut 6.4–5.
[58]Deut 6.6–7.
[59]Twelfth-century ascetic writer.
[60]St Peter of Damaskos, *Book 1: A Treasury of Divine Knowledge*, "How God's Speech is not Loose Chatter" (*Philokalia* III, 175).

between loving the Lord God and the blessings of life is made over and over again, "that you may live and multiply," "that you may gather in your grain and your wine and your oil."[61] Jesus refers to the Shema as the "great and first commandment" in the law.[62] Along with Leviticus 19:18 ("you shall love your neighbor as yourself"), he says that "on these two commandments depend all the law and the prophets."[63]

Despite the explicit commandments and the promise of blessings, man continually seeks after other lovers. Man is cautioned against this infidelity continually throughout the law and the prophets, in the strongest of terms. For example, "If you forget the Lord your God and go after other gods and serve them and worship them, I solemnly warn you this day that you shall surely perish."[64]

Yet despite strong imprecations against this unfaithfulness, the Prophet Hosea poignantly remarks: "She . . . went after her lovers, and forgot me, says the Lord."[65] Even in the face of this adultery, the Lord God remains faithful in his steadfast love, saying: "Therefore, behold, I will allure her, and bring her into the wilderness, and speak tenderly to her. . . . I will betroth [her] to me in righteousness and in justice, in steadfast love, and in mercy . . . [and] faithfulness."[66] The steadfast love and forbearance of God is strikingly evident further on in Hosea: "When Israel was a child, I loved him, and out of Egypt I called my son. The more I called them, the more they went from me. . . . I will heal their faithlessness; I will love them freely, for my anger has turned from them."[67] This prophecy is fulfilled in the Lord Jesus Christ, the bridegroom who endures all things, even death on the cross, to allure his unfaithful bride to return to that relationship of love commanded by the Lord God in the old covenant.

The love which is commanded in the old covenant is made possible for us by the coming of Christ. The only-begotten Son has opened the door of

[61] Deut 8.1, 11.14.
[62] Mt 22.38.
[63] Mt 22.40.
[64] Deut 8.19.
[65] Hos 2.13.
[66] Hos 2.14, 19–20.
[67] Hos 11.1–2; 14.4.

love for us and given us that love as a gift: "As the Father has loved me, so I have loved you; abide in my love."[68] That love, now commanded by Jesus, shows forth power if we follow him: "A new commandment I give to you, that you love one another; even as I have loved you, that you also love one another. By this all men shall know that you are my disciples, if you have love for one another."[69] The Lord Jesus truly fulfilled the Shema of Israel by going to the cross: "I do as the Father has commanded me, so that the world may know that I love the Father."[70] These words of Jesus speak for all of us, in that he loved the Father so much that he did the Father's will in ascending the cross.

The songs of human love for God are set forth most intensely in the Psalms, for poetry is best equipped to speak the words of love. A few examples: "I love thee, O Lord, my strength";[71] "Love the Lord, all you his saints";[72] "I love the Lord, because he has heard my voice and my supplications."[73] St Paul recalls Isaiah's vision when he declares, "As it is written, 'What no eye has seen, nor ear heard, nor the heart of man conceived, what God has prepared for those who love him.'"[74] In the Divine Liturgy, just before the Nicene Creed (symbol of faith), the priest bows three times before the altar, each time echoing the opening verses of Psalm 18: "I will love Thee, O Lord, my strength. The Lord is my firm foundation, my refuge, and my deliverer."[75] These are love songs par excellence.

Love, however, is sometimes hard to come by. We have issues expressing it. Our own self-love gets in the way. The fathers of the Church can help us, if we listen to their advice. For those of us having difficulty in loving God, St Maximos the Confessor[76] counsels: "Stop loving yourself and

[68]Jn 15.9.

[69]Jn 13.34–35.

[70]Jn 14.31.

[71]Ps 18.1.

[72]Ps 31.23.

[73]Ps 116.1.

[74]1 Cor 2.9. When I was a counselor at St Andrew's Camp in upstate New York in the late 1960s, a visiting priest served in our chapel. He preached on this passage. When he spoke these words, he lifted up his eyes to heaven and his face shone. He understood within his soul this love of God.

[75]*Divine Liturgy*, 54.

[76]Seventh-century theologian and confessor (i.e., one tortured while defending the faith).

you will love God."[77] St Peter of Damaskos refers to the teaching of St Basil the Great: "To love God with all your soul means to love nothing together with God."[78] In other words, what is required is a complete concentration of love upon God, with no distractions from oneself, nor any other thing. Jesus indicated this when he said that anyone who loves family more than him is not worthy of him.[79]

This statement poses a great difficulty for many people, for does God not wish us to love others? Yes, but not more than God, to whom our love must be directed first. The foundation of love must be established so that we can transmit the love of God to others. This concept comes to mind every time the flight crew on a plane advises the adults to "put on your own oxygen mask before helping your children put on theirs." You cannot help your children when you yourself cannot breathe. Similarly, we can't love others with full, sacrificial, and complete love before first loving God.

How then can we acquire this love for God? St Macarios of Egypt[80] advises: "Let him continually beseech the Lord to send this love into his heart ... augmenting it by grace day by day through the ceaseless and unbroken remembrance of God. Through diligence and effort, concern and struggle, he becomes capable of acquiring love for God, given form within him by the grace and bounty of Christ."[81] Orthodox Christians wear crosses on their chests and display icons in their homes. They remember God every time they sense the cross around their neck, or when their eyes see the icons on the wall. They consider what they are doing, thinking, and feeling. I knew a man who refused to allow whistling in his house because "you are not supposed to whistle in front of icons." Because he was prone to become angry at times with his family, I added, "Yes, and you're not supposed to argue in front of icons, either." The presence of God is a promise of both love and of judgment.

[77]St Maximos the Confessor, *Four Hundred Texts on Love* 4.37 (*Philokalia* II, 104).
[78]St Peter of Damaskos, *Book 1: A Treasury of Divine Knowledge*, "How God's Speech is not Loose Chatter" (*Philokalia* III, 175).
[79]Mt 10.37.
[80]Fourth-century Egyptian monk and spiritual writer.
[81]St Symeon Metaphrastis, *Paraphrase of the Homilies of St Makarios of Egypt*, "Spiritual Perfection" 1.1 (*Philokalia* III, 288–89).

In conclusion, to love God is the greatest commandment to mankind, and it stands at the very center of our faith. The Son of God loves the Father, and his love dwells in us. He gives us the gift of that love, commanding us further to love one another as he loves the Father in obedience, even to the cross. Our love for God is a gift that requires constant attention: we must avoid the distractions of the world, constantly call upon the grace of the Lord, and place our love for him above all else.

SERVE THE LORD YOUR GOD

Several New Testament writers, namely Paul, James, Peter, Jude, and John, frequently refer to themselves by way of salutation as "servants of God," as in "Paul, a servant of Jesus Christ. . . ."[82] Likewise, during communion in the Orthodox Church, the priest or deacon calls each communicant "the servant of God."[83]

The Lord God himself bestowed this title upon several Old Testament persons, among them Abraham,[84] Moses,[85] David,[86] Job,[87] and the unnamed Servant of the Lord mentioned in Isaiah 42–53. We will focus here briefly on Abraham, Moses, and the Servant.

The Old Testament servants of God fulfilled God's commands. Abraham was noted for his complete faith and trust in God, even to the point of willingness to sacrifice his only son according to God's instruction.[88] St Paul extols Abraham's faith as that of one who hoped "against hope" and whose faith "did not weaken," even when the Lord's promise conflicted with the evidence of his own eyes.[89] Abraham's faith was borne out by the birth of his son Isaac when he reached advanced years, and in the founding of many nations. St Maximos the Confessor notes that Abraham sought God first above all things, including his native land and his family: "The

[82]Rom 1.1.
[83]*Divine Liturgy*, 81.
[84]Gen 26.24.
[85]Num 12.7–8; Josh 1.7; 2 Kg 21.8.
[86]2 Sam 7.4, 8; 1 Kg 11.34; 1 Chr 17.4.
[87]Job 1.8, 2.3; 42.8.
[88]Gen 22.
[89]Rom 4.18–19.

person . . . with the clear eye of faith . . . in times of temptation and conflict . . . rises above nature because he has put the Cause of nature first, just as Abraham put God before Isaac."[90]

Service to God necessarily implies service to his people. During a hot day under the oak of Mamre, Abraham, as a self-described servant, offered the hospitality of the coolness of his tree and the food from his tent for the refreshment and rest of three visitors.[91] He interceded for the people of Sodom (unsuccessfully, as it turned out, but that was not his own fault).[92] St Theodoros the Great Ascetic[93] sets Abraham forward as an example of hospitality, "inviting all who passed by . . . his table laden for all comers including the impious and barbarians, without distinction. Hence, he was found worthy of that wonderful banquet when he received angels and the Master of all as his guests."[94]

Moses was the instrument of God in the liberation of the people of Israel from the tyranny of Pharaoh. As servant, Moses did whatever God asked of him. He was *active*.

- He was the *voice* of the Lord before Pharaoh: "The Lord said to Moses, 'See, I make you as God to Pharaoh. . . . You shall speak all that I command you. . . .'"[95]

- He *exercised God's mercy* in opening the Red Sea for the Israelites to pass over as on dry land, and then closed the waters upon Pharaoh's pursuing army.[96]

- He *endured ungrateful murmurings* from the people: "Is it because there are no graves in Egypt that you [Moses] have taken us away to die in the wilderness? . . . For it would have been better for us to serve the Egyptians than to die in the wilderness."[97]

[90]St Maximos the Confessor, *Various Texts on Theology, the Divine Economy, and Virtue and Vice* 2.50 (*Philokalia* II, 197).
[91]Gen 18.1–8.
[92]Gen 18.22–29.
[93]Ninth-century Syrian bishop and ascetic writer.
[94]St Theodoros the Great Ascetic, *A Century of Spiritual Texts* 85 (*Philokalia* II, 32).
[95]Ex 7.1–2.
[96]Ex 14.
[97]Ex 14.11–12.

- He *suffered the anger* of the people he was guiding: "And Moses cried to the Lord, 'What shall I do with this people? They are almost ready to stone me.'"[98]

- He *interceded* with the Lord on behalf of the people: "O Lord . . . I pray thee, go in the midst of us, although it is a stiff-necked people; and pardon our iniquity and our sin, and take us for thy inheritance."[99]

- He *transmitted* to the people the law of God which he had received on Mount Sinai.[100]

Throughout these events, the Lord spoke with, guided, and commanded Moses. From the time of the Burning Bush to the tent of meeting outside the camp, to the plains of Moab where he died, the Lord spoke "with Moses face to face, as a man speaks to his friend."[101] When he died, "his eye was not dim, nor his natural force abated."[102] St Gregory of Nyssa, commenting on this description in his famous work *The Life of Moses*, declares:

> From this, we learn that, when one has accomplished such noble actions, he is considered worthy of this sublime name, to be called servant of Yahweh. . . . This for him is the end of the virtuous life. . . . History speaks of "death," a living death, which is not followed by the grave, or fills the tomb, or brings dimness to the eyes and aging to the person.[103]

St Gregory continues: "What then are we taught through what has been said? To have but one purpose in life: to be called servants of God by virtue of the lives we live."[104]

Centuries after Moses, the prophecy of Isaiah introduces "the mysterious figure of a 'Servant' . . . to whom God has assigned a prominent role

[98]Ex 17.4.
[99]Ex 34.9.
[100]Ex 20.
[101]Ex 33.11.
[102]Deut 34.7.
[103]St Gregory of Nyssa, *The Life of Moses* 2.314 (*The Life of Moses* [Mahwah, NJ: Paulist Press, 1978], 135).
[104]Ibid.

in the reconciliation and restoration of mankind," according to Georges Barrois.[105] Four poems in Isaiah (Is 42.1–9; 49.1–6; 50.4–11; 52.13–53.12) develop this concept of the Servant. Of these, the most familiar to Orthodox Christians are the last two. The first of these is read at vespers of Great and Holy Thursday and at the third hour of Great and Holy Friday. The second and best-known is read at the sixth hour and vespers of Great and Holy Friday. The identity of the "Servant" in these prophesies is a subject of much discussion and varied opinions among biblical scholars.[106] However, for the Church, "the final identification of the Servant is with Jesus Christ, sent, suffering, triumphant."[107]

These servant poems (or "songs"[108]) provide intimate insight into what it means to serve God. In the first (Is 42.1–9), the Lord speaks about his Servant. He is chosen and supported by the Lord, and the Holy Spirit is placed upon him. The Lord delights in him! The Servant will "bring forth justice to the nations" but he will do this calmly ("not cry or lift up his voice"), peacefully ("a bruised reed he will not break"), and faithfully with perseverance ("will not fail or be discouraged"). In the second (Is 49.1–6), the Servant speaks about himself. As in the first song, the Lord calls him "from the womb." The Servant knows that the Lord has given him weapons (a "mouth like a sharp sword" and a "polished arrow"), but these weapons are hidden ("in the shadow of his hand"; "in his quiver he hid me away"), recalling the calm and peace we hear in the first song.

The third song (Is 50.4–11) reveals the trials and suffering to be endured by the Servant.[109] Isaiah here foretells the passion of Christ: "I gave my back to the smiters. . . . I hid not my face from shame and spitting." But despite the adversity, the Servant twice declares: "The Lord God helps me." In the end, the Servant will triumph over those who contend with him:

[105]Georges A. Barrois, *The Face of Christ in the Old Testament* (Crestwood, NY: St Vladimir's Seminary Press, 1974), 113.

[106]A Monk of the Eastern Church [Lev Gillet], *The Year of Grace of the Lord: A Scriptural and Liturgical Commentary on the Calendar of the Orthodox Church*, Deborah Cowan, trans. (Crestwood, NY: St Vladimir's Seminary Press, 2001 [1st ed. 1980]), 170.

[107]Barrois, *Face of Christ*, 120.

[108]Georges A. Barrois, *Scripture Readings in Orthodox Worship* (Crestwood, NY: St Vladimir's Seminary Press, 1977), 93.

[109]Barrois, *Face of Christ*, 114.

"Behold, all of them will wear out like a garment; the moth will eat them up." This faithfulness, confidence, and trust would be impossible without an intimate personal relationship between the Servant and his Lord. The Servant awakens in the morning to face the day and his mission to others "to sustain with a word those who are weary," all the while knowing that he himself will be spat upon and beaten for his efforts. Yet he is not alone with the rising sun; the Lord is there with him: "Morning by morning he wakens, he wakens my ear to hear as those who are taught."

The fourth and final song (Is 52.13–53.12) "could be entitled: 'The Passion according to Isaiah'— an evangelist rather than a prophet, wrote St Jerome."[110] In this song, the Lord announces the triumph of his Servant—although not according to the way of the world. Yes, "he shall be exalted and lifted up, and shall be very high" according to the prophecy, but lifted up in the sense of ascending the cross, as Jesus said: "'And I, when I am lifted up from the earth, will draw all men to myself.' He said this to show by what death he was to die."[111] The person of the Servant does not possess the qualities desirable to the world: good looks, popularity, pride, independence, eloquent speaking, or a good reputation. Rather, the Servant had no beauty, was despised and rejected, and not esteemed. He not only sympathized with, but also physically and emotionally bore, the sorrows of others. He was wounded for their wrongs. He was silent before his oppressors. His grave was with the wicked.

Was all this the foretelling of an unfortunate accident, or God's will? Isaiah answers: "It was the will of the Lord to bruise him; he has put him to grief; when he makes himself an offering for sin, he shall see his offspring, he shall prolong his days; the will of the Lord shall prosper in his hand; he shall see the fruit of the travail of his soul and be satisfied." These verses did not remain a prophecy forever; the image of the Servant in Isaiah was made real and tangible[112] in the person of Jesus Christ, who "came not to be served but to serve."[113]

[110]Barrois, *Scripture Readings*, 93f.
[111]Jn 12.32–33.
[112]1 Jn 1.1.
[113]Mt 20.28.

In conclusion, to serve the Lord God is, first and foremost, to share in a relationship of servant to Master, one which is not formal and distant, but intimate and face-to-face. The servant loves the Master and does what he tells him to do. His ear is always open to the voice of the Master. He serves the Master's people according to the Master's instructions. The servant is the voice and hands of the Master. He is calm, peaceful, faithful, and persevering. He suffers complaints, ingratitude, and insults from the people he serves, all in the name of the Master, "for his name's sake."[114] The servant serves at the cost of losing his own life.

KEEP THE COMMANDMENTS

Keeping a set of commandments might seem to imply nothing more than a ritualistic observance or rote repetition of prescriptive instructions. However, Moses' declaration goes far beyond that. The verb "to keep" as uttered by Moses (and translated in the Greek Septuagint as *phylassesthai*) is repeated in the New Testament numerous times. Its inherent meaning is made clear by the simple statement of Jesus: "'Blessed rather are those who hear the word of God and keep (*phylassontes*) it!'"[115] One must live the word, the commandments and statutes, and not simply hear them. St John of Kronstadt advises: "Take the trouble to spend a single day according to God's commandments, and you will see and feel for yourself how good it is to fulfill God's will, which for us is life, eternal blessedness."[116]

At Orthodox vespers, following the augmented litany, we say: "Blessed art thou, O Lord; teach (*didaxon*) me thy statutes. Blessed art thou, O Master; make me to understand (*sinetison*) thy statutes. Blessed art thou, O Holy One, enlighten (*phōtison*) me with thy statutes." During the small doxology at daily matins, we repeat the same verses.[117] The verses preceding these petitions are essentially the same for both services: we ask God

---

[114]Mt 5.11.

[115]Lk 11.28.

[116]St John of Kronstadt, *Spiritual Counsels of Father John of Kronstadt: Select Passages from My Life in Christ*, W. Jardine Grisbrooke, ed. (London: James Clarke & Co, Ltd., 1967), 204.

[117]*Holy Cross Service Book*, Kallistos G. Samaras, ed. (Brookline, MA: Holy Cross Orthodox Press, 1978), 63f, 20f.

to protect us from sin; we bless, praise, and glorify his name; we ask for his mercy and declare that we hope in him. In each petition, the Lord is the actor and we are the subjects.

- "Teach" (*didaxon*) is used widely throughout the New Testament to mean "to instruct" or impart wisdom to those who wish to learn. It is used in this sense particularly when Jesus is teaching in the synagogues.[118]

- To "understand" (*sinetison*) represents the next level of learning, distinguished from simple hearing or listening to the words of the teacher. The parable of the Sower explains: "When anyone hears the word of the kingdom and does not understand (*synientos*) it, the evil one comes and snatches away what is sown. . . . As for what was sown on good soil, this is he who hears the word and understands it."[119]

- To "enlighten" (*phōtison*) represents a higher level of learning still, namely, to be filled with the very light of God. Psalm 34, recited at the end of the Divine Liturgy, tells us to "look to him, and be radiant (*phōtisthēte*)," that is, full of light.[120] The face of Moses "shone because he had been talking with God."[121] In his commentary on 1 Thess 4:2–3, Fr Paul Tarazi states that:

> God's will for the believers is summed up in their "sanctification—ἁγιασμός (*hagiasmos*)," in their becoming saints. . . . He calls the faithful to be sanctified, i.e., to become like Him, to become divine, to be such that the people would see God's light reflected in their faces. Thus "Thy will be done on earth as it is in heaven" is a prayer that God's presence may fill the whole earth through our holiness, us the Christians.[122]

[118]Mt 13.54, Jn 7.14.
[119]Mt 13.19, 23.
[120]Ps 34.5.
[121]Ex 34.29. In the Septuagint Greek, the verb "shone" here goes even further to the meaning of "glorified" (*dedoxastai*) as is used of Christ "now is the Son of man glorified" in Jn 13.31.
[122]Paul Nadim Tarazi, *I Thessalonians: A Commentary* (Crestwood, NY: St Vladimir's Seminary Press, 1982), 136.

St Theodoros the Great Ascetic, at the beginning of his hundred spiritual texts, emphasizes the importance of keeping the Lord's commandments, since not only does our "profession demand this of us, but it is also our natural duty, for since we were originally created by God as 'very good' (Gen 1.31), we owe it to God to be such."[123] He sees this action as a normal consequence of our love for and belief in God, rather than anything special on our part. The Pharisees were proud of carrying out the Mosaic law with all its ritualistic and dietary commandments. However, for us the central commandment is given in the Shema, and all others follow from that.

According to the fathers, keeping the commandments is not optional, even for monastics who maintain contemplative prayer.[124] Prayer requires fulfillment through action, which echoes the words of St James on faith and works: "If a brother or sister is ill-clad and in lack of daily food, and one of you says to them, 'Go in peace, be warmed and filled,' without giving them the things needed for the body, what does it profit?'"[125] Archbishop Dmitri Royster, in his commentary on Romans 4.4–5, circles back to the original requirement in Deuteronomy to keep the commandments: "Our Lord had answered the question, 'What must I do to inherit eternal life' with 'thou knowest the commandments'; on hearing the claim of the man, he further advises him, 'Yet lackest thou one thing . . . sell all, and distribute to the poor' (Lk 18.18–22)."[126] The new commandment given by Jesus is "that you love one another as I have loved you."[127] We had already received the commandment to love our neighbor,[128] but Jesus clarified this by saying that we must love as he loved us, which means giving our very life for the other.

We become proficient in keeping the commandments of God precisely by keeping them—or trying to keep them. We observe when we fall short of their demands, repent of our inadequacies, and resolve to do better with God's help. St Peter of Damaskos encourages us:

[123]St Theodoros the Great Ascetic, *A Century of Spiritual Texts* 1 (*Philokalia* II, 14).
[124]Ibid., 200, 230.
[125]Jas 2.15–16.
[126]Archbishop Dmitri Royster, *Romans*, 99.
[127]Jn 15.12.
[128]Lev 19.18, Lk 10.27.

Through grace He has given all men the power to become sons of God (cf. Jn 1.12) by keeping the divine commandments. Or, rather, these commandments keep us, and are the grace of God, since without his grace, we cannot keep them. . . . Let us set to work undistractedly, as though beginning lessons at school.[129]

The forty-day lenten season in the Orthodox Church is sometimes called a school for repentance. Step by step, week by week, lessons are offered in the hymns and scriptural readings of the lenten services. These teachings draw us closer to an inner transformation within our soul, mind, and body enabling us to more readily keep the commandments of God. Each day, when we say our prayers and read the Holy Scriptures, we have the opportunity to hear God's teachings, to sit at his feet as he proclaims his word.

The Lord himself reminded us that his "yoke is easy, and [his] burden is light,"[130] if only we rely on the love that he has for us. Even after commenting on the struggle that keeping the commandments entails, St Makarios of Egypt concludes: "The fulfillment of the commandments presents no difficulty or trouble to us when it is facilitated by the love of God, and when this love relieves it of all that is burdensome."[131]

CLOSING REFLECTION

Each of us, in striving to fulfill the will of God described in the above requirements, acts within different environments: physical, emotional, mental, spiritual, etc. The parable of the sower amply demonstrates this principle in its description of the rocky ground, the thorns, the weeds, the shallow earth, and the good soil. One wishes the seed to grow into a healthy and fruitful plant, but sometimes things seem to just get in the way. The Church fathers recognized this and tempered their counsel to people at different stages of their spiritual journey.

[129]St Peter of Damaskos, *Book 1: A Treasury of Divine Knowledge*, "Introduction" (*Philokalia* III, 89).

[130]Mt 11.30.

[131]St Symeon Metaphrastis, *Paraphrase of the Homilies of St Makarios of Egypt*, "Spiritual Perfection" 1.14 (*Philokalia* III, 290).

At the same time, we cannot ignore Christ's command to be perfect as our Father in heaven is perfect, to be holy as he is holy. How do we know when we are just going through the motions versus when we are true servants of God who love him, walk in his ways, and keep his commandments? Abba Dorotheus[132] offers a useful reflection to close out our discussion on discerning the will of God.

> The Apostle commanded us to "prove what is that good, and acceptable, and perfect, will of God" (Rom 12.2), in order thereupon to act in accordance with it. What is this good will of God? To love one another, to be compassionate, to be merciful and so on; this is the *good will of God*.
>
> And what is the *acceptable will of God*? Not everyone who does something good does it in a manner acceptable to God. It may happen, for example, that someone finds an orphan, poor and good-looking; her beauty pleases him and so he takes her in and brings her up, because she is poor but also because of her beauty. This is the will of God which is *good* but not *acceptable*. It is *acceptable* when he does an act of mercy not from some human impulse, but for the sake of God who has commanded this, for the sake of the good itself, from compassion alone—and this is acceptable to God.
>
> Finally, the *perfect* will of God is when someone does an act of mercy not grudgingly, not indolently, not contemptuously, but with his whole strength and his whole will, bestowing mercy as though he himself were receiving it, and being bountiful as though he himself were receiving the bounty; then the perfect will of God is fulfilled. This is how man fulfills the good, and acceptable and perfect will of God.[133]

---

[132]Sixth-century ascetic writer and abbot in Gaza.

[133]Abba Dorotheus, *Directions on Spiritual Training* 99 (*Early Fathers from the Philokalia*, 175).

PART TWO

Strategic Leadership

In the introduction of this book, we considered the following definition of leadership:

> *Christian leadership is the conscious working together in faith and in love, in a community of brothers and sisters, to do God's will on earth as it is in heaven, and to attain to the kingdom of God, in the love of God the Father, the grace of our Lord Jesus Christ, and the communion of the Holy Spirit.*

Leadership is not a matter of exercising influence for one's own purposes. It is not about trying to attract followers or to acquire power. Rather, it is working together with others who may also be leaders in their own right. It is working towards a common goal: to do God's will. It is not leading aimlessly or distractedly, but rather leading strategically.

WHY SHOULD LEADERSHIP BE STRATEGIC?

The adjective "strategic" implies that the "leading" in question is directed towards defining and realizing a strategy to accomplish a vision or mission, systematically planned and carefully developed. The word "strategy" itself derives from the Greek *stratēgia*, which is used only once in the Bible, in Judith 5.3, with the sense of "generalship," i.e., leading an army, expedition, or campaign. Again considering the example of Moses, we see that his "campaign" for the people of Israel was at all times under the direction of the Lord God and his strategy, whether in his dealings with Pharaoh, in his gathering the people by the Red Sea, or in his taking them across the water into Sinai. His "generalship" was completely in accordance with and transparent to the Lord God: "Moses came and told the people all the words of the Lord and all the ordinances; and all the people answered with one voice, and said, 'All the words which the Lord has spoken we will do.'"[1]

Strategic leadership must have a *vision* that is greater than the individual leader. God revealed his vision to Moses, "'Come, I will send you to Pharaoh that you may bring forth my people, the sons of Israel, out of Egypt.' But Moses said to God, 'Who am I that I should go to Pharaoh, and bring the sons of Israel out of Egypt?' He said, 'But I will be with you. . . .'"[2]

Strategic leadership must recognize the inherent *weaknesses* of the leader and develop ways of compensating for those. Moses did not want to speak for God: "Oh, my Lord, I am not eloquent . . . but . . . slow of speech and of tongue. . . . Send, I pray, some other person."[3] So, God appointed Aaron to help Moses in speaking with the people.

Strategic leadership must consider *obstacles*, such as the murmurings and complaints of the people of Israel who would have rather remained as the slaves of the Egyptians than encounter the uncertainty of the exodus to the Promised Land. "They did not listen to Moses, because of their broken spirit and their cruel bondage."[4]

Strategic leadership implies discipline and proper *organization*, with everyone pulling together in community. St Clement of Rome explains:

> We must march under [God's] irreproachable orders. Let us note with what discipline, readiness and obedience those who serve under our generals carry out orders. Not everybody is a general, colonel, captain, sergeant, and so on. But "each in his own rank" carries out the orders of the emperor and his generals. The great cannot exist without the small; neither can the small exist without the great. All are linked together.[5]

---

[1]Ex 24.3.
[2]Ex 3.10–12.
[3]Ex 4.10, 13.
[4]Ex 6.9.
[5]Clement of Rome, I Clement 37 (*Early Christian Fathers*, Cyril C. Richardson, ed. [New York, NY: Macmillan, 1970], 60–61).

In addition, St Gregory Nazianzen emphasizes that there should be progression within the ranks as one gains experience, for example, "for a brave soldier to be made a captain, and a good captain to become a general, and have committed to him the conduct of the whole campaign."[6]

Strategic leadership is not for the faint-hearted, nor for the one who seeks only to advance himself or herself. Leaders have power to heal or to injure others, to create well-being or to inflict pain, to send a person home happy and ready to greet his or her family in love and peace, or unhappy and bitter, ready to strike out at a minute's impulse at spouse or child. Leadership is an awesome responsibility, of which St Gregory Nazianzen warns:

> But [even if] a man is free from vice, and has reached the greatest heights of virtue: I do not see what knowledge or power would justify him in venturing upon this office. For the guiding of man, the most variable and manifold of creatures, seems to me in very deed to be the art of arts and science of sciences.[7]

[6] St Gregory Nazianzen, *Oration* 2.5 (NPNF[2] 7:206).
[7] St Gregory Nazianzen, *Oration* 2.16 (NPNF[2] 7:208).

3

Who Are the Leaders?
Lessons from the Prophets

Who, exactly, is the leader of an organization or institution, whether it be a parish, diocese, seminary, church ministry group, or nonprofit? Is it the pastor, the president, the council or board members, the bishop, the dean, the chairperson, or perhaps the faculty? Confusion and misunderstandings arise over the question of leadership roles more frequently than one might imagine. Egos can be bruised easily, and people may be offended. People who take on what might be considered "leadership" responsibilities without being granted an "official" position are often resented. The reaction of the Pharisees to the man born blind, who spoke the truth simply and straightforwardly in defense of Jesus, is an excellent example: "They answered him, 'You were born in utter sin, and would you teach us?' And they cast him out."[1]

One might suppose that in the Church, and in many other institutions, the leadership definition would be quite simple. We have (or we think that we have) a set of well-defined hierarchies. On one hand, there are people who decide and lead, and on the other the people who obey and follow. However, in many institutions leadership responsibility is frequently delegated. The bishop delegates to the priest, who in turn delegates to parish council and individual ministry leaders. In seminaries, the governing board delegates to administration and faculty, staff, and students; in other organizations, the management committee or board delegates to individual managers and supervisors.

[1] Jn 9.34.

An example of delegation is provided by Moses' father-in-law. Following the exodus from Egypt, Moses became very tired of dealing with all the disputes arising among the people, who "stood about Moses from morning till evening."[2] His father-in-law recommended that Moses "choose able men from all the people, such as fear God, men who are trustworthy and who hate a bribe; and place such men over the people. . . . Let them judge the people at all times; every great matter they shall bring to you, but any small matter they shall decide themselves. . . ."[3] Moses listened to his father-in-law and did "all that he had said."[4]

Three lessons can be derived from this event. First, Moses chose not to keep his leadership responsibilities to himself, but shared them with others. Second, his father-in-law acted as a leader in giving Moses uninvited, straightforward, and unapologetic advice: "Listen now to my voice; I will give you counsel, and God be with you!"[5] Third, Moses acted as a true leader in listening to advice, for he "gave heed to the voice of his father-in-law"[6]

In many organizations, subordinates are very wary of recommending to superiors that they should delegate their work to others. They are reluctant even to suggest to their bosses that they might not be supermen or superwomen. However, supervisors who are true leaders will welcome good advice, especially if it comes with a well-thought-out delegation plan.

Leaders step up to assist other leaders. This is key. When Israel fought against Amalek, Moses stood at the top of the hill overlooking the battle, holding the rod in his hand. When "the people saw the hands of their lawgiver lifted up, they prevailed over the enemy in battle; but if they saw them hanging limp, they fell back."[7] Moses' arms became tired. Aaron and Hur stood on either side of him and held up his arms, so that "his hands were steady until the going down of the sun. And Joshua mowed down Amalek and his people with the edge of the sword."[8]

[2]Ex 18.13.
[3]Ex 18.21–22.
[4]Ex 18.24.
[5]Ex 18.19.
[6]Ex 18.24.
[7]St Gregory of Nyssa, *The Life of Moses* 2.149 (*Life of Moses*, 90).
[8]Ex 17.12–13.

How often do we take the time to observe our leaders, whether they be our superiors, peers, or subordinates, to see whether or not they need help? If they do, do we pitch in and assist without being asked? Sometimes the assistance we offer may not be physical, but rather emotional. Simply asking, "How are things going today?" can be uplifting and show that someone cares. And if we are able to hold up a leader's arms, as Aaron and Hur did, we have forged a connection that will last for a long time.

All of us, whether we are at the top of the organization or at the bottom, are called to become leaders in the sense of taking responsibility for the organization and its vision.[9] A story is told of three bricklayers working at the site of the construction of St Paul's Cathedral in London. The architect, Sir Christopher Wren, was inspecting the construction works when he asked each one what he was doing. The first said, "I'm laying bricks." The second one explained, "I'm building a wall." The third proudly declared, "I'm helping Sir Christopher Wren build St Paul's Cathedral." Which of these bricklayers was the leader? The third obviously saw beyond the bricks and mortar, even beyond the structural unit he was building, to perceive the edifice being erected to the glory of God. Noteworthy in this little anecdote is the kinship and partnership the third bricklayer felt with the noble architect. He was not merely following orders, but also assumed special responsibility for the straightness and strength of that wall as they built it brick by brick, and working spiritually side by side with the great man.

St Paul spoke frequently of his "fellow workers [*synergous*] in Christ Jesus."[10] The entire last chapter of the Epistle to the Romans is devoted to one thing: praising his co-workers. He knew that he could not accomplish his apostolic task alone. He depended on many others to help him and mentions over twenty individuals by name, as well as their families. "St John Chrysostom . . . laments the fact that lists of names such as this (in vv. 3–15 and 21–23) are passed over quickly and without much attention by many readers, 'For it is possible even from bare names to find a great

[9]Despite this broad responsibility of leadership, specific leaders who exercise authority in the sense of "ruling," "presiding," or "governing" must exist; cf. St Gregory Nazianzen's comment that it is "wrong and disorderly that all should wish to rule, and that no one should accept [that rule]" (St Gregory Nazianzen, *Oration* 2.4 [NPNF² 7:205]).

[10]Rom 16.3.

treasure.'"[11] Martyrs, deaconesses, fellow prisoners, future bishops, men and women, all labored together with St Paul. According to Archbishop Dmitri Royster, among them were twenty-five of the seventy apostles appointed by Christ who had preceded him in his journeys from town to town, "as lambs in the midst of wolves," healing the sick and proclaiming the kingdom. It is noteworthy that Jesus identified these fellow workers completely with himself: "He who hears you hears me, and he who rejects you rejects me."[12]

In the secular world, one's background, position, and title are often the critical determinants of whether or not one is viewed as a leader. From the Christian perspective, little of this matters. The Prophet Isaiah was a self-described "man of unclean lips."[13] The Prophet Amos was "a herdsman, and a dresser of sycamore trees."[14] The Prophet Jeremiah was "only a youth."[15] St Paul "persecuted the church of God" and "this Way" to the death.[16]

In fact, the gift of prophecy is given to the most unlikely and varied of characters. Comparing the disparate backgrounds of two great prophets, Georges Barrois writes: "Isaiah was an aristocrat, at ease at the court and among the peers of the gentry . . . [while] Amos was an uncouth shepherd and migrant farm laborer."[17] However, the prophets shared one characteristic in common: they experienced an encounter with God so overwhelming as to grant extraordinary powers of speech and courage.

In Isaiah's case, he had a vision of the Lord God enthroned in the midst of the six-winged seraphim, who sang the thrice-holy song of praise to the Lord of hosts. Smoke filled the Lord's temple, and the foundations shook with the voice of the seraphim. Isaiah was awestruck and terrified, and immediately confessed his unworthiness: "Woe is me! For I am lost; for I am a man of unclean lips, and I dwell in the midst of a people of unclean

---

[11] Archbishop Dmitri, *Romans*, 389.
[12] Lk 10.16.
[13] Is 6.5.
[14] Am 7.14.
[15] Jer 1.6.
[16] 1 Cor 15.9; Acts 22.4.
[17] Barrois, *Face of Christ*, 106.

lips; for my eyes have seen the King, the Lord of hosts!"[18] The account then relates how a seraphim touched Isaiah's mouth with a fiery coal from the altar, pronouncing the same words now pronounced during the Divine Liturgy by the priest after taking communion: "Behold, this has touched your lips; your guilt is taken away, and your sin forgiven."[19]

But for this leader the story does not end there, for he did not "depart in peace" and go back to his home. He "heard the voice of the Lord saying, 'Whom shall I send, and who will go for us?' . . . [Isaiah responds] 'Here am I! Send me.'"[20] This "noble man," as St Jerome described him, "of urbane elegance, without the slightest tinge of rusticity in his discourse" became a prophet whose "early prophetic utterance are," according to Barrois, "oracles of woe, denouncing the social disorders which threatened the kingdom of Judah . . . when the rich grew richer and the poor poorer, when the leadership was failing or corrupt, the priests greedy and arrogant."[21]

Amos, on the other hand, was a simple shepherd and seasonal orchard laborer. The latter work involved pricking the skin of the fruit of sycamore trees to foster growth.[22] When confronted by a demand by the priest Amaziah that he leave Israel because of his damning prophecy against King Jeroboam, Amos declares that he is "no prophet, nor a prophet's son." Rather, he is a "herdsman, and a dresser of sycamore trees" taken by the Lord "from following the flock" and told by the Lord himself to prophesy.[23] Amos' humble background starkly differentiates him from that of the professional prophets who "were the yes-men of government circles, encouraged and granted an official status . . . [who] made it their business to tell the ordinary citizens the 'smooth things' they delighted to hear," according to Old Testament scholar Eric William Heaton.[24] It is a great temptation to be a yes-man, to tell superiors what they want—or what we think they want—to hear. It takes the courage of an Amos to act differently.

[18]Is 6.5.

[19]Is 6.6.

[20]Is 6.8.

[21]Barrois, *Face of Christ*, 105f.

[22]Philip J. King, *The Jerome Biblical Commentary*, Raymond E. Brown, Joseph A. Fitzmyer, and Roland E. Murphy, eds. (Englewood Cliffs, NJ: Prentice-Hall, Inc., 1968), 251.

[23]Am 7.14–15.

[24]E. W. Heaton, *The Old Testament Prophets* (Baltimore, MD: Penguin Books, 1961), 37.

The Lord speaks to Amos directly, as "the Lord used to speak to Moses face to face, as a man speaks to his friend."[25] Amos is able to be a leader and even to persuade the Lord to change his mind. This is an amazing icon of how the subordinate can lead the superior. Amos sees "the Lord standing beside the altar."[26] The Lord shows him the locusts and the fire of judgment, to be visited upon Israel. Amos intercedes for Jacob and begs God for forgiveness. And the Lord changes his mind ("repented") and says, "It shall not be."[27]

Jeremiah was a young man when he received his call from the Lord, and therefore felt unprepared to assume responsibility.[28] He objects to the call, despite the direct and intense four-fold declaration of the Lord: "I formed you . . . I knew you . . . I consecrated you . . . I appointed you a prophet to the nations."[29] His demurral is similar to that of many of us when we are called upon to assume responsibility: "Ah, Lord God! Behold, I do not know how to speak, for I am only a youth."[30] The Lord does not accept this excuse:

> "Do not say, 'I am only a youth'; for to all to whom I will send you, you shall go, and whatever I command you you shall speak. Be not afraid of them, for I am with you to deliver you," says the Lord. Then the Lord put forth his hand and touched my mouth; and the Lord said to me, "Behold, I have put my words in your mouth."[31]

The latter dialogue and action is reminiscent of the ordination of an Orthodox deacon or priest. The ordaining bishop lays his hand upon the candidate and says,

> The grace divine, which always heals that which is infirm, and completes that which is wanting, elevates through the laying on of hands [name] the most devout subdeacon/deacon to be a deacon/priest.

[25]Ex 33.11.
[26]Am 9.1.
[27]Am 7.3.
[28]Couturier, *Jerome Biblical Commentary*, 305.
[29]Jer 1.5.
[30]Jer 1.6.
[31]Jer 1.7–9.

Wherefore let us pray for him, that the grace of the all-holy Spirit may come upon him.[32]

The key here is that all of us are wanting and in need of God's mercy and grace. As the Lord said to Paul: "'My grace is sufficient for you, for my power is made perfect in weakness.'"[33] St Paul took this promise to its ultimate conclusion: "I will all the more gladly boast of my weaknesses, that the power of Christ may rest upon me. For the sake of Christ, then, I am content with weaknesses, insults, hardships, persecutions, and calamities; for when I am weak, then I am strong."[34]

St Paul surely earned the award for the most unlikely Christian leader and follower of the Way. He was a zealous and strict Pharisee, likely in training to become a rabbi.[35] He admits in his own words: "I persecuted this Way to the death. . . . I punished them often in the synagogues . . . and in raging fury against them, I persecuted them even to foreign cities."[36] Paul's response to the great sermon of the deacon Stephen, whose "face was like that of an angel" while being judged by the council,[37] was to hold the clothes of those who stoned Stephen and consent to his death.[38] He continued to ravage the church, "breathing threats and murder against the disciples of the Lord."[39] His demeanor was not only one of anger, but also cold hostility and malice against the Way. He devised a plan to obtain letters to synagogues in Damascus in order to find disciples and arrest them.

What could possibly turn such a person around and make him one of the foremost apostles of Christ? Neither intellectual persuasion, nor emotional appeal, nor threat of punishment, nor promise of reward, but simply the encounter with God.

[32]Hapgood, *Service Book*, 312, 316.
[33]2 Cor 12.9.
[34]1 Cor 12.9–10.
[35]Joseph A. Fitzmyer, *Jerome Biblical Commentary*, 217.
[36]Acts 22.4, 26.11.
[37]Acts 6.15.
[38]Acts 8.1.
[39]Acts 9.1.

Jesus Christ appeared to Paul in a blinding flash of light, as the Lord God appeared to Moses in the burning bush. A voice addressed him, and Paul immediately called out, "Who are you, Lord?"[40] The Lord had a special mission for Paul: "He is a chosen instrument of mine to carry my name before the Gentiles and kings and the sons of Israel; for I will show him how much he must suffer for the sake of my name."[41] In the same manner as the prophets already mentioned here, Paul was chosen, taken out of his previous life to become a spokesman for God, to turn the hearts of the people to God and away from sin and evil. But in this case, Paul was specifically called to suffer for Christ, and to take up that same cross that Christ ascended. The promises to the people of Israel in the Old Testament are fulfilled in the New, but in a way unanticipated by many. The promise to the people in the New Testament is the coming of the kingdom: through Christ and his ultimate resurrection, but first via the cross. "Through the cross is joy come into all the world" as we sing at matins.[42]

Each of the above leaders—Isaiah, Amos, Jeremiah, and Paul—displayed characteristic reactions to an encounter with God: surprise at being chosen, and at finding themselves able, despite their disparate backgrounds, to speak God's word. According to St Paul, the grace of God "was given to each of us. . . . [So] that some should be apostles, some prophets . . . some pastors and teachers."[43]

Leadership, from a Christian perspective, means first and foremost an honest opening of ourselves to God: hearing his voice whatever the situation in which we find ourselves, and then responding to that voice in obedience and faith, in openness and courage, ready to do his will, whoever and wherever we are. Without this foundation, without the love of God as our cornerstone, leadership becomes, to borrow the words of St Paul, "a noisy gong and clanging cymbal."[44]

[40] Acts 9.5.
[41] Acts 9.15–16.
[42] Hapgood, *Service Book*, 31.
[43] Eph 4.7, 11.
[44] 1 Cor 13.1.

4

Foundations of Christian Leadership: Six Goals

M any secular systems exist for analyzing leadership character-istics, and some may be of interest to those who are trying to better understand their personal leadership styles.[1] These systems usually address outward aspects of behavior, however, and may not have the internally transformative power to enable the true leader to lead in every situation, whether favorable or unfavorable. The Christian understanding of leadership has as its foundation the person of Christ.

St Paul declares the newness of the person in Christ: "If anyone is in Christ, he is a new creation; the old has passed away, behold, the new has come."[2] To be in Christ, to have the root of our being in him, is a radical new beginning, a restart of our life, a cataclysmic change, a "transition, a great change . . . from sins and impieties . . . to a life of virtue."[3] Our outward behavior is changed, but more importantly, we are intimately reconnected with God. We become like Adam in the garden, for, in the words of Alexander Bogolepov, "the ultimate goal of man's re-creation is to lead him back to his original condition, 'to restore the lost image of God.'"[4]

---

[1]See especially Douglas McGregor, *The Human Side of Enterprise* (New York: McGraw-Hill, 1960) and Daniel Goleman, "What Makes a Leader?" *Harvard Business Review* (November/December 1998) and *Emotional Intelligence* (New York, NY: Bantam Books, 1997).

[2]2 Cor 5.17.

[3]St John Chrysostom, Homily 11.4 on 2 Corinthians (NPNF[1] 12:583 [amended by the author]). Chrysostom is commenting on 2 Cor 5.17 ("Therefore if any one is in Christ, he is a new creation; the old has passed away, behold, the new has come").

[4]Alexander A. Bogolepov, *Orthodox Hymns of Christmas, Holy Week, and Easter* (New York, NY: Russian Orthodox Theological Fund, Inc., 1965), 16.

It is to begin again, fresh and new, to see the glory of God present in his renewed creation, and to give thanks for it.[5] A radical and life-changing transformation takes place, relative to God, mankind, and the world. We see things completely differently from before, and we have the power to act accordingly.

In baptism, we clothe ourselves with Christ: "As many as have been baptized into Christ, have put on Christ."[6] The "clothes" referred to here are not mere outward coverings, as though we were coat hangers or mannequins performing a masquerade. Rather, they incarnate and bring into reality a transformation of our personhood, in the new creation. Nicholas Cabasilas reminds us that St Paul "at one time . . . speaks of Christ being engraved and formed on Christians, at other times being wrapped around them like a garment."[7] When putting on their vestments before celebrating the Divine Liturgy, the clergy of the Orthodox Church recite verses from the psalms and the prophets to remind them that their bodies are no longer their own, but members of Christ. As an example, when placing the cuffs on their wrists, they say: "Thy right hand, O Lord, is glorified in power. . . . Thy hands have made and fashioned me. Give me understanding that I may learn thy commandments."[8] As we walk through each day, we must remind ourselves that "it is no longer I who live, but Christ who lives in me."[9]

The true foundation of Christian leadership is Christ. To be a Christian leader is, first, to be renewed in Christ, to strip away old baggage and clothe oneself with him. The following sections of this chapter reflect upon six leadership goals, or building stones, that stem from this foundational renewal in Christ. The cornerstone of one's efforts is Christ and his kingdom; nothing can be built without that rock. A second and a third foundation stone is also needed: an unflinching and brutally frank knowledge

[5]See Alexander Schmemann, *Of Water and the Spirit* (Crestwood, NY: St Vladimir's Seminary Press, 1974), 47.

[6]Gal 3.27.

[7]Nicholas Cabasilas, *The Life in Christ* (Crestwood, NY: St Vladimir's Seminary Press, 1974), 67.

[8]*Divine Liturgy*, 8f; Ex 15.6; Ps 119.73.

[9]Gal 2.20.

of oneself, and an unceasing and intensely focused love for others. We need to connect ourselves to others. Our relationship bridge with others is built upon the final three stones of humility, service, and steadfastness. These qualities allow us to be transparent to Christ so that his humility, service, and steadfast love, even to death on the cross, shine through us to others. We will reflect on these six foundational leadership goals in the rest of this chapter.

FIRST GOAL: CHRIST AND HIS KINGDOM

The Christian leader has the number one goal of seeking God's will and his kingdom. "Seek first his kingdom and his righteousness"[10] was the advice of the Lord when confronted by the people's worries concerning the clothes they would wear, what they would eat, and the everyday cares of this life. There can be no other starting point nor ending point, not even the success of the parish, diocese, seminary, or organization in material terms, nor in supposedly spiritual terms, such as the number of services or people, the size of the sanctuary, the beauty of the temple, etc. We begin and end with Jesus Christ and his kingdom. St Seraphim of Sarov emphasized this focus on the "one thing necessary" in his plea to his disciple Motovilov: "Always ask yourself: Am I in the Spirit of God or not?" Nothing else matters at that point, only Christ and his Holy Spirit. In other words, without Christ "all is vanity."[11]

The clear and unmistakable message of Jesus is to place God first in one's life, even to the extent of loving God more than our family. "He who loves father or mother more than me is not worthy of me; and he who loves son or daughter more than me is not worthy of me; and he who does not take up his cross and follow me is not worthy of me."[12] For many, this is a shocking statement that makes it sound almost as if God is jealous of the love we have for others. However, if we are honest with ourselves, we know that our love for our spouses, our children, and our family is weak. We know this to be true the moment they oppose us, fail to do what we

[10]Mt 6.33.
[11]Eccl 1.2.
[12]Mt 10.37–38.

want them to do, or perhaps do not treat us with the respect we think is due to us. Then we become irritated, sulky, and perhaps angry, and the feeling of love disappears. It is only through the love of God, as foundation and source of our love for others, that we can be dispassionate, patient, and truly loving and caring, despite all the obstacles and difficulties that we face every day.

St Paul goes further in his desire for God: "I count everything as loss because of the surpassing worth of knowing Christ. . . . For his sake I have suffered the loss of all things, and count them as refuse, in order that I may gain Christ."[13] What is required of us is to place God first and all other things second without exception, whether they be family, career, knowledge, anything. This is admittedly not an easy task. Eve found it quite difficult to refuse the blandishments of the serpent when he offered her the fruit of the tree, which "was good for food . . . a delight to the eyes . . . to be desired to make one wise."[14] The only trouble was that the Lord God told them not to eat the fruit from that tree. Eve did not fear God. She did not respect his wishes. She did not place God first. She was tempted, and yielded to that temptation. The counterexample is Abraham's obedience to God. Abraham is counted as the father of many nations because of his faith—a superabundant faith sufficient not only for him to obey God, but to be willing to sacrifice his only son. These hard sayings[15] point to the necessity, for those of us who call ourselves Christian leaders, to place God first in our lives not only in words but also in deeds.

For many Christian leaders, this perspective may represent a radical change in the way we view our daily responsibilities. It forces us to go back to the beginning, back to basics. Such an overwhelming love for and unwavering commitment to Christ is how many of us began our Christian life, perhaps as idealistic young people who were caught up in a vision of Christ and love for him and his Church.

So often, however, these motivations become lower priority for a variety of reasons. Everyday responsibilities and stresses, including putting

[13]Phil 3.8.
[14]Gen 3.6.
[15]Cf. Jn 6.60.

food on the table for the family, can overwhelm a person. Some of us may so enjoy the respect, even adulation, that we have as priests, bishops, teachers, supervisors, or managers, that we are be tempted to look not to Christ but at ourselves. There are some in the Church for whom a leadership position is simply a job. The striving for the kingdom can become a saying to mouth, parroting the words of the gospel or the fathers, without fundamental belief within one's heart. This is a far more dangerous situation, in which our striving becomes a robot-like exercise in external piety and speech.

The first prayer said every morning by an observant Jew is the Modeh Ani, which offers thanksgiving for the continued gift of life from God, that God has returned his soul to him. The first prayer for the Orthodox Christian is "in the name of the Father, and the Son, and the Holy Spirit," which declares our commitment that everything we do, think, and feel this day will be in God's name. We then call down the Holy Spirit to abide in us, that we may be granted God's grace to do what we must do in his name. We beg the Holy Trinity to have mercy on us, to wash away our sins, to pardon our transgressions, and to visit and heal our infirmities, all for God's sake. We pray the Lord's Prayer, declaring our willingness to do God's will—not at some future time or place, but here and now. These words are not our words; we did not make them up. They are the words of the Church, God's words, placed in our mouth as the Lord God placed words in Jeremiah's mouth.[16]

Once we have heard the word of the Lord, we cannot act as if it had not been said, nor as if we did not hear it. According to Metropolitan Philaret of Moscow,[17]

> The creative word is like an adamantine bridge upon which creatures are placed, and they stand under the abyss of the Divine Infinite, over the abyss of their own nothingness . . . because the word of God must not be imagined as like the spoken word of man, which, when it has been pronounced, straightway desists and vanishes in air. In God there

---

[16]Jer 1.9.
[17]Nineteenth-century bishop of Moscow and saint of the Orthodox Church.

is nothing of cessation, nothing of vanishing. His word proceeds but does not recede: *the word of the Lord endureth forever* (1 Pet 1.25).[18]

The word of God stands as help, but also as judge. Those of us who are Christian leaders need to take care that we do not hear these words of Christ spoken to us: "If you were blind, you would have no guilt; but now that you say, 'We see,' your guilt remains."[19]

Jesus himself points to the structural relationship between us and him: "I am the vine, you are the branches."[20] Everything in our life, including our relationship to others and our leadership responsibilities in the Church and other institutions, must be centered in Christ. It can be nothing else. This means that every decision, every action, every word, must be referred constantly and without fail to Christ and his gospel. This point cannot be emphasized enough: without a primary focus on Christ, all else is doomed to fail, perhaps not in the eyes of the world, but certainly in the eyes of God.

SECOND GOAL:
EXAMINE AND REDISCOVER OUR VALUES

The second goal of Christian strategic leadership is akin to the examination of conscience that every Orthodox Christian is supposed to undertake prior to going to the priest for confession.[21] It is not an automatic exercise, but rather a true soul-searching that plumbs the depths of our entire relationship with God. It asks the question: "What are my values as a Christian, and more specifically as a leader in Christ's Church?" It is too simple to answer, "Why, it's self-evident that my values are the same as Christ and the Church. I am a believer. What more do I have to say?"

We all take our status as Christians for granted sometimes. We assume that we love God and follow Christ. We assume that our values are the

[18]Quoted in Georges Florovsky, *Creation and Redemption* (Belmont, MA: Nordland Publishing Company, 1976), 45.

[19]Jn 9.41.

[20]Jn 15.5.

[21]This is analogous to the analysis of our strengths and weaknesses in the strategic plan, to be discussed in Part Four.

same as his. But when we look deep inside and honestly examine the values that govern our daily lives, activities, and relationship with others, we may come to a different conclusion.

The life of St Herman of Alaska includes a wonderful account of a conversation between the saint and the captain and officers of a vessel from St Petersburg. He asked the question, "Should we not love God above all else, desire him more than anything, and search him out?" They all replied, "Why yes, that's self-evident!" St Herman went on to say that in fact we do not love God in the way that we should, remembering him at all hours of the day, trying to please him and to obey his commandments. The officers admitted that they did not do these things. St Herman then said these famous words: "Let us from this day forth, from this hour, from this minute, love God above all and fulfill his holy will!"

St Herman recognized how easily people can delude themselves into thinking they are one with God while in fact acting quite differently. The only way that we can be in tune with God is to reestablish that connection with him each day, each hour, each minute. It becomes all too easy for us to let each day slip into the next without self-examination. And once we are out of tune with God, it becomes very easy to be out of tune with others, especially the ones whom we love and who love us.

We know that we need to set priorities. Yet far too often, the urgency of the moment takes precedence over the truly important things in our lives. We need only bring to mind the familiar sight of the family breadwinner who plunges endlessly into work, neglecting the physical and emotional aspects of family relationships. Similarly, the priest of a church may have so many activities, including services, that he has no time for the people who really need his pastoral attention. In fact, he may not even know who those in need are, since he has not made time to get to know them. The values that we imprint in our minds and hearts govern our behavior, especially in such conflict situations.

St Gregory Nazianzen reflects on the need for a Christian leader to constantly and objectively review the state of his soul and never be satisfied. He must continuously examine what the Lord wishes from him and strive unceasingly for that.

He should know no limits in goodness or spiritual progress, and should dwell upon the loss of what is still beyond him, rather than the gain of what he has attained, and consider that which is beneath his feet a step to that which comes next: and not think it a great gain to excel ordinary people, but a loss to fall short of what we ought to be: and to measure his success by the commandment and not by his neighbors.[22]

As Christians, we know that we were created in the image and likeness of God. We know that our true home is with God. We were created to love God and care for others, according to God's commandments. However, it is rare for us to pause and consider our path in life and whether we are on the right loving and caring road. Often, we simply proceed from day to day, taking life as it comes.

At times, however, we wonder whether this life is all it seems to be. This questioning can be a frightening event. Perhaps we've experienced a tragedy within the family, such as the death of a close relative or a parent. Such moments are especially painful if we are young. We ask ourselves if this life is all there is. Sometimes we are forced to recognize the person we have become, and are not happy about what we see. We may have deeply offended someone we love, perhaps inadvertently but seemingly almost beyond our powers to have avoided that offense. We ask ourselves, "Why do I always do that?"

Sometimes the soul-searching that follows such events takes years to complete. It may never be finished. St Mary of Egypt, who lived a dissolute life in fourth-century Alexandria, experienced this when she attempted to enter the Church of the Holy Sepulchre in Jerusalem. She was held back by an invisible force emanating from the icon of the most pure Mother of God. She spent the next forty years of her life in self-searching in the desert.

Asking critical and fundamental questions and attempting to find the answers will be extremely difficult. St Isaac the Syrian maintained that to really know oneself as one really is, is a greater act than raising the dead.[23]

---

[22]St Gregory Nazianzen, *Oration* 2.14 (NPNF[2] 7:208).
[23]Cf *Ascetical Homilies*, Homily 68.

Abba Evagrius the Monk[24] posited self-knowledge as a condition for divine knowledge: "Do you wish to know God? Learn first to know yourself."[25]

How can we know ourselves? We can seek counsel of others, people who have insight and wisdom and whom we trust to tell us the truth. The very act of asking advice breaks down the barriers which separate us from others, exposing the hidden things of which even we are not aware. But sharing our thoughts, fears, and desires with those closest to us is not easy. In the Orthodox Church, the priest, who serves as father confessor, can fulfill this role of spiritual physician. Discussing this role, St Gregory Nazianzen notes the resistance that many offer to the diagnosis and the healing process.

> Human prudence and selfishness, and the want of training and incli-
> nation to yield ready submission are a very great obstacle to advance
> in virtue, amounting almost to an armed resistance to those who are
> wishful to help us. And the very eagerness with which we should lay
> bare our sickness to our spiritual physicians, we employ in avoiding this
> treatment, and shew our bravery by struggling against what is for our
> own interest, our skill in shunning what is for our health.[26]

Sometimes there are good friends who have been through the same experiences. St Mark the Ascetic[27] advises that one "should also question other servants of God who are of the same mind and engaged in the same ascetic struggle, so that he does not travel in the dark without a light, not knowing how or where to walk."[28]

Many years ago, I heard a story about a farmer who attended church with his wife. When she died, he stopped coming to church. His pastor noticed this and went to visit him at his home. The man was a laconic New Englander who did not say much to anyone. It was winter. The two men sat together quietly on the couch in front of a blazing fire in the fireplace, just

---

[24]Fourth-century monastic writer.

[25]Abba Evagrius the Monk, *Miscellaneous Sayings from Various Texts* 3 (*Early Fathers from the Philokalia*, 109).

[26]St Gregory Nazianzen, *Oration* 2.19 (NPNF[2] 7:209).

[27]Fifth-century Egyptian monk.

[28]St Mark the Ascetic, *Letter to Nicolas the Solitary* (*Philokalia* I, 151).

looking at the flaming logs. The pastor stood up, took the tongs, and separated one flaming piece of wood from the others. He then put it to one side and retook his seat. They continued looking at the fire, and especially at that one piece of wood. Little by little, the separated ember turned from blazing red to cold, dark gray. The pastor rose, took the tongs, and put the ember back in the fire with the rest of the logs. The ember immediately blazed up. The farmer turned to the pastor and said, "I'll see you in church Sunday."

And that's a good segue to our next goal.

THIRD GOAL:
FOCUS ON, CARE FOR, AND LOVE OTHERS

The third goal of strategic leadership is to see each person as a child of God for us to focus on, care for, and love. This act is a tremendous spiritual exercise that takes all of one's powers, attention, and discipline. To focus on others means to recognize them as of ultimate importance to God and hence of ultimate importance to oneself. Each person is to be seen as a child of God not just theoretically, but with intensity of feeling, as St Paul says in Philippians 4.1: "My brethren, whom I love and long for, my joy and crown."

We often hear the verb "to love" spoken in a "churchy" way, since love is expected of Christians, but sometimes it can become a hollow word. Note how St Paul adds the words "to long for." To long for someone means to keep that person in our hearts and minds constantly, returning again and again in our thoughts to that person and aching in our hearts until we see him or her again. St Paul's feelings were echoed by St Seraphim of Sarov, who greeted everyone he met with the salutation: "Christ is risen, my joy!" What purity of heart, what humility, what grace is required to see everyone we meet as "my joy"! Yet this is the desire of the Christian leader who loves those whom he serves.

This feeling for and relationship to others is clearly a gift of God; it does not happen spontaneously unless we become a "little child" again. This joy was at the center of the life of Fr Alexander Schmemann, who again and again saw this joy as light reflected in the faces of others and in nature's quiet splendor, but most especially in the liturgy and the celebration of the Eucharist.

The pages of his journal, however, illustrate the struggle he went through to realize and rediscover that joy while in the midst of his responsibilities as the dean of St Vladimir's Seminary and a leader in the Church.[29] How difficult it must have been for Fr Alexander to receive yet another group of seminary students year after year with all their attendant problems, issues, and spiritual baggage, and to concentrate on, focus on, and care for them. Yet the Christian leader is called to do just this. It is part of the responsibility we shoulder yet easily forget in the endless whirl of chores, meetings, deadlines, and other concerns. As Jesus said to Martha: "You are anxious and troubled about many things; one thing is needful."[30]

Our ego frequently gets in the way of the need to focus on others. As a result, our person-to-person relationships and group communications are adversely impacted. We often seek to assert ourselves at the expense of hearing others. We want at minimum to be well-thought of, and at best praised for our qualities, whatever we believe them to be. These inner motivations build a wall between us and others.

To truly hear others without immediately exerting pressure on them to adopt our (often pre-formulated) solutions to their problems is extraordinarily difficult. It requires patience to refrain from telling others what they should do. It also demands that we be willing to accept the fact that they may know more than we do, especially with regard to their own feelings, motivations, fears, and hopes. The author of *Unseen Warfare* offers the advice that "one should never trust oneself in anything."[31] This counsel is applicable not only to our own decisions but doubly so to any advice that we may offer to other people. The Lord Jesus Christ reserved some of his most powerful rhetoric for the "blind guides"[32] who cared not for the people, but rather for themselves—for outward appearance, praise, and glory.

[29]Alexander Schmemann, *The Journals of Father Alexander Schmemann 1973–1983* (Crestwood, NY: St Vladimir's Seminary Press, 2000).
[30]Lk 10.41–42.
[31]*Unseen Warfare*, 81.
[32]Mt 23.24.

Assuming that we are working to free ourselves from egotism and self-assertion in dealing with others, how should we then proceed as leaders in our duty to focus on, care for, and love others? St Gregory Nazianzen emphasizes the need to discover and understand the inner foundation of the other. Everyone has "baggage," which in St Gregory's words is like a wax seal that has been imprinted by past experiences. With some, the seal is fresh and smooth; for others, it is rough and bears the marks of struggles. We cannot understand another through a simple question-and-answer session, nor can we hope to know someone's inner feelings without a heartfelt desire to do so for the single purpose of loving that other person. Perhaps we can help them, perhaps they can help us. In helping others, many times we help ourselves.

There are times when we explicitly know that others need help. We see that they are struggling, that they need a friend, that they need some form of guidance. St Paul declares that we should "become all things to all men, that [we] might by all means save some."[33] The Christian leader cares for others as a physician cares for his or her patients. The physician attempts every treatment to cure the patient's maladies and diseases, and does not give up until the end. The Christian leader does not try only one approach to serving others, but is flexible and knowledgeable about those he or she serves so "by all means to save some." St Gregory Nazianzen extends the comparison with the physician of bodies to the physician of souls.

> I allege that our office as physicians far exceeds in toilsomeness, and
> consequently in worth, that which is confined to the body; and further,
> because the latter is mainly concerned with the surface, and only in a
> slight degree investigates the causes which are deeply hidden. But the
> whole of our treatment and exertion is concerned with the hidden man
> of the heart, and our warfare is directed against that adversary and foe
> within us.[34]

Are we as leaders really called to be spiritual physicians? This may seem far-fetched. However, we have all had the experience of someone saying,

[33]1 Cor 9.22.
[34]St Gregory Nazianzen, *Oration* 2.21 (NPNF[2] 7:209).

"You made my day," after we did something kind or said something complimentary. Was the other person just being polite, or did he or she mean it? I think the words are sincere, because we recognized the person, we cared for him or her, we touched the "hidden heart." In some way the other received a gift of healing, and all because we loved that person.

FOURTH GOAL: BE HUMBLE

The fourth goal of strategic leadership is the absolute requirement to be humble. To be humble is a fundamental attitude and a deep foundation of one's soul. St Paul describes Christ as having "emptied himself" (*eauton ekenōsen*).[35] According to one ancient commentator, this "consists not in any loss or privation of his power, but in the fact that he lowered himself to the basest level and condescended to the meanest tasks."[36] A critical question that the Christian leader needs to ask himself is whether he is capable of being like Christ in this ultimate sense, or whether "lowering and condescending" is too difficult for him or, to put it more frankly, "beneath him."

The transition to this objective of "emptying oneself" may be easier if we reflect on the King James translation of Phil 2.7, which reads "he made himself of no reputation." A former president of an American Baptist seminary made this action of Christ the central point of his reflection on his five-year tenure:

> In reflecting on these past five years, I have come to believe that true Christian leadership is an ongoing, disciplined practice of becoming a person of no reputation, and thus, becoming more like Christ in this unique way. In his reflections on Christian leadership, Henri Nouwen refers to this as resisting the temptation to be relevant. He says, "I am deeply convinced that the Christian leader of the future is called to be completely irrelevant and to stand in this world with nothing to offer but his or her own vulnerable self."[37]

[35]Phil 2.7.

[36]Marius Victorinus ("Amrosiaster"), *Epistle to the Philippians* 2.8.1 (*Ancient Christian Commentary* VIII, 243).

[37]R. Scott Rodin, "Becoming a Leader of No Reputation," *Journal of Religious Leadership* 1.2 (2002): 105–119.

The above quote from Henri Nouwen is taken from a remarkable book entitled *In the Name of Jesus: Reflections on Christian Leadership*. It provides, in part, an in-depth reflection on the three temptations of Christ as expressed in those of Christian leaders: the temptation to be relevant, the temptation to be spectacular, and the temptation to be powerful.[38] Nouwen was a brilliant scholar with twenty years at Notre Dame, Yale, and Harvard, but then he was called to minister to a small community of handicapped people who cared little about his past, his positions, or his titles. They cared only about him as a person. The more vulnerable he became, "of no reputation," the more that he was able to care for and love others in his ministry—and the more he learned about himself.

Many of us first become leaders in school or professional life. We are taught to guard our reputation and our good name. But when we try to become leaders using Christ's servant example, the need for a good reputation is a hindrance. We care what people think about us. We emphasize our good qualities. We get irritated or perhaps angry when others belittle us, or fail to recognize us for the good people that we are. These personal and usually unconscious reactions erect a barrier between us and the ones we hope to serve. These walls can only be demolished—or at least lowered— by our consciously becoming persons "of no reputation" who frankly do not care what others think of us. Such leaders do care what others think, but not about themselves. Otherwise, any time someone opposes them the barriers go up, and every previous effort is of no use.

To be humble, paradoxically, enables us to be courageous. Sometimes, when faced with an ethical issue, we might ask ourselves, "Should I speak out or not?" We may not say anything because we are afraid of offending someone, or worried that others will think less of us—or worse, that "higher-ups" might become angry or annoyed. If we do not care about our reputation, then we are free to say what we want to say, since reactions of others will not concern us.

But isn't it important to have a reputation if we want others to listen to us (since, presumably, we have something to offer)? Reputation is a

[38]Henri J. M. Nouwen, *In the Name of Jesus: Reflections on Christian Leadership* (New York, NY: Crossword Publishing, 1989).

two-edged sword. Reputation is undeniably important in this fallen world if we want people to hear us. Unfortunately, someone who lacks an important-sounding title or credentials will often not be taken seriously. However, reputation can kill our moral resolve if we try to preserve it. Fear of damaging our precious reputation can make us afraid to speak the truth openly and courageously . As Jesus said, "whoever loses his life for my sake will find it."[39]

Can we find an instance in the Gospels in which Jesus takes care to protect his reputation? How irrelevant for the world is the sight of Jesus hanging dead upon the cross? What does he say to those who want stones turned into bread, who wish to be relevant to the needs of the world as they see them? In response to the devil's temptation, he says, "Man shall not live by bread alone, but by every word that proceeds from the mouth of God."[40]

St Paul understood this very well. He said that we Christians must be the refuse, the castoffs, the scum and garbage of the world. As Jesus' disciples complained elsewhere, "This is a hard saying. Who can listen to it?"[41] This is clearly one of those things that are impossible with men, but made possible with God's grace—the grace of the One who shed the glory he had with the Father, and was made sin and death for us. We must become transparent to God. Those whom we serve must see Christ himself through us. In the words of John the Baptist: "He must increase, but I must decrease."[42]

Fr Paul Tarazi, a retired professor of Old Testament at St Vladimir's Seminary, puts the question of reputation quite simply and bluntly. He is fondly quoted by his students as offering the following advice: "When you awake every morning, I want you to go into the bathroom, stand in front of the mirror, look at yourself, and say 'I am not a big deal.'"

[39]Mt 16.25.
[40]Mt 4.4.
[41]Jn 6.60.
[42]Jn 3.30.

The Fathers stress that humility is the most important virtue, one without which no other virtue is possible. St Abba Dorotheus quotes a certain staretz,[43] who said, "Above all we need humility."

> Why did he say this? Why did he not say that above all we need self-mastery ... the fear of God ... mercy or faith? ... He shows us by this that neither fear of God, nor mercy, nor faith nor self-mastery, nor any other virtue can be achieved without humility.

Abba Dorotheus continues: "Humility attracts God's grace to the soul ... [and] delivers the soul from every passion and temptation." Humility rejects the common temptation to blame others for problems and, conversely, lays the blame upon oneself. Thus, the humble man "endures everything that may befall untroubled, without grief, with perfect calm; and so he is angered by no one and angers no one."[44]

To be humble means to be able not only to suffer criticism but also to welcome it. We will see shortly how this plays a critical part in the strategic planning process. St Mark the Ascetic warns those who are not prepared:

> He who does not understand God's judgments walks on a knife edge and is easily unbalanced by every puff of wind. When praised, he exults; when criticized, he feels bitter. He quarrels with those who reprove him, and those who forgive him he regards as fools.[45]

Asking for frank and honest input is necessary, but it is a dangerous enterprise. As St Paul says, "It is a fearful thing to fall into the hands of the living God."[46] By opening up to others and placing ourselves in their hands, we place ourselves in his hands.

The acquisition of humility is impossible to describe, yet simple to experience. Abba Dorotheus claims that "no one can describe in words

---

[43] A monastic elder who serves as a spiritual advisor.

[44] Abba Dorotheus, *Directions on Spiritual Training* 11–12 (*Early Fathers from the Philokalia*, 155–56).

[45] St Mark the Ascetic, *On Those who Think that They are Made Righteous by Works* 193 (*Philokalia* I, 142).

[46] Heb 10.31.

what humility is and how it is born in the soul, unless he learns this from experience." He quotes the staretz again: "The ways to humility are bodily labors done intelligently, considering oneself below all others, and cease-less prayer to God."[47]

Ceaseless prayer to God is the foundation of humility. The one who engages in this prayer offers himself totally to God, thanking him for every-thing which he receives as a blessing, entreating his help and mercy in all that he does, and ascribing any achievement or good of his to the grace of God. To be humble is to be totally a servant of God, dedicated to doing his will in everything and denying one's own will in order to truly love others.

FIFTH GOAL: DESIRE TO SERVE, NOT TO BE SERVED

The relationships and leadership characteristics that Jesus shows forth are best represented by Isaiah's Old Testament image of the Suffering Servant, the man for others.[48] Jesus bluntly states that "the Son of man came not to be served but to serve,"[49] and "I am among you as one who serves."[50] St Paul emphasizes the personal servanthood of Jesus Christ by saying he "emptied himself, taking the form of a servant."[51]

The pure desire to serve rather than be served is the most important characteristic of the Christian leader. Without this, little can be done. The Christian leader sees a need and wants to help. The Prophet Isaiah gives us an example. When he heard the Lord asking, "Whom shall I send, and who will go for us?" he said those famous words spoken by every servant of God: "Here am I! Send me."[52] Isaiah's response was immediate. He neither pon-dered the question nor evaluated his ability to perform the tasks desired by God. He volunteered to serve. He did not hang back, waiting to see if others would volunteer first. He wanted to serve. In the New Testament,

[47] Abba Dorotheus, *Directions on Spiritual Training* 15–16 (*Early Fathers from the Philokalia*, 156).
[48] Is 53.
[49] Mt 20.28.
[50] Lk 22.27.
[51] Phil 2.7.
[52] Is 6.8.

St Peter counsels the elders, the overseers, the first bishops, to be eager to serve.[53] The prophet has no idea to whom he is being sent or what is in store for him, yet he desires to do whatever the Lord asks of him.

One serves not for the sake of reward, whether physical or emotional, but to serve, pure and simple. One must not be a hired servant, ready to flee at the moment of danger or difficulty, nor one who murmurs and complains, but rather one who seeks to do the work and will of the Lord. This is a tall order for leaders who are motivated to work for money, glory, career advancement, or other personal compensation. It is certainly true that people must be compensated properly according to the advice of St Paul, who quotes Scripture: "You shall not muzzle an ox when it is treading out the grain" and "The laborer deserves his wages."[54] However, neither money, status, nor position can be the motivation for the daily work of the Christian leader. Higher principles and values must take priority.

In the corporate world, it becomes quite evident to all when someone has his own personal interests in mind and not the interests of the organization of which he is a part. This sort of person may decline or be reluctant to accept tough assignments because he might not perform well, and his chances for advancement might thereby be hindered. Similarly, he may seek to outshine others by subverting their efforts in the hopes of getting ahead. Difficult economic times may cause him to complain about his personal situation and lead him to lose enthusiasm for his work.

In a seminary, the "hired servant" on the faculty balks at taking on additional coursework or advising additional students. The hired servant on the staff complains constantly about working conditions, even though the administration is doing the best it can under the circumstances. The hired servant in administration complains about the faculty, the trustees, and the pressures of life dealing "with those people." In each of these theoretical cases the notion of Christian service is completely absent.

In a parish, the desired situation of true Christian service can sometimes be turned on its head. A priest told me that he once received the following words of advice from a senior priest on the occasion of his taking

[53] 1 Pet 5.2.
[54] 1 Tim 5.17–19.

on his first pastorate: "Always remember that the people in the parish are there to serve *you*." This statement is the complete reverse of what should have been said. Service should indeed be mutual but someone must be the initiator, just as Christ initiated the washing of the feet of the disciples. However, the disciples' betrayal, denial, and desertion of Jesus still occurred *after* the washing of their feet.[55] This example shows that we can neither demand nor expect others to learn from our service as though it were something special. We can only quietly serve, and as leaders say, "We are unworthy servants; we have only done what was our duty."[56]

It is critical for us as leaders to recognize that Jesus Christ shows himself primarily as servant. Some icons in Orthodox churches depict Christ as the high priest, vested in episcopal robes. It is not uncommon for people to regard the bishop as an authority figure. This mistaken understanding might translate into also seeing Jesus Christ as an authority figure who wishes to be served. However, nothing could be further from the truth. As Jesus said, "The Son of man came not to be served but to serve."[57] In fact, Jesus offers us a very blunt example of reversing the roles of greater and lesser, asking: "Which is the greater, one who sits at table, or one who serves? Is it not the one who sits at table? But I am among you as one who serves."[58]

Jesus is no ordinary man. He is the Son of God. By the force of his divine person, he enables us to be accounted righteous and to have our iniquities taken up by him: "By his knowledge shall the righteous one, my servant, make many to be accounted righteous; and he shall bear their iniquities."[59] Not only does he serve us, give us his knowledge, and bear our iniquities, but he dies for us. "I am the good shepherd. The good shepherd lays down his life for the sheep."[60] Similarly, as Christian leaders we must, as in Jesus' instruction to St Peter, feed Christ's sheep.[61] Indeed, we must lay down our lives for them.

---

[55]Lk 13.15.
[56]Lk 17.10.
[57]Mt 20.28.
[58]Lk 22.27.
[59]Is 53.11.
[60]Jn 10.11.
[61]Jn 21.17.

SIXTH GOAL: REMAIN STEADFAST IN TOUGH TIMES

The image of the steadfast leader is exemplified by Christ's stilling of the wind and waves in Matthew 8, and by his calmness and resolve on his path to the cross. The steadfast leader hears the words of Christ, "Do not be anxious about tomorrow," while at the same time recalling that Jesus adds, "Let the day's own trouble be sufficient for the day."[62] When a leader feels that he is weak and near his end, he hears these words of St Paul: "[God's] power is made perfect in weakness."[63] How easily we forget that as Christians, and especially as Christian leaders, we are called to take up our cross. That cross will necessarily produce suffering, be it physical, emotional, or psychological. That suffering should lead us, as St Paul again advises, to endurance, character, and hope.[64]

The starkest depiction of what awaits the Christian leader appears in our Lord's prophecy immediately preceding the Passover and his passion. In Luke 21, Jesus describes the troubles that will befall his followers: earthquakes, wars, famines, pestilence, every sort of terror and destruction. The most shattering consequence of following Christ will come in the form of betrayal, persecution, and even death at the hands of friends and relatives. Nevertheless, Jesus promises to enable his disciples to speak with power despite these troubles and in the midst of their enemies—not with their own words, crafted beforehand with logic and reason, but as a direct gift of his wisdom. However, his followers must remain on guard against the cares and pleasures of worldly life that might weaken their resolve and inhibit their ability to be alert to the day of the coming of the Lord. Jesus calls his followers to endurance and steadfastness: "Watch at all times, praying that you may have strength to escape all these things that will take place, and to stand before the Son of man."[65]

Despite the tribulations that Jesus tells us to expect in this world, he proclaims: "Be of good cheer, I have overcome the world."[66] Through

---

[62]Mt 6.34.
[63]2 Cor 12.9.
[64]Rom 5.4.
[65]Lk 21.36.
[66]Jn 16.33.

baptism and chrismation, we have been given the gift of the Holy Spirit and have spiritual powers available to us as "fruits of the Spirit."[67] Among these fruits are patience and self-control, which taken together enable us to avoid reacting negatively to trials or tribulations.

A common affliction among leaders is complaining about their job assignment, profession, working conditions, career, the people around them, etc.[68] Complaining is a highly negative trait. It detracts from work performance. Spreading one's gloomy outlook also adversely affects others. St Peter of Damaskos teaches that the "patient endurance of afflictions" is a gift from God which enables us to "become an imitator of Christ, of his holy apostles, and of the martyrs and saints."[69] In fact, St Peter does not advise us to merely endure the problem, but rather to give thanks for it: "He who has been found worthy of this great gift should give thanks to God."[70] To give thanks for an uncomfortable situation is to completely give oneself over to the will of God. It opposes the "natural" inclination of man to rail against everything he considers unfair, unjustified, and uncalled for in his working situation.

Complaining often arises from the expectation of a reward (usually for a job well done or a good deed) that is not forthcoming. This expected reward might take the form of monetary compensation, praise, or even a simple word of thanks. St Mark the Ascetic speaks bluntly about the

---

[67]Gal 5.22–23.

[68]In the corporate world, it is normal for candidates for higher management to prove themselves, or rather be proven in the sense of tested or refined in fire, by taking on extremely difficult assignments. These could be under harsh physical and cultural living conditions. They could be working with very trying people. They could be working to turn around an organization which is on the ropes and ready to founder. A refinery general manager I knew was confronted with the case of a head office manager who was given a developmental position in the refinery. Now an oil refinery is a place filled with tough people who are working in an inherently dangerous environment of flammable substances at high temperatures and pressures. It is not for the faint-hearted. The head office individual was not used to dealing with these conditions and complained about the difficulties. The general manager turned to him and said: "We put you into the refinery to find out what kind of mouse you are—are you Mighty Mouse or Mickey Mouse?" Nothing else was said, and no more complaints were made.

[69]St Peter of Damaskos, *Book 1: A Treasury of Divine Knowledge,* "God's Universal and Particular Gifts" (*Philokalia* III, 172).

[70]Ibid.

presupposition underlying such expectations: "He who does something good and expects a reward is serving not God but his own will."[71]

We must refuse to entertain thoughts of discontent, even when it concerns "the loss of what is desirable," as Abba Evagrius the Monk has commented. How often do we think to ourselves when times get rough, "If only I had done this, or had not done that, things could have been different." The mind dwells on what could have been, according to Evagrius:

> Certain thoughts come first and bring to the soul memories of home, relatives and the old way of life. When they see that the soul does not oppose them but goes with them and mentally spreads itself in enjoying them, they seize it and immerse it in discontent.[72]

St Paul ends his letter to the Ephesians with a frank prophecy of what awaits the Christian in the world. It will not be comfortable. It will be violent in hidden ways that others will not see. We will be assailed by the powers of darkness and evil, of untruth and unrighteousness. Nevertheless, he calls upon us to take up the armor of God as a warrior of prayer, "strong in the Lord and in the strength of his might. . . . And having done all, to stand."[73]

---

[71]St Mark the Ascetic, *On Those who Think that They are Made Righteous by Works* 57 (*Philokalia* I, 130).

[72]Abba Evagrius the Monk, *To Anatolius: On Eight Thoughts* 5 (*Early Fathers from the Philokalia*, 110–11).

[73]Eph 6.10, 13.

PART THREE

Ministerial Leadership

In previous chapters we discussed the foundations and goals of Christian leaders. We now turn to the question of what Christian leaders *do*, specifically. Christian leaders are called to be active ministers and servants of God, as Christ was minister and servant. The people of God are called to be kings, priests, and prophets as Christ is King, Priest, and Prophet. The practical day-to-day implication for Christian leaders is that we are to be benefactors, intercessors, speakers, and doers.

The fundamental Christian ministry belongs to the people of God (*laos tou Theou*), to whom God has promised "I will take you for my people (*laon*), and I will be your God."[1] Even when the people departed from God and were driven away because of their evil and abominations, the Lord brought them back under his protection, declaring: "They shall be my people, and I will be their God. I will give them one heart and one way. . . ."[2] St Paul recalls these promises when he reminds the Corinthians that they "are the temple of the living God . . . and [God's] people."[3] St Peter describes the new people of God as "a chosen race, a royal priesthood, a holy nation, God's own people, that you may declare the wonderful deeds of him who called you out of darkness into his marvelous light. Once you were no people but now you are God's people [*laos Theou*]. . . ."[4]

Unfortunately, in some circles the term "laity" has come to imply someone who is inferior to someone else, e.g., layperson versus expert, laity

[1]Ex 6.7.
[2]Jer 32.38–39.
[3]2 Cor 6.16.
[4]1 Pet 2.9–10 (cf. Ex 19.6; Hos 2.23).

versus clergy. This is not the Christian, and specifically not the Orthodox, understanding of the term. A "layperson" is a member of the people (*laos*) of God. All clergy, including bishops, are members of the people of God by virtue of their baptism and chrismation, their initiation into the Church. Their ordination and consecration to their particular offices in the Church neither diminish nor erase, nor otherwise alter their initiation as members of the people of God.

We will consider first what it means to be initiated into the Church, to be part of the people of God, and then reflect upon the special charisms and responsibilities of the deacons, priests, and bishops. We will also discuss the implications of their vocations and what they have to teach us by their lives.

5

King, Priest, and Prophet: Leadership in Action

All ministries, whether of the clergy or the laity, are rooted in the person of Christ. It cannot be otherwise. We are all created in the image and likeness of God. Christ, the incarnate Son of God, assured us that we will do even greater works than he did because he goes to the Father.[1] Metropolitan John Zizioulas explains:

> It is not an accident that in the New Testament writings there is hardly any ministerial title known to the primitive Church that is not attributed to Christ. He is the Apostle (Heb 3.1), the Prophet (Mt 23.8; Jn 18.13), the Priest (Heb 5.6; 8.4; 10.21; 2.17), the Bishop ἐπίσκοπος [episkopos] (1 Pet 2.25; 5.4; Heb 13.13), the Deacon (Rom 15.8; Lk 22.27; cf. Phil 2.7), etc. Christ is "pre-eminent in everything" (Col 1.18).[2]

None of these "functions," "roles," and "offices" are intended as ends in themselves. Rather, they exist to ensure that Christ's presence is realized in the Church, and that his ministry as priest, bishop, deacon, prophet, and apostle is manifested throughout the world.

---

[1]Jn 14.12.

[2]Metropolitan John Zizioulas, *The One and the Many: Studies on God, Man, the Church, and the World Today* (Alhambra, CA: Sebastian Press, 2010), 181.

THE ENTRANCE INTO THE CHURCH: BAPTISM AND CHRISMATION

The person who desires to enter the Orthodox Church meets the priest and his or her sponsor in the vestibule of the Church. The priest lays his hand upon the catechumen's[3] head, an act reminiscent of the laying on of hands of the Apostles Peter and John on the multitude in Samaria.[4] In the prayers immediately following, the catechumen is dignified by increasingly noble titles: "servant . . . a reason-endowed sheep in the holy flock of Christ, an honorable member of the Church, a consecrated vessel, a child of the light, and an heir of the kingdom."[5] All of this takes place during the preamble to the sacrament of baptism!

During the prayers following the procession of priest, catechumen, and sponsor into the center of the church, the priest prays that the person to be baptized will be "a child of the light, an heir of eternal good things, a member and partaker of the death and resurrection of Christ our God." He is anointed with the oil of gladness "unto the healing of soul and body . . . unto the hearing of faith . . . that he may walk in the way of God's commandments." He is baptized "in the name of the Father, and of the Son, and of the Holy Spirit" into Christ's death and resurrection. He is "clothed with the robe of righteousness, in the name of the Father, and of the Son, and the Holy Spirit." He is granted "the seal of the gift of the holy, and almighty, and adorable Spirit." He is prayed for: "preserve his soul in purity and uprightness . . . that he may please thee in every deed and word." He hears the word of the Lord to "go and teach all nations . . . baptizing them . . . teaching them" (Mt 28.19–20). He is endowed with "the garment of incorruption." He bows his head to allow "a first offering shorn from the hair of his head," that he may be ever "a warrior invincible in every attack of those who assail him." He is blessed by the hand of the priest, "inspiring the newly illumined with the Holy Spirit."

---

[3]One who is preparing for baptism through instruction.

[4]Acts 8.17.

[5]All quotations from the baptism and chrismation services, unless otherwise specified, are from Hapgood's *Service Book*, 271–85.

This sequence of incredible and continuing elevations of the human person, who was once in the grip of the evil one, to a transformed existence on the divine plane of the Father, Son, and Holy Spirit, is truly mind-boggling. The words of St Peter ring in our ears: "He has granted to us his precious and very great promises, that through these you may escape from the corruption that is in the world because of passion, and become partakers of the divine nature."[6] We are given what properly belongs to Christ, as a gift of the grace of God. Fr Alexander Schmemann powerfully declares:

> In Christ . . . we belong to the Father, are adopted as sons. In Christ, the true and unique Temple, we become the temple of the Holy Spirit. In Christ, who is the King, the Priest, and the Prophet, we are made kings, priests, and prophets and, in the words of St. John Chrysostom, "abundantly possess not one but all three of these dignities."[7]

We are here quite far from a conventional, worldly, and secular view of the "laity." The people who belong to the body of Christ, who have been made members of that body through baptism and chrismation, are called to the highest commitment: to fulfill the will of God, to fear him, to serve him, to be filled with light, to be followers of Christ in every act and word, to be carriers of his cross who are willing to suffer and die for his sake. In the words of St Macarios of Egypt we are called upon to "meditate on [our] own nobility. . . . By the anointing, all have become *kings, priests* and *prophets* of the heavenly mysteries."[8]

THE KINGLY MINISTRY

St Gregory of Sinai[9] notes that "all the faithful are truly anointed priests and kings in the spiritual renewal brought about through baptism, just as priests and kings were anointed figuratively in former times."[10] We are

[6] 2 Pet 1.4.

[7] Schmemann, *Of Water and the Spirit*, 80–81; Chrysostom, Homily 3.4 on 2 Corinthians.

[8] St Macarios of Egypt quoted in Paul Evdokimov, *The Struggle with God* (Glen Rock, NJ: Paulist Press, 1966), 205.

[9] Fourteenth-century monastic and ascetical writer.

[10] St Gregory of Sinai, *On Commandments and Doctrines, Warnings and Promises* 133 (*Philokalia* IV, 250).

accustomed to hearing how we are made part of the kingdom of God, where God rules and we are his subjects. However, the concept of our being anointed as kings may seem a bit incongruous.

In the story of creation, God said to Adam and Eve: "Be fruitful and multiply . . . have dominion over the fish of the sea and over the birds of the air and over every living thing that moves upon the earth."[11] In other, less symbolic terms, man is to govern everything in the whole world. This vocation was the one God intended man to fulfill: to take care of the world, to do good to and for it, to be its benefactor—in short, to be its king. He was created in God's "own image, and this means in the image of the King of kings, of the One who has all power and authority."[12]

Man failed in this vocation, not realizing that to be king of creation required him to obey and be subject to the Creator King. "Instead of leading [creation] to its fulfillment, he wants to benefit from it, to have and possess it for himself."[13] He saw the beauty of nature, the attractiveness of food, and even the desire for knowledge not as gifts from God, but as a reality separate and independent from him.[14]

In Christ, this fallen king is redeemed by the rebirth of water and the Spirit. The world revealed in the blessing of the waters[15] is transfigured in Christ, ready once again to receive the dominion of the recreated king. We acknowledge the preeminence and dominion of God: "Great art thou, O Lord, and marvelous are thy works, and there is no word which sufficeth to hymn thy wonders."[16] The words of prayer acknowledge that the nature of the world is subject to God: the elements, seasons, heavenly powers, sun, moon, stars, light, waters, sea, air. And we proclaim, as Adam did not: "We confess thy grace. We proclaim thy mercy. We conceal not thy gracious acts."[17]

In practical terms, we recognize the goodness of the gifts that have been given to us, including the inherent goodness within our own soul,

[11]Gen 1.28.
[12]Schmemann, *Of Water and the Spirit*, 82.
[13]Ibid., 83.
[14]Cf. Gen 2.6.
[15]Blessing of the water in the font as part of the baptismal service.
[16]Hapgood, *Service Book*, 277.
[17]Ibid., 278.

misdirected and distorted though it may be. Fr Schmemann declares: "The misuse of [man's] creativity in art, in science, in the whole of life leads him to dark and demonic dead ends; but his creativity itself, his need for beauty and knowledge, for meaning and fulfillment, is *good*."[18] In the baptismal service, a glimpse of the new kingdom of God is projected, in which we are to become filled with light and partake of the death and resurrection of Christ. Emerging from that service as newly enlisted warriors of Christ, how are we then to react to the world, complicated and complex as it is, yet which we proclaim to be good?

Jesus began to teach his disciples about his coming passion, death, and resurrection immediately after Peter's declaration that Jesus was the Christ. Peter did not like what Jesus predicted, and he rebuked Jesus. In turn, Jesus rebuked Peter and called him Satan, on the side of man rather than God. Jesus then summoned his disciples and said to them, "If any man would come after me, let him deny himself and take up his cross and follow me. For whoever would save his life will lose it; and whoever loses his life for my sake and the gospel's will save it."[19]

This radical teaching is a stumbling block for many today, who wish for a more carefree life than Jesus is indicating. Some may even wish for glory, either in their life in the Church or in the world. The icon of the crucifixion often bears the title "King of Glory."[20] The glorification of Jesus comes from the Father, with whom Jesus was glorified from eternity. Now Jesus calls upon the Father in the presence of his disciples so that they might know that this death which he is to suffer is indeed glory: "Now, Father, glorify thou me in thy own presence with the glory which I had with thee before the world was made."[21] The glory and kingship of Jesus is revealed by the cross. As St John Chrysostom says, "I call him King, because I see Him crucified: it belongs to the king to die for His subjects."[22]

---

[18]Schmemann, *Of Water and the Spirit*, 85.

[19]Mk 8.34–35.

[20]Michel Quenot, *The Resurrection and the Icon* (Crestwood, NY: St Vladimir's Seminary Press, 1997), 173.

[21]Jn 17.5.

[22]From Leonid Ouspensky and Vladimir Lossky, *The Meaning of Icons* (Boston, MA: Boston Book & Art Shop, Inc., 1969), 180; Chrysostom, *De cruce et latrone*, Homily 2 (PG 49, 413).

We recover our own kingship by taking up Christ's cross. Fr Alexander Schmemann remarked, "The cross, being Christ's enthronement as King, is revealed to us as the only way to our enthronement with Him, to our restoration as kings."[23] St Paul speaks about our glory in accepting the cross when he says: "But far be it from me to glory except in the cross of our Lord Jesus Christ, by which the world has been crucified to me, and I to the world."[24] The world is crucified to me by being revealed as ultimately shallow and empty. "Vanity of vanities! All is vanity," said the Preacher.[25] On the other hand, "while revealing the self-condemnation and thus the *end* of 'this world,' the cross . . . makes possible the true *acceptance* of the world as God's creation, as the object of God's infinite love and care."[26]

How is this seemingly contradictory attitude towards the "world" possible? How are we to avoid both the pull towards an uncritical acceptance of the world, and its opposite—rejection of the world and withdrawal into isolation from it? We know that the world was created by God as good. We know that man fell through his sin and continues to fall through sin, which is separation from God. Man continually disobeys God's commandments; he loves and serves other gods, walking in ways different from his. But the Lord came to set us free from sin and death by his cross. Although the world has been reclaimed for God, the final victory still eludes us, at least visibly. The victory is won by Christ, but the battles continue in the heart of each of us. Fr Boris Bobrinskoy observed, "The Church will be engaged in the battle against Satan—against the evil one—until the end of time. She will face ordeals that await all of Christ's disciples."[27] This is the meaning of the second part of St Paul's statement that he is crucified to the world. Fr Schmemann personalizes this battle: "Only in me, in my faith, in my life, and in my action can this doctrine become life and the cross of Christ become power. . . . The world [is] given to me by God as my life and

---

[23]Schmemann, *Of Water and the Spirit*, 90.

[24]Gal 6.14.

[25]Eccl 1.2.

[26]Schmemann, *Of Water and the Spirit*, 91.

[27]Boris Bobrinskoy, *The Mystery of the Church: A Course in Orthodox Dogmatic Theology* (Crestwood, NY: St Vladimir's Seminary Press, 2012), 167.

my vocation, my calling, my work, my responsibility."[28] If we take up these responsibilities, we are kings in service to God and his people.

THE PRIESTLY MINISTRY

Let us repeat St Gregory of Sinai's statement that "all the faithful are truly anointed priests and kings in the spiritual renewal brought about through baptism, just as priests and kings were anointed figuratively in former times."[29] While being called a "king" may strike a resonant chord within us based on the above reflection, the title "priest" may seem inappropriate. However, we are certainly called to be such by the Apostle Peter:

> Come to him, to that living stone, rejected by men but in God's sight chosen and precious; and like living stones be yourselves built into a spiritual house, to be a holy priesthood, to offer spiritual sacrifices acceptable to God through Jesus Christ. . . . You are a chosen race, a royal priesthood, a holy nation, God's own people, that you may declare the wonderful deeds of him who called you out of darkness into his marvelous light.[30]

Sacrifices have been offered to God since the dawn of creation by such men as Cain and Abel, Noah, Abraham, Isaac, and Jacob. Following the exodus from Egypt, Moses was instructed by the Lord to construct the tabernacle and altar, and to appoint Aaron "and his sons . . . from among the people of Israel, to serve me as priests."[31] Sacrifices and offerings were necessary to reconcile the relationship between man and God, between servant and master, between the sinner and the one who forgives sin.

Man was created, in the words of Fr Alexander Schmemann, to be *homo adorans*, the one who praises God, giving him thanks for all that he created, offering up all things to God and receiving them back from God with thanksgiving, dedicating all to God and thus leading the world, which

[28]Schmemann, *Of Water and the Spirit*, 92.
[29]St Gregory of Sinai, *On Commandments* 133 (*Philokalia* IV, 250).
[30]1 Pet 2.4–5, 9.
[31]Ex 28.1.

was placed under his dominion, onto the right track.[32] He was called upon to continuously pray for creation and to glorify God through his appreciation of the good things which God had made.

The epitome of this glorification is poetically expressed in Psalm 104 (Ps 103 LXX), which is liturgically chanted at the beginning of vespers as the Church remembers and gives thanks for creation. We remember and give thanks for the light, the heavens, the waters, the clouds, the wind, fire and flame, the mountains, the valleys, the birds, animals, and "plants for man to cultivate, that he may bring forth food from the earth, and wine to gladden the heart of man, oil to make his face shine, and bread to strengthen man's heart."[33] We recognize the need for man to work, and to acknowledge his complete dependence upon God. We glorify God and rejoice with him in his creation: "May the glory of the Lord endure forever, may the Lord rejoice in his works. . . . I will sing to the Lord as long as I live; I will sing praise to my God while I have being."[34]

As part of our priestly responsibilities, we are called as the people of God to make "supplications, prayers, intercessions, and thanksgivings . . . for all men."[35] The Church offers a special evening prayer of intercession to be prayed by all the faithful, which follows an examination of conscience and prayers for oneself:

> Forgive, O Lord, lover of men, those who hate and wrong us. Do good to those who are doers of good. Grant the petitions of our brethren and friends which are for their salvation and eternal life. Visit those who are sick and give them healing. Guard those at sea. Travel with those who travel. Give thy support to our rulers. To those who help us and are merciful to us grant forgiveness of sins. On those who charge us, in our unworthiness to pray for them, have mercy according to thy great mercy. Be mindful, O Lord, of our parents and brethren who have already fallen asleep, and give them rest where the light of thy

---

[32]Schmemann, *For the Life of the World: Sacraments and Orthodoxy* (Crestwood, NY: St Vladimir's Seminary Press, 1995), 15.

[33]Ps 104.14–15.

[34]Ps 104.31, 33.

[35]1 Tim 2.1.

countenance visiteth them. Be mindful, O Lord, of those who bring forth fruit, and do good works in thy holy churches, and grant to them their petitions that are for their salvation and eternal life. Be mindful, O Lord, also of us thy humble, sinful, and unworthy servants, and lead us into the path of thy commandments, by the prayers of thy most pure Mother, our Lady, Mother of God, and ever-virgin Mary, and of all thy saints, for thou art blessed unto the ages of ages. Amen.[36]

This prayer is said by all Orthodox Christians, whether lay or clergy, without exception, and shows the priestly character of all the baptized. We ourselves are lifted up in this intercession by God himself, for "the Spirit helps us in our weakness; for we do not know how to pray as we ought, but the Spirit himself intercedes with us with sighs too deep for words."[37]

THE PROPHETIC MINISTRY

As we have seen, the role of the prophet in the Old Testament was to go forth for God and speak his words to the people. Professor George Cronk explains, "The Greek word *prophetes* means 'one who speaks for another,' and especially for God. And the Hebrew word for 'prophet' is *nabi*, 'a person who communicates, or pours forth the divine will.' "[38] The prophet may have been prepared before taking on this responsibility, but then again he may not have been. He might be simple or sophisticated, a friend of God or an enemy. One thing was clear: he was neither self-proclaimed nor a trained professional, but someone appointed by God via a direct experience and encounter with him.

Immediately following the triple immersion in the sacrament of baptism, the Lord's words in Psalm 32 are read: "I will instruct you and teach you the way you should go; I will counsel you with my eye upon you."[39] At baptism and chrismation each of us encounters God, who promises to give us understanding and look upon us. Further, the priest prays:

[36] *Manual of Eastern Orthodox Prayers* (Crestwood, NY: St Vladimir's Seminary Press, 1991), 17f.

[37] Rom 8.26.

[38] George Cronk, *The Message of the Bible: An Orthodox Christian Perspective* (Crestwood, NY: St Vladimir's Seminary Press, 1982), 94.

[39] Ps 32.8.

Deliver him (her) from the evil one and all his devices; preserve his (her) soul, through thy saving fear, in purity and righteousness, that in every deed and word, being acceptable before thee, he (she) may become a child and heir of thy heavenly kingdom.

Every word uttered by the newly enlisted warrior of Christ is to be acceptable to God. As the newly chrismated servant of God circles the life-giving font in procession with the priest, we sing the hymn: "As many of you as have been baptized into Christ, have put on Christ. Alleluia." If we have put on the Word of God, Jesus Christ, does it not stand to reason that we have also been given the possibility and the power to speak the words of God? Metropolitan Anthony Bloom exhorts us to go even further and become an *act* of God:

> Amos said that a prophet is one with whom God shares his thoughts and who not only receives the thoughts of God but, like a true prophet, proclaims them, lives them, witnesses to them, becomes an act of God. And it is to this that we are called in the Church, to be an act of God in the world. This is the special activity of the Church, which means that in all domains, political, social, economic, educative, the Christian's role has a peculiarity that makes it different from all the other functions in the world: it is an act of God. . . . We are called to be that divine act by which God reveals himself to the world, and, as such, our destiny can only be that of Christ.[40]

We heard previously the call of the Lord to the Prophets Amos, Isaiah, and Jeremiah, and their response to that call. The Lord calls to each one of us to speak his words, perhaps not in such extreme circumstances as these, but perhaps in quieter and more intimate environments. Who would argue with the fact that a mother and father speak the words of the Lord and transmit his message of love and protection to their children? The book of Proverbs stresses this obligation to teach in exceedingly tender terms:

[40]Archbishop Anthony Bloom, *God and Man* (Crestwood, NY: St Vladimir's Seminary Press, 1983 [1st ed. 1971]), 116–17.

Hear, my son, your father's instruction, and reject not your mother's teaching; for they are a fair garland for your head, and pendants for your neck.... When you walk, they will lead you; when you lie down, they will watch over you; and when you awake, they will talk with you.[41]

The comforting words of Christ's love and forgiveness are expressed in our own lives when, as his prophets, we speak these words to our loved ones, friends, and colleagues. We speak most effectively when we mesh with others' souls—when we understand them, sympathize with them, and share their sufferings and their difficulties as Christ has shared our sufferings. Only then can we speak to them with authentic words that come more from the heart than the lips. But as was the case with Christ's words, our own words may meet with opposition and anger. Jeremiah prophesied in the name of the Lord in order to save the people. In return he was beaten and imprisoned: "'Denounce him! Let us denounce him!' say all my familiar friends, watching for my fall. 'Perhaps he will be deceived, then we can overcome him, and take our revenge on him.'"[42] Professor Heaton notes that Jeremiah was not only willing to speak the words of the Lord, but more importantly "had also undertaken to bear in his own life the burden of God's grief at his people's sin."[43] In this, Jeremiah certainly acted like Christ, the Suffering Servant.

The vocation of prophet, which is given to all of us at chrismation, is "the gift of that *sobriety* which in Christian ascetical literature always is posited as the first and the essential foundation of all true spirituality,"[44] according to Fr Schmemann. Sobriety in everyday terms can be equated with "groundedness," i.e., subject neither to the winds of opinion nor the clashing forces of others' judgments, but rather guided by "the still small voice" of God.[45] In the *Philokalia*, sobriety is described as *nēpsis*, or "watchfulness." Watchfulness is that constant attention to thoughts

[41]Prov 1.8–9; 6.22.
[42]Jer 20.10.
[43]Heaton, *Old Testament Prophets*, 49.
[44]Schmemann, *Of Water and the Spirit*, 102.
[45]1 Kg 19.12.

and actions, placing everything in reference to Christ and his gospel, and rejecting everything contrary to it. According to St Hesychios the Priest,[46] "Watchfulness is a continual fixing and halting of thought at the entrance of the heart."[47]

The gospel vision of sobriety is best described in the Sermon on the Mount, wherein Jesus speaks about those who hear his words and either do them or not. It is of no use to hear God's words and pretend to honor them, then go about our business as though we had not heard them, or worse, not to be guided in our actions by them. In that case our house is built upon sand and will fall, according to Jesus, in the event of strong winds and rain. The one who hears and does "will be like a wise man who built his house upon the rock; and the rains fell, and the floods came, and the winds blew and beat upon that house, but it did not fall, because it had been founded on the rock." [48]

---

[46]Dates of life unknown; likely sixth to ninth century.
[47]St Hesychios the Priest, *On Watchfulness and Holiness* 6 (*Philokalia* I, 163).
[48]Mt 7.24–27.

6

Family, Community, and Vocation: Leadership of the Laity

In light of these reflections, the ministry of the laity, the people of God, cannot be seen as other than of highest significance and importance in the life of the Church. Anyone who minimizes the mission and responsibility of the laity either has not heard or is untrue to the words of Christ, the apostles, and the Church. Sometimes clergy or other leaders in the Church look down upon the laity, especially those parishioners who may be in a position to question or perhaps even challenge them—for example, parish and diocesan councils or other organs of governance in the church. This attitude is obviously wrong.

The laity's leadership is the work of every Christian. We are to be soldiers of Christ, his reason-endowed sheep, and show forth his love in this world. We do this, first and foremost, in our private spiritual life, in the prayer closet, at quiet moments of the day, in the night watches, when all the troubles and worries of the world beset us. At such times we need to remind ourselves of the abiding love of God, his demands on us for love and mercy and steadfastness, and remind ourselves that one thing is necessary and we are to continuously choose the better part. In this way we suffer from our inadequacies, shortcomings, and sins, and at the same time rejoice in the boundless mercy, forgiveness, and co-suffering of God.

THE LEADERSHIP OF THE LAITY IN THE FAMILY

One who is blessed to have a family begins with the mission of bringing God's love to those persons, those children of God for whom one bears a special responsibility of love, compassion, and understanding. In particular, the love of a husband for his wife, and the wife for her husband, is the highest form of godly and sacrificial love that exists in the Church. The words of the Apostle Paul need to echo in the ears of every married person every second of the day: "Be subject to one another out of reverence for Christ. Wives, be subject to your husbands, as to the Lord. . . . Husbands, love your wives, as Christ loved the church and gave himself up for her."[1] This subjection to the Lord is neither slavish, nor silent, nor obsequious. It is an honorable subjection, as a servant subjects himself to a master who is loved and cherished.

The last chapter of Proverbs presents the image of the "good wife" in glowing terms: more precious than jewels, strong, charitable, industrious, dignified, full of wisdom and kindness, blessed, praiseworthy. The relationship between husband and wife is built upon complete trust in one another: "The heart of her husband trusts in her, and he will have no lack of gain. She does him good, and not harm, all the days of her life."[2] The woman calls forth the miracle, as did Mary at the wedding in Cana with the conversion of water into wine, for she converts her human activity into the physical and spiritual nurture of the family. Her work is unending but exceedingly fruitful:

> She works . . . with willing hands . . . [and] brings her food from afar. . . .
> She rises while it is yet night. . . . [and] plants a vineyard. . . . She . . .
> reaches out her hands to the needy. . . . makes linen garments and sells
> them. . . . She opens her mouth with wisdom, and the teaching of kindness is on her tongue. . . . She does not eat the bread of idleness. . . . [3]

---

[1]Eph 5.21–22, 25.
[2]Prov 31.11–12.
[3]Prov 31.13–16, 20, 24, 26–27.

Despite these efforts, she neither complains nor worries, for "strength and dignity are her clothing, and she laughs at the time to come."[4] As a result, her husband is secure and "is known in the gates, when he sits among the elders of the land."[5]

The husband, rather than being a person of privilege, is called to give himself in love, the love of the cross: to sacrifice himself completely, without restraint, for the sake of the other. St John Chrysostom expresses in very clear terms the implication of this command when he says to the husband:

> Even if it shall be needful for thee to give thy life for her, yea, and to be cut into pieces ten thousand times, yea, and to endure and undergo any suffering whatever—refuse it not. Though thou shouldest undergo all this, yet wilt thou not, no, not even then, have done anything like Christ.[6]

The wife's "submission" to her husband's "authority and forethought" (in the words of St John Chrysostom[7]) is transformed from a purely human relationship into a spiritual relationship, i.e., through the husband to Christ himself. In this spiritual relationship, positive changes on the part of the husband may occur due to the wife, according to the Apostle Peter: "You wives, be submissive to your husbands, so that some, though they do not obey the word, may be won without a word by the behavior of their wives, when they see your reverent and chaste behavior."[8]

In spite of these counsel of St John Chrysostom and the Apostle Peter, differences between husband and wife sometimes lead to disagreements and quarrels. According to Fr Alexander Elchaninov,

> Family quarrels . . . often result from the wife's reproaches, borne reluctantly by the husband even though they may be deserved. . . . [and] often come from the wife's desire to see her husband better than he is in

---

[4]Prov 31.25.
[5]Prov 31.23.
[6]St John Chrysostom, Homily 20 on Ephesians (NPNF[1] 13:144).
[7]Ibid.
[8]1 Pet 3.1–2.

reality. . . . In this sense, in the new human being, in which two persons have merged, the wife plays the role of conscience.[9]

The clear teaching of the Church is that marriage is the mutual union of the two with Christ, crowned as king and queen in a new little kingdom as both warriors and martyrs.

The significance of the indwelling of Christ within the marriage relationship and under the roof of the family cannot be emphasized enough. Paul Evdokimov remarks:

> Clement of Alexandria calls marriage the "House of God" and applies to it the words about the presence of the Lord, "I am in the midst of them" (Mt 18.20). According to St Ignatius of Antioch, then, "Where Jesus Christ is, there is the universal Church," which enables us to clearly see the ecclesial nature of the nuptial community.[10]

The relationship of parents to their children is a perfect example of the Church at work, the "church in their house," to use the words of St Paul.[11] Fr Thomas Hopko observes:

> Doing God's work at home . . . consists in parents loving each other and caring for their children in the obvious ways: spiritually, intellectually, emotionally, and physically. It consists of children honoring their parents with proper obedience, respect, and care.[12]

The Apostle Paul softens his advice to fathers concerning their children, for after advising children to obey their parents, he counsels fathers to not provoke their children to anger. He appears to be quite aware of what can transpire in a child's growing up, and how the parents respond. St John Chrysostom comments:

[9]Alexander Elchaninov, *The Diary of a Russian Priest* (Crestwood, NY: St Vladimir's Seminary Press, 1982), 90.

[10]Paul Evdokimov, *The Sacrament of Love: The Nuptial Mystery in the Light of the Orthodox Tradition* (Crestwood, NY: St Vladimir's Seminary Press, 1985), 121–22.

[11]Rom 16.5.

[12]Thomas Hopko, *Speaking the Truth in Love: Education, Mission, and Witness in Contemporary Orthodoxy* (Crestwood, NY: St Vladimir's Seminary Press, 2004), 110.

He does not say, "Love your children." Nature itself takes care of this by implanting this in us against our will. So that interpretation would be superfluous. Instead, what does he say? *Do not make your children angry.* So many parents do this. They do this by depriving them of their portion of the inheritance and their promises, by oppressing them with burdens, by treating them not as though they were free but as slaves.[13]

Despite our stated love for those around us, whether heartfelt or not, these practical attitudes of mutual service and subjection, even between those of disparate ages and stations in life, should be continuously reinforced.

All of the above requires leadership, which needs to be deliberately undertaken, ruthlessly evaluated, and continuously improved as a foundational step for the Christian who also leads outside the home. The one who is unloving at home will be unloving outside. The one who cannot understand others at home will not be able to understand others outside. The one whose home is full of bitterness, anxiety, and disagreement will never find harmony, peace, nor unanimity without. St John Chrysostom underscores this truth:

When they are in harmony, and their children are being reared well and their household is in good order, their neighbors will smell the sweet fragrance of harmony, along with all their friends and relatives. But if the contrary is true, everything is overturned and thrown into confusion.[14]

The home is both a training and a proving ground. We are trained and proven (sometimes with tragic results) with those we love and can hurt the most. Clement of Alexandria comments: "The prize in the contest of men is shown by him who has *trained* himself by the discharge of the duties of marriage; by him, I say, who in the midst of his solicitude for his family shows himself *inseparable from the love of God*."[15]

---

[13]St John Chrysostom, Homily 21 on Ephesians (*Ancient Christian Commentary* VIII, 203).

[14]St John Chrysostom, Homily 20 on Ephesians (*Ancient Christian Commentary* VIII, 194).

[15]Clement of Alexandria, *Stromateis* 7.12.70 (PG 9, 297) quoted in Evdokimov, *Sacrament of Love*, 118.

In his meditation on the wedding at Cana, Metropolitan Anthony Bloom describes the miracle of one person's openness to and faith in God:

> [Mary] turns to the servants and says to them: "Whatever he tells you to do, do it." She makes a total, integral, unlimited act of faith, the faith on which the Annunciation was founded; the faith that she bore witness to in being the mother of the Child-God now comes to light in all its fullness. Because she believed in a perfect way, she established at this instant, in this village wedding, the kingdom of God. For the kingdom of God is that which we offer to God with a pure heart, a faith without blemish. There is an old saying of Israel: "God is everywhere man permits him to enter. . . ." You see what this presence and this holiness can be: the presence of God, because one person was present to God.[16]

THE LEADERSHIP OF THE LAITY AT WORK

The first example of work in the Bible is that of the creation, for after "God finished his work which he had done . . . he rested on the seventh day from all his work. . . ."[17] All of this—the creation of the light, the earth, the vegetation, the heavens, the creatures in the sea and on the land, of male and female—was good work. "And God saw everything that he had made, and behold, it was very good."[18] The fall of Adam and Eve brought a burdensome aspect to work which did not exist in the garden, namely, toil, thistles, thorns, dust, and sweat. Even the offerings from that work might not be received by God in uniform ways, depending on the heart of the giver. Abel's offering was accepted; Cain's was not. Noah's work in building the ark was blessed; the builders of the tower of Babel were scattered throughout the earth.

We have already addressed the builders of the tabernacle, whose work is explicitly described in Exodus. Another example of common work is provided by Nehemiah in his account of the rebuilding of the wall of

---

[16]Bloom, *God and Man*, 101.
[17]Gen 2.2.
[18]Gen 1.31.

Jerusalem: "So we built the wall. . . . For the people had a mind to work."[19] Nehemiah's description of work is different in tone from that of the tabernacle detailed in Exodus 35–39 in that its emphasis is on the people. Granted, the design and workings of the tabernacle were highly specified, and a wall a far simpler matter than that glorious structure, but Nehemiah's description of the people involved is still remarkable. He names some forty individuals and a dozen groups that participated in the rebuilding. Clearly, joy is being expressed in the common work.

Few people work well by themselves. Most of us need to work with other people, or are compelled to do so by circumstance. This necessity can lead us either to heaven or hell, as was the case for one of Jean-Paul Sartre's characters in *No Exit*, who states famously, "Hell is other people." The key connection is the source and content of the relationships between people. Our primary relationship as Christians is with God; all other relationships flow from this.

In the opening lines of Psalm 104 (103 LXX), read at the beginning of vespers, we hear twenty-two verses glorifying the work of God in great and poetic detail. We finish with the exultant refrain: "O Lord, how manifold are thy works! In wisdom hast thou made them all. . . ."[20] Note, however, that immediately before this crescendo of feeling—a fulsome and ascending praise of the trees, birds, mountains, badgers, wild goats, the moon, the sun, and the beasts, even the young lions who roar—we say rather flatly and meekly: "Man goes forth to his work and to his labor until the evening."[21] Is this all there is, just work, all day long? Surely there must be some joy, some satisfaction, some redemption to be found in work. But what is the content and basis of this work?

Even as an Orthodox icon reveals the underlying truth and substance of the persons or events depicted, so also Orthodox architecture and iconography provides us with insight into the nature of work. Leonid Ouspensky comments on the nature of church architecture:

---

[19]Neh 4.6.
[20]Ps 104.24.
[21]Ps 104.23.

Unlike classical architecture which, starting with the exterior, moves to the interior and gives content to form, Orthodox architecture starts with the content and gives it form, hereby moving from the interior to the exterior.[22]

In the same way, man's work proceeds from within himself, from the foundations of his spirit and person and the values which define him. The principles that form his person flow naturally from him in all his activity and especially in his work, whatever it may be. In the case of the Christian who has put on Christ and been sealed with the Holy Spirit, these principles take on a living and vital character, active and evident in everything one does. Ouspensky continues, addressing the role of the iconographer:

The painter must be acutely aware of the responsibility that rests upon him when creating an icon. His work must be informed by the prototype it represents in order for its message to become a living, active force, shaping man's disposition, his view of the world and of life.[23]

From the perspective of the ontology of the human person, the heart contains the vital principles which direct every work that one does. As Jesus said: "The good man out of the good treasure of his heart produces good, and the evil man out of his evil treasure produces evil; for out of the abundance of the heart his mouth speaks."[24] The one who is open to God and who desires and thirsts for God will, according to the prophecy of Ezekiel, indeed receive a new heart: "A new heart I will give you, and a new spirit I will put within you; and I will take out of your flesh the heart of stone and give you a heart of flesh."[25]

[22]Leonid Ouspensky, *Theology of the Icon* (Crestwood, NY: St Vladimir's Seminary Press, 1992), 2:220.

[23]Ouspensky, *Theology of the Icon*, 2:270. Ouspensky was true to his principles, according to Metropolitan Anthony Bloom, who said of him: "You could read him, revealed, in the icons he painted. For him an icon was the projection in line and colors of an experience of things eternal; an experience that was personal; that of a person, a living member of the mysterious body of Christ, not of a separate individual projecting, as it were, himself for others to see and admire" in Patrick Doolan, *Recovering the Icon: The Life and Work of Leonid Ouspensky* (Crestwood, NY: St Vladimir's Seminary Press, 2008), 9.

[24]Lk 6.45.

[25]Ezek 36.26.

This incredible promise was not made to an obedient and faithful people as a reward for good works, but rather to the people of Israel, who were unclean and evil, and profaned the name of the Lord God among the Gentiles. The Lord does this purely for the sake of his good name, that it may be vindicated in its holiness and never despised by the Gentiles because of the sins of Israel, and so that the Gentiles will know that God is the Lord. The lesson for us here is that without God the heart, along with the person within whom it dwells and everything he or she does, is insufficient and inadequate. The Lord God wills to renew the heart not by small modifications, but by a complete transplant.

During the Divine Liturgy in the Slavic tradition, immediately before the consecration of the holy gifts as the body and blood of Christ, the priest and deacon antiphonally call upon the Lord to renew the Holy Spirit in them and all the people. In particular, the deacon recites the words of Psalm 51 (50 LXX): "Create in me a clean heart, O God, and renew a right spirit within me. Cast me not away from thy presence and take not thy Holy Spirit from me."[26]

In addition to prayer, a primary vehicle for enabling that good heart to prepare the person for work is Scripture, which, as the Apostle Paul counsels, "is . . . profitable for teaching, for reproof, for correction, and for training in righteousness, that the man of God may be complete, equipped for every good work."[27] St Ignatius Brianchaninov advises, "As often as possible read the gospel, and learn in it the will of your Lord and Savior."[28] The saints teach that the garden of the heart is to be continually fertilized by the gospel, softened and watered by prayer, and weeded by constant remembrance of God and his commandments. "If we constantly observe the Lord's commandments, then by our spirit we shall be united with him."[29]

We work in community, and yet even in the midst of many people and surrounded by activity, we can continue to be inspired by God.

[26]Ps 51.10–11 (Ps 50 LXX), from Hapgood's *Service Book*.
[27]2 Tim 3.16–17.
[28]Bishop Ignatius Brianchaninov, *On the Prayer of Jesus* (Liberty, TN: Saint John of Kronstadt Press, 1995), 98.
[29]Ibid.

Metropolitan Theoliptos[30] advises: "When you work with the brethren, let your hands do the work while your lips keep silence, and let your intellect be mindful of God."[31] The key is to remember God regardless of what is being done. Nicholas Arseniev relates this story about St Anthony:

> [Anthony] once prayed to God that he would show him someone who was better than he, who could serve as his example. He told Anthony to go to Alexandria; the first man that he met at the entrance to the city would be the one that God had sent in answer to his prayer. Indeed, he did meet a man at the entrance to the city and questioned him. Who are you? I am a tanner. And what do you do? I am busy at my tannery and serve my customers. But what are your works before God, your forms of self-denial? I have none. But what do you do then? How do you spend your day? I spend my day working. And what do you do then? How do you serve God? Describe your day to me. Well, in the morning, after I get up, I place myself for several moments before the face of God, and I think that in this whole great city of Alexandria there can be no one who is as great a sinner as I. And in the evening, before going to bed, I again place myself for a few moments before the face of God, and again I think that in all this great city of Alexandria there is no one who is as great a sinner as I. Such was the lesson God sent to St. Anthony.[32]

It was said of St Pachomius,[33] the founder of coenobitic (communal) monasticism and head of a monastic community, that he showed the way "by example rather than precept, himself looking after all the cares of the 'station' (μονή)—preparing the table, sowing and watering the vegetables, answering the door, tending the sick—wanting his disciples to be free from care."[34] A

---

[30]Fourteenth-century bishop and mystical theologian.

[31]Metropolitan Theoliptos, *On the Inner Work in Christ and the Monastic Profession* (*Philokalia* IV, 186).

[32]Nicholas Arseniev, *Russian Piety* (Crestwood, NY: St Vladimir's Seminary Press, 1975), 35–36. Cf. Saying 24 in *Give Me a Word: The Alphabetical Sayings of the Desert Fathers*, John Wortley, trans. (Yonkers, NY: St Vladimir's Seminary, 2014), 37.

[33]Fourth-century founder of coenobitic (community) monasticism in Egypt.

[34]Derwas J. Chitty, *The Desert a City: An Introduction to the Study of Egyptian and Palestin-

story related by St Tikhon of Zadonsk's[35] servant illustrates the saint's attitude toward work:

> One day he went for a walk behind the monastery and he told me, on returning to his cell: "I saw a dead tree in the forest which would make two cart-loads of firewood, maybe more. Bring the axe for chopping." We went into the forest and began chopping; he took off his cassock and began to work in his shirt. He would often say, "He who lives in idleness never stops sinning."[36]

Leadership is first formed by the work we perform internally, unknown to others: silent prayer, continual thirst for the living God, fervent intercession for others both known and unknown, loved and unloved. It is also, according to St Gregory the Great,[37] formed within us when we are not yet in an acknowledged leadership position. "If one recalls how he acted as a layperson, he suddenly knows if he will be able, as a leader, to do well. For no one is able to acquire humility while in a position of authority if he did not refrain from pride when in a position of subjection."[38]

Leadership is formed by continually educating ourselves through the reading of sacred Scripture and other holy books. It is formed by remembering God throughout each moment of the day and seeing his face in everyone we encounter. It is formed by exercising the virtues revealed to us by God and observing his commandments, especially that of love for one another. It is formed by living simply even when surrounded by plenty. It is formed by serving others both in action and by example, performing our jobs with discipline and competence. It is formed by allowing God to work through us to build the community around us and to sustain mutual love, care, and concern.

---

ian Monasticism under the Christian Empire (Crestwood, NY: St Vladimir's Seminary Press, 1966), 21.

[35]Eighteenth-century Russian bishop and teacher.

[36]Arseniev, *Russian Piety*, 127–28.

[37]Sixth-century bishop of Rome, liturgist, and pastoral theologian.

[38]Gregory the Great, *The Book of Pastoral Rule* 1.9. In *The Book of Pastoral Rule*, George E. Demacopoulos, trans. (Crestwood, NY: St Vladimir's Seminary Press, 2007), 42.

7

Service: Leadership of the Deacon

We have already spoken about one of the most important characteristics of the Christian leader: the desire to serve rather than be served. The fundamental duty of the deacon is to re-present Christ as servant and thus be an example of service to everyone he encounters. In this way we understand that the duty of service is not drawn from an abstract moral imperative, but rather from Jesus Christ, whose service is manifested in the person of the deacon. Metropolitan Anthony Bloom describes the service provided by St Vladimir to the poor of Kiev as "living, active love, the diaconate of Christ."[1] This extraordinary responsibility is visited upon those who are capable of receiving it. It is an indelible charism that penetrates deeply into the soul and body of the deacon and realizes itself not only in a church environment, but in every situation.[2]

The deacon is given the responsibility to serve without separating himself from the people of God. He remains at all times a baptized and chrismated member of the body of Christ. All of the people of God bear a responsibility to show forth Christ in our lives, to love one another so that all will know that we are sent by God. The deacon, while not shirking in any way this responsibility, takes on the additional focus of Christ as servant. In this function, he leads the people in discovering and living out the servanthood of Christ. St John of Damascus says: "If anyone wants to know about your faith, place him before the icons." In the same way, if anyone wishes to

---

[1]Bloom, *God and Man*, 78.

[2]For an extensive and insightful study on the Diaconate, see John Chryssavgis, *Remembering and Reclaiming Diakonia: The Diaconate Yesterday and Today* (Brookline, MA: Holy Cross Orthodox Press, 2009).

know and to experience the servanthood of Christ, he or she should look to the deacon. St Ignatius of Antioch goes so far as to say: "Everyone must show the deacons respect. They represent Jesus Christ. . . ."[3]

Clearly, this is a daunting responsibility, but when cheerfully accepted it becomes a joy. Jesus said: "Learn from me; for I am meek and lowly of heart, and you will find rest for your souls. For my yoke is easy, and my burden is light."[4] The task is only difficult when we shrug off his yoke and believe that service to others is beneath us. This temptation needs to be acknowledged by all who wish to follow Christ as servant, whether as an ordained deacon or not. In fact, this possibility is clearly recognized in the prayer of the laying on of hands by the bishop upon the head of the man to be ordained deacon:

> The grace divine, which always healeth that which is infirm, and completeth that which is wanting, elevateth, through the laying-on-of-hands, (name), the most devout subdeacon, to be a deacon: Wherefore, let us pray for him, that the grace of the all-holy Spirit may come upon him.[5]

The candidate for ordination is surprisingly deemed "infirm" and "wanting," and yet in a few minutes the bishop proclaims him "Axios! Worthy!," which is repeated three times by the people. The candidate is unworthy at the beginning, since nothing that he has entitles him to this ministry. There are no "rights" in the ministry of service. All that the deacon has is his humility and the prayers of the people for the visitation of the Holy Spirit, that through these he may be made worthy. The prayers are fervent and direct: "O Lord our God . . . send down the fullness of the Holy Spirit. . . . Preserve this man . . . vouchsafe to him the grace which thou didst grant unto Stephen, thy first martyr . . . make him worthy. . . . Manifest him as wholly thy servant." The last sentence of this prayer does not suggest that he should manifest *himself*, but that God should manifest *him*—not partially, but *wholly*, i.e., not part-time but full-time.

---

[3]St Ignatius of Antioch, Epistle to the Trallians 3 (Richardson, *Early Christian Fathers*, 99).
[4]Mt 11.29–30.
[5]Hapgood, *Service Book*, 312.

The first deacons were selected for practical reasons. The apostles were hampered in their preaching by duties such as the daily distribution of food to the widows. Seven assistants were accordingly selected by the people to perform these tasks. The candidates had to be "of good repute, full of the Spirit and of wisdom."[6] While their fundamental task was the daily administration, at least two of the seven were active in other forms of service.

Stephen was "full of grace and power, [and] did great wonders and signs among the people." He became the first martyr for the new faith.[7] Philip preached the word in Samaria, did signs, healed, and baptized. In his service, Stephen manifested the self-emptying servanthood of Christ. He did not seek to preserve his person, but offered himself up as a living sacrifice to God. When he was arrested for blasphemy as a result of his preaching, he did not try to plead his way out but courageously spoke the truth, caring nothing for himself. Philip was similarly a servant, doing whatever needed to be done. When an angel spoke to him telling him to go down a desert road, he obeyed and went. And when the Spirit told him to join up with a chariot on that road, he did so. And in so doing he converted the Ethiopian eunuch. He neither delayed nor asked questions; he did what he was told.

The Apostle Paul gives guidance to Timothy regarding the desired characteristics of deacons:

> Deacons likewise must be serious, not double-tongued, not addicted to much wine, not greedy for gain; they must hold the mystery of the faith with a clear conscience. And let them also be tested first; then if they prove themselves blameless let them serve as deacons. . . . Let deacons be the husband of one wife, and let them manage their children and their households well; for those who serve well as deacons gain a good standing for themselves and also great confidence in the faith which is in Christ Jesus.[8]

[6] Acts 6.3. The word "deacon" is not bestowed upon the Seven in the book of Acts. Rather, it is implied in the service (*diakonein*) that is provided to the widows. This more general term "service" is also applied in Acts 6.4 to the work of the apostles in the "ministry of the word" (*diakonia tou logou*). The term "deacons," as specifically applied to the Seven and their successors, is mentioned in Phil 1.1 and 1 Tim 3.8.

[7] Acts 6.8.

[8] 1 Tim 3.8–10, 12–13.

The word "likewise" that appears in the first sentence refers to the prior chapter of this epistle, which speaks about bishops. St John Chrysostom confirms that deacons "should have the same qualities as bishops. And what are these same? To be blameless, sober, hospitable, patient, not brawlers, not covetous."[9] He goes on to comment on the word "double-tongued": "Nothing so debases a man as deceit, nothing is so pernicious in the Church as insincerity."[10] The common requirement for bishops and deacons to be neither covetous nor greedy, but to have integrity, live above reproach, and manage their households well indicates that both ministries were occupied with the business of community administration.[11]

From the viewpoint of today's parish, the primary duty of the deacon is to assist the priest and bishop in conducting the liturgical services, and to lead the people in prayer. This perspective is not far from the truth, as these duties represent both the pinnacle and the foundation of the deacon's life in Christ.

The deacon's service at the altar is evidence of God's love for him, as well as his love for God and his service to him and his people. He is placed openly in an environment that demands concentration and focus on God: among the holy icons, at the holy altar, in the presence of the holy cross and the gospel. The very goal of our faith is announced clearly at the beginning of the Divine Liturgy: "Blessed is the kingdom of the Father, and the Son, and the Holy Spirit." The content of every prayer and action points to the intimate and loving relationship between God and his people. And the deacon is there as minister and servant of the mysteries, along with the bishop and the priest. The mutual dialogues, prayers, remembrances, and blessings are all constant and vital connections between the servitors as members of the body of Christ. Although the deacon is subordinate to the other clergy, he still leads them in the actions they must undertake. He even indicates with his orarion[12] what they should do: "Master, give the blessing! Master, bless the high place! Master, bless the holy bread! Master,

---

[9]St John Chrysostom, Homily 11 on 1 Timothy (NPNF[1] 13:441).

[10]Ibid.

[11]J. L. Houlden, *The Pastoral Epistles* (Harmondsworth, Middlesex, England: Penguin Books, 1976), 80.

[12]This is also known as a "stole" in the West. It is emblematic of the service of the deacon.

bless the holy cup!" In a very real sense there is co-leadership in the service, and not only among the clergy.

A primary liturgical function of the deacon is to lead the people in prayer. He declares: "In peace, let us pray to the Lord!" The fundamental assumption and hope is that the deacon himself is praying with a fervent heart, not superficially or out of habit, or with a sense of performing, but purely out of love for God and his people. When one prays inwardly, without concern for pitch or cadence, it is certainly easier to concentrate on the meaning of the prayer and one's response to it, as the prayer beats within one's heart. It is more difficult to concentrate when one prays outwardly, especially in the case of leading others in public. St John of Kronstadt[13] speaks about this difficulty: "The prayers of many of the clergy who read rapidly become quite untrue: with their lips they seem to pray; in appearance they are pious, but their hearts are asleep, and do not know what their lips say. . . . We must pray gladly, with energy, from the whole heart."[14] The saint advised his deacons to fan the hearts of the people in prayer, just as they fan the coals in the censer. In the tradition of co-leadership, St John encouraged the people: "We must pray for them, as they pray for us; we must pray that their words may penetrate into their hearts and breathe warmth into them. They pray for us in the words of holy persons, and we must pray for them also."[15]

In today's church environment, few deacons are employed in church occupations alone; some are tradesmen and professionals, others counselors, businessmen, accountants, or teachers, and carry many other responsibilities. The work that they provide for the Church, *qua* Church, is done strictly on a volunteer, pro bono basis. Fr Thomas Hopko notes that clergy are forbidden to take up certain occupations which "compromise or harm their ecclesial ministries . . . [including] politicians, lawyers, judges, businessmen, bankers, or soldiers. They may, however, be farmers and physicians, and, in some cases, teachers, counselors, and social

---

[13]Russian priest in St Petersburg; lived at end of nineteenth and beginning of twentieth centuries.

[14]St John of Kronstadt, *My Life in Christ*, in George P. Fedotov, *A Treasury of Russian Spirituality* (Belmont, MA: Nordland Publishing Company, 1975), 358.

[15]Ibid.

workers."[16] Entrance into one of these occupations, or seeking ordination while a member, is a subject for discussion between the deacon and bishop, with the bishop making the decision in each case. Regardless, in any occupation there can be no divide between the vocation of the deacon as re-presenting Christ as servant and his vocation in that outside occupation. Should there be, one of these alternatives needs to go.

However, if the deacon remains true to his diaconate throughout all the days and hours of his life, then any worthwhile occupation can be enlightened by the image of Christ as servant, which the deacon represents. A so-called "secular" occupation can be an excellent opportunity for the deacon to re-examine his own values. As a businessman or industrialist with an imposing title, does he still have the sense of serving his employees, customers, and suppliers and acting with love and concern for them? Can a judge or a lawyer serve others, administering justice and the law with humility and care, without arrogance or self-centeredness? These are important questions. If a deacon, who has been granted the charism of service in Christ, cannot show that Christ-like service in his profession, what can be expected of "ordinary" people? The deacon shows the way and leads others in giving service to one another.

Within the Church, there are many works of service that can be undertaken by deacons, especially those trained in disciplines like administration, education, accounting, finance, law, construction, engineering, trades, etc. In each case the deacon brings to the effort a "bridge" function, showing others in Church leadership positions the professional standards that need to be instituted.

In all his efforts the deacon remains faithful to the ultimate goal of Christ to love and care for others—in other words, he leads by serving. The holy Theotokos exercised leadership at the marriage in Cana when she told the servants "Do whatever he tells you to do." She pointed the way to Christ, passing over herself. In the same way, the deacon in his service leads by pointing always and being completely transparent to the Suffering Servant, the one who is the Servant of all, Jesus Christ.

[16]Hopko, *Speaking*, 111.

8

Sacrifice: Leadership of the Priest

In the early Church, there was no significant distinction between the offices of presbyter and bishop. In fact, St John Chrysostom comments in his homily on First Timothy that St Paul deliberately skips over the presbyters, going directly from bishops to deacons.

> The reason for this omission was that between presbyters and bishops there was no great difference. Both had undertaken the office of teachers and presidents in the Church, and what he has said concerning bishops is applicable to presbyters. For they are only superior in having the power of ordination, and seem to have no other advantage over presbyters.[1]

There is a body of literature explaining the development of the presbyterate and the episcopate which we will not delve into at this juncture. Suffice it for now to say that the original "priest" (*iereus*) was the bishop (*episkopos*). As the community grew, the bishops relied upon the elders or presbyters (*presbyterous*), who were empowered by the bishops to preside at the Eucharist and perform the sacred mysteries (with the exception of ordination). In this chapter, we will concentrate on the specific priestly character of both the bishop and presbyter. We will defer discussion on the governance and overseeing character to the next chapter on the leadership of the bishop. However, it should be emphasized, both here and later, that the foremost responsibility of the bishop, his *sine qua non*, is his presiding

---

[1] St John Chrysostom, Homily 11 on 1 Timothy (NPNF[1] 13:441).

at the Eucharist and calling together the Church, the body of Christ, from whom and in whom all ministries in the Church flow.

The offices of both bishop and presbyter possess the specific sacramental role of leading the congregation in the liturgical remembrance of the saving acts of God, most especially the Eucharist. The priest is the presider (*proistamenos*) of the assembly.[2] It is he who celebrates the Eucharist and calls upon the Holy Spirit to transform the bread and the wine, the offerings of the lives of the people of God, into the life-giving body and blood of the savior, Jesus Christ. This special ministry, not vouchsafed to the deacons, elevates the priest above the rank of servant to one whose actions, together with the prayers of the people, manifest the glory of God and his intimate presence among his people.[3]

The prayer spoken by the ordaining bishop follows the same prayer used at the ordination of the deacon ("The grace divine, which always completes that which is wanting . . .") and gives a list of the particular responsibilities of the priest: "that he may be worthy to stand in innocency before thine altar; to proclaim the gospel of thy kingdom; to minister the word of thy truth; to offer unto thee spiritual gifts and sacrifices; to renew thy people through the laver of regeneration."[4] Clearly, this ministry involves the first place at the altar, the offering of the holy gifts, the preaching of the word of God, and the baptism of the people.

According to Fr Alexander Schmemann, the priest "manifests the power of the priesthood of Christ, who consecrated himself for us and who is the one priest of the New Testament. . . . The priest is neither a 'representative' nor a 'deputy' of Christ: in the sacrament he is Christ himself, just as the assembly is his body."[5] The prayers of the Divine Liturgy emphasize the priest's awareness of his sacred and awesome responsibility. In the prayers of entrance before the liturgy, the priest asks: "O Lord, stretch forth Thy

---

[2] Alexander Schmemann, *The Eucharist: Sacrament of the Kingdom* (Crestwood, NY: St Vladimir's Seminary Press, 1988), 15.

[3] Note, however, that ordination to the holy priesthood in no way expunges or obliterates the charism of servant bestowed upon the deacon. In the words of Fr Boris Bobrinskoy to a newly ordained priest, "The priest must never stop being deacon" (personal communication).

[4] Hapgood, *Service Book*, 317.

[5] Schmemann, *Eucharist*, 25.

hand from Thy holy dwelling place on high, and strengthen me for this, Thine appointed service, that standing without condemnation before Thy throne, I may offer the bloodless sacrifice."[6] Before the entrance with the Holy Gifts, he prays: "O Lord our God . . . by the power of the Holy Spirit enable me, who am endowed with the grace of the priesthood, to stand before this, Thy holy table, and perform the sacred mystery of Thy holy and pure Body and precious Blood."[7]

The grace of the priesthood mentioned here is simply the priesthood of Christ, the "high priest of our confession."[8] This grace is visited upon the entire Church and, according to Fr Boris Bobrinskoy, "is a part of the Church's entire life, of every ecclesial ministry, of every consecration of the Spirit, whether diaconal, didactic, kerygmatic, pastoral, or administrative. . . . But some vocations are ultimately priestly, such as those concerning the eucharistic celebration, and the sanctification of the faithful."[9] These responsibilities are reserved purely to the priest as priest, whether he is a presbyter or bishop.

> The term *priest* was extended from the person of Christ, for whom alone it is used in the New Testament, to the bishop, for whom again it was used until about the fourth century. In being the head of the eucharistic community and offering in his hands the Eucharist—a task of the episcopate *par excellence* in the first four centuries—the bishop, and later on the presbyter precisely and significantly enough when he started offering the Eucharist himself, acquired the title of priest.[10]

The ultimate character of priestly service is revealed in the life-giving sacrifice of Christ: loving, caring, healing, serving, and giving. All these characteristics are subsumed under the category of pastoral attitude and practice. The people see Christ re-presented through the life and person of the priest, and so, under the leadership example of the priest, themselves

[6]*Divine Liturgy*, 5.
[7]Ibid., 48.
[8]Heb 3.1.
[9]Bobrinskoy, *Mystery*, 190.
[10]Metropolitan John Zizioulas, *Being as Communion: Studies in Personhood and the Church* (Crestwood, NY: St Vladimir's Seminary Press, 2002), 231.

receive practical example and guidance in their own loving, caring, healing, serving, and giving.

The priest himself has as the foundation of his ministry the sacrifice of
Christ, in taking up his cross and following Christ to Golgotha and beyond.
The very hands which bless the bread and wine to become the broken Body
and shed Blood of Christ must be willing to be spread upon the cross and
transfixed with nails. Immediately before the martyrdom of St Polycarp of
Smyrna,[11] the saint "looked up to heaven and said: 'Lord God Almighty . . .
thou hast deemed me worthy of this day and this hour, to take my part in
the number of the martyrs, in the cup of thy Christ . . . among whom may
I be received in thy presence this day as a rich and acceptable sacrifice.'"[12]
The ordained priest by grace participates in the divine life of God, and
his ordination becomes "transfiguration" (*metamorphōsis*) according to
St Gregory of Nyssa.[13] In the transfigured person, loving and giving are no
longer mechanical, artificial behaviors but rather actions flowing naturally
from the inner person, from the one who has participated in the death
and resurrection of Christ and who, in offering up that sacrifice which is
uniquely Christ's, becomes himself capable of revealing that willingness to
suffer and die in his own life.

Metropolitan Anthony Bloom, in his meditation on holiness, describes
the work of the monasteries founded by St Joseph of Volotsk[14] in northern
Russia. The monks lived in great privation, without heat in the coldest
of weather, and worked long hours to feed the peasants who lived about
them, and built orphanages, schools, and homes for the aged.

> Hunger, cold, ignorance, neglect of the aged, neglect of the young: all
> this became the object of love. And if you read the works and life of
> St Joseph, there is no doubt that there was nothing else but love, for
> he had no concern for anything else. He did not care about the con-
> sequences, nor did it matter what people thought about the folly of
> these things. What he said was that these people were hungry and in

[11]Second-century bishop and martyr.
[12]Martyrdom of Polycarp 14.1–2 (Richardson, *Early Christian Fathers*, 154).
[13]Quoted in Zizioulas, *Being*, 228.
[14]Fourteenth or fifteenth-century Russian monastic.

need of help, and that we who have known Christ, who know who He is, must bring Him to them. And if it costs you your life, well, it costs you your life![15]

St Paul said: "If we live, we live to the Lord, and if we die, we die to the Lord; so then, whether we live or whether we die, we are the Lord's."[16] The testimony of the early Christian martyrs gave credence to this message. They were willing to suffer and to die for Christ, in a "martyrdom conformable to the gospel."[17] St Paul appeals to his brethren "to present your bodies as a living sacrifice, holy and acceptable to God. . . . Be imitators of God, as beloved children. And walk in love, as Christ loved us and gave himself up for us, a fragrant offering and sacrifice to God."[18] St John Chrysostom refuses to attribute a theoretical or symbolic meaning to these words, saying, "He suffered on his enemies' behalf. This is the fragrant offering, the acceptable sacrifice. If you suffer for your enemies as a fragrant offering, you too become an acceptable sacrifice, even if you die. This is what it is to imitate God."[19]

> What was Christ's love like? Did it withhold anything? Did it observe
> or measure its own spiritual gifts? What did it regret? Where was it
> ever stingy? Christ's humanity was spat upon, struck, crucified. Christ's
> divinity was incarnate fully and to the end in his spat-upon, battered,
> humiliated, and crucified humanity. The cross—an instrument of
> shameful death—has become for the world a symbol of self-denying
> love. And at no time or place—neither from Bethlehem to Golgotha,
> neither in sermons nor parables, nor in the miracles he performed—
> did Christ ever give any occasion to think that He did not sacrifice

---

[15]Bloom, *God and Man*, 81.

[16]Rom 14.8.

[17]Martyrdom of Polycarp 1.1 (Richardson, *Early Church Fathers*, 149). Richardson comments, "Christian martyrdom was . . . nothing less than a mystic communion and conformation with One who died for our sins that he might raise us eternally unto a life of holiness and everlasting joy" (ibid., 141–42).

[18]Rom 12.1; Eph 5.1–2.

[19]St John Chrysostom, in *Ancient Christian Commentary*, VIII, 183. The *Nicene and Post-Nicene Fathers* translation is stronger on the necessity of death: "And if thou shalt die, then wilt thou be indeed a sacrifice" (NPNF[1] 13:130).

Himself wholly and entirely for the salvation of the world, that there was in him something held back, some "holy of holies" which he did not want to offer or should not have offered.[20]

The above reflection is by Mother Maria Skobtsova, the martyr of Ravensbrück.[21] Her life was consumed by love and sacrifice for her neighbor, for the least of Christ's brethren, and not in theory only, but in practice. In her essay "On the Imitation of the Mother of God," she calls upon us to follow the sacrificial example of the Mother of God in her co-suffering with Christ.

> Here the most important thing is to feel what the Son's Golgotha is for the Mother. He endures his voluntary suffering on the cross—she involuntarily *co*-suffers with him. He bears the sins of the world—she *co*llaborates with him, she *co*-participates, she *co*-feels, *co*-experiences. His flesh is crucified—she is *co*-crucified.[22]

She accepts the cross that was given to her and receives the sword which pierces her heart.[23] As mother, she also co-suffers with us and accepts the crosses and swords of every soul who has been given to her by her son and Lord: "Woman, behold, your son! Behold, your mother!"[24] Mother Maria calls us to imitate the Mother of God as we imitate Christ.

> The first founder of the deed of love teaches us the humble acceptance of these other crosses. She calls every Christian soul to repeat tirelessly after her: 'Behold the handmaid of the Lord,' even to shedding one's blood, even to feeling as if a sword has pierced one's heart. This is the measure of love; this is the limit to which the human soul should aspire. We can even say that this is the only proper relation of one person to another. Only when one's soul takes up another person's cross, his

[20]Mother Maria Skobtsova, "Types of Religious Life," *Mother Maria Skobtsova: Essential Writings* (Maryknoll, NY: Orbis Books, 2003), 179f.

[21]Twentieth-century Russian nun living in France during World War II; died in 1945 taking the place of a woman being sent to the gas chamber.

[22]Skobtsova, "On the Imitation of the Mother of God," *Writings*, 68.

[23]Cf. Lk 2.34.

[24]Jn 19.26–27.

doubts, his grief, his temptations, falls, sins—only then is it possible to speak of a proper relation to another.[25]

The priest lifts up his hands in imitation of the Lord's being lifted up on the cross; he blesses and breaks the bread, and remembers our most holy lady, the Mother of God. He stands for the people in offering the holy gifts "on behalf of all and for all." He it is who most intimately co-suffers with Christ and is co-crucified with Christ. He is the one who re-presents the crucified Christ in his priestly person, bearing the crosses of others and pierced in his heart with the swords which pierce theirs. In so doing, he leads the people to become co-crucified with Christ and co-sufferers with others. Mother Maria continues:

> Here it is possible to speak of the whole of Christianity as an eternal offering of the divine liturgy beyond church walls. What does this mean? It means that we must offer the bloodless sacrifice, the sacrifice of self-surrendering love not only in a specific place, upon the altar of a specific temple; the whole world becomes the single altar of a single temple, and for this universal liturgy we must offer our hearts, like bread and wine, in order that they be transformed into Christ's love, that He may be born in them, that they may become "God-manly" hearts, and that He may give these hearts of ours as food to the world, that He may bring the whole world into communion with these hearts of ours that have been offered up, so that in this way we may be one with Him, not so that we may live anew but so Christ would live in us, becoming incarnate in our flesh, offering our flesh upon the cross of Golgotha, resurrecting our flesh, offering it as a sacrifice of love to Himself. Then truly in all ways Christ will be in all.[26]

To be a leader, the priest must be a follower and imitator of Christ. He must imitate the Mother of God in being transparent to Christ, pointing toward Christ, co-suffering with Christ, and accepting the crosses and

---

[25]Skobtsova, "On the Imitation of the Mother of God," *Writings,* 69f.
[26]Skobtsova, "Types of Religious Life," *Writings,* 185.

swords borne by the people. In this way he becomes an example for us of
how to co-suffer and be co-crucified for others.

The many other desired characteristics of the priest (preaching, teaching, counseling, confessing, liturgizing, etc.) must stem from his acceptance
of the cross of Christ and the sword of the Mother of God. Otherwise,
the temptation is for all these activities to become self-affirming exercises
expressing his own authority, power, and goodness. If this is the case, then
any criticism, any lack of affirmation, appreciation, or praise from others
will have a negative impact on the priest and on those he pretends to serve.
If he is not serving God and God's people absolutely and without limit,
then he is serving only himself; he has built his house upon the sand, and
when the wind blows and the storms come, the house will be destroyed.

Clergy and laity are called to the mutual subjection commanded by the
Apostle Paul in Ephesians. St Jerome bluntly declares:

> Let bishops hear this, let priests hear, let every rank of learning get this
> clear: In the church, leaders are servants. Let them imitate the apos-
> tle. . . . The difference between secular rulers and Christian leaders is
> that the former love to boss their subordinates whereas the latter serve
> them. We are that much greater if we are considered least of all.[27]

In the same way as the priest sacrifices himself for the people, the
people he inspires must in turn sacrifice themselves for the priest. In the
service of ordination, following the consecration of the bread and wine to
become the body and blood of Christ, the bishop places the consecrated
lamb into the hands of the newly ordained priest and says: "Receive thou
this pledge, and preserve it whole and unharmed until thy last breath,
because thou shall be held to an accounting therefore in the second and
awesome coming of our great Lord, God, and Savior, Jesus Christ." According to some interpretations, this action exhorts the priest to ensure that
communion is not given to those who are unworthy. However, the lamb is
the body of Christ. The Church is the body of Christ. The priest thus holds

---

[27]St Jerome, Epistle to the Ephesians 3.5.21 (PL 26, 530A–C). In *Ancient Christian Commentary* VIII, 194.

the Church, and her people, in his hands. He is called to preserve it whole and unharmed, as the prayer says.

Who holds the priest in his or her hands? Certainly, the bishop has responsibility for overseeing all that the priest does in his service. That is without question. But in a more intimate and immanent sense, the people whom the priest serves hold him in their hands. That is their responsibility, day in and day out. They are called to show sacrificial love to him just as he is called to show that love to them. They are called to focus on him, care for him, and love him—and not only him, but also his wife and children. The people are called to be their friends, to have open ears, hands, and hearts, to "love one another with brotherly affection [and to] outdo one another in showing honor."[28]

---

[28]Rom 12.10.

9

Shepherd and Overseer:
Leadership of the Bishop

The development of the episcopacy, or office of the bishop, has been the subject of much historical study. According to Metropolitan John Zizioulas, "It is important to draw, right from the start, a line of demarcation between two periods of the early Church, namely that of the first three centuries and that of the fourth century and beyond."[1] For the first of these two periods, we will review references to the episcopacy in the New Testament epistles and writings of the apostolic fathers such as Clement of Rome, Ignatius of Antioch, and Cyprian of Carthage We will then review the service of consecration of a bishop to see how the apostolic tradition has unfolded to the present day.

THE NEW TESTAMENT ON THE BISHOP

As noted previously, the source of every ministry, including that of the bishop, is Christ. St Peter notes: "For you were straying like sheep, but have now returned to the Shepherd and Guardian (*episkopon*) of your souls."[2] The word *episkopos* in the Septuagint Old Testament refers to the function of an "overseer" such as Eleazar, son of Aaron, who was placed in charge of the sanctuary.[3] In the New Testament, the word appears in the book of Acts, where St Paul exhorts the elders of the assembly (*presbyterous*

---

[1]Zizioulas, "Ἐπισκοπὴ and Ἐπίσκοπος in the Early Church," *One and Many*, 221.
[2]1 Pet 2.25. The King James translation renders *episkopon* as "bishop."
[3]Num 4.16.

tis ekklēsias) to attend to the needs of the flock of which the Holy Spirit has made them overseers (*episkopous*).[4] When the apostles established communities of Christians, those communities chose elders to be their leaders, in keeping with the established custom in both Jewish and civil society. St Paul reminds Titus that he left him in Crete to appoint elders (*presbyterous*) in every town.[5] He further comments on the qualifications of these elders and refers to them as bishops: "a bishop [*episkopon*], as God's steward [*oikonomon*], must be blameless . . . not arrogant or quick-tempered. . . ."[6] Hence there was no distinction in the very early Church between presbyters and bishops; the terms were used interchangeably.

To the responsibility of "overseer" St Paul adds the qualification of "steward," which meant a manager to whom the master entrusted his affairs. Further uses of the verb derived from *episkopos*, suggesting what the bishop/presbyter should be doing in his role of overseer, are found in Acts 7.23, Acts 15.36, and James 1.27. The actions indicated are to look after, care for, and visit in order to see how someone is doing. In James, the reference is to visiting orphans and widows. In Acts, the first reference expresses the desire of Moses to visit his brothers, while in the case of the second Paul desires Barnabas to visit the brethren "in every city where we proclaimed the word of the Lord, and see how they are." The overseeing role of the bishop thus included visitations, inspections, and caring for others.

It was normal in the early Church "for all the faithful of a certain city to come together in one place (*epi to auto*) for the celebration of the Eucharist" under the presidency of the city's bishop.[7] As communities became larger and spread into the countryside, presbyters began to assume the leadership role at the eucharistic celebration and were "ordained for the specific purpose of presiding over and offering the Eucharist."[8] As this phenomenon increased, the role of the bishop by the fourth century had

---

[4]Acts 20.17, 28.

[5]Titus 1.5.

[6]Titus 1.7.

[7]Zizioulas, "The Bishop in the Theological Doctrine of the Orthodox Church," *One and Many*, 236.

[8]Ibid., 237.

become less and less that of president of the assembly, for practical reasons, and more and more concerned with overseeing the work of the Church, including the establishment of new churches and the ordination of presbyters to serve them.

THE APOSTOLIC FATHERS ON THE BISHOP

The responsibility of the episcopate ranges from ensuring continuity with apostolic tradition to fostering the unity of the Church, both locally and at large, and building up the faith and conduct of the local congregations. St Clement of Rome, in a letter written at the end of the first century, takes care to focus on the continuous connection between God, Christ, the apostles, and the bishops and deacons.

> The apostles received the gospel for us from the Lord Jesus Christ; Jesus, the Christ, was sent from God. Thus Christ is from God and the apostles from Christ. In both instances the orderly procedure depends on God's will. And so the apostles . . . preached in country and city, and appointed their first converts, after testing them by the Spirit, to be the bishops and deacons for future believers.[9]

St Ignatius of Antioch, writing around the same time, similarly emphasizes the need for the bishop to be completely consistent with the mind of Jesus Christ: "For Jesus Christ—that life from which we cannot be torn—is the Father's mind, as the bishops too, appointed the world over, reflect the mind of Jesus Christ."[10] Further, the great martyr encourages all to "act in one accord with the bishop's mind . . . form yourselves into a choir, so that with perfect harmony and taking your pitch from God, you may sing in unison and with one voice to the Father through Jesus Christ."[11]

Regrettably, Christians have from time to time transgressed against this ideal of unity and harmony. The church at Corinth was particularly identified as suffering from this sin by St Paul and St Clement in their respective

---

[9] 1 Clement 42.1–5 (Richardson, *Early Christian Fathers*, 62).
[10] St Ignatius of Antioch, Letter to the Ephesians 3.2 (Ibid., 88).
[11] St Ignatius of Antioch, Letter to the Ephesians 4.1–2 (Ibid., 89).

epistles to the Corinthians. St Paul had been informed of quarrels within the Corinthian church that had led to various parties or factions being formed. The apostle expresses his desire for unity in no uncertain terms: "I appeal to you, brethren, by the name of our Lord Jesus Christ, that all of you agree and that there be no dissensions among you, but that you be united (*katērtismenoi*) in the same mind and the same judgment."[12] The Greek word for "united," according to one modern commentator, "suggests a mutual adjustment and adaptation, a readiness to give into one another in the interests of harmony."[13] The King James translation uses "perfectly joined together," while the NPNF translation of St John Chrysostom's commentary has "perfected together."[14] St Paul laments the foolishness of quarrels within the Church, even when they are couched in eloquent language and structured in logical arguments: "Where is the wise man? Where is the scribe? Where is the debater of this age? Has not God made foolish the wisdom of the world?"[15] Every ecclesiastical controversy, quarrel, and schism is, according to St Paul, due to the simple fact that Christians have forgotten the cross of Christ and the love of God for man that the cross represents. He reminds the Corinthians that everything has been given to them as gift, "that none of you may be puffed up in favor of one against another."[16]

Some forty years later, St Clement of Rome heard of dissension in the Corinthian church, this time involving church members who succeeded in overthrowing the ruling presbyters. St Clement recalls the counsel of St Paul in chastising the Corinthians in very strong terms:

> Pick up the letter of the blessed apostle Paul. What was the primary thing he wrote to you, "when he started preaching the gospel?" To be sure, under the Spirit's guidance, he wrote to you about himself and Cephas and Apollos, because even then you had formed cliques. Factiousness, however, at that time was a less serious sin, since you

---

[12] 1 Cor 1.10.

[13] Richard Kugelman, "The First Letter to the Corinthians," *Jerome Biblical Commentary*, 256.

[14] St John Chrysostom, Homily 3.2 on 1 Corinthians (NPNF1 12:11).

[15] 1 Cor 1.20.

[16] 1 Cor 4.6.

were partisans of notable apostles and of a man they endorsed. But think now who they are who have led you astray and degraded your honorable and celebrated love of the brethren. It is disgraceful, exceedingly disgraceful, and unworthy of your Christian upbringing, to have it reported that because of one or two individuals the solid and ancient Corinthian church is in revolt against its presbyters. . . . The result is that the Lord's name is being blasphemed because of your stupidity, and you are exposing yourselves to danger.[17]

St Clement continues, advising that those "who are responsible for the revolt must submit to the presbyters. . . . Learn obedience, and be done with your proud boasting and curb your arrogant tongues."[18] The words of the Lord Jesus come to mind: "That they may all be one; even as thou, Father, art in me, and I in thee, that they also may be in us, so that the world may believe that thou hast sent me."[19] Any strife or lack of unity constitutes abject disobedience to the injunction of Christ that all should be one. The Lord died to make us one: "And I, when I am lifted up from the earth, will draw all men to myself."[20] The critical nature of the absolute requirement for unity cannot be overemphasized. The underlying assumption is that the bishops and presbyters who were confronted with rebellion have, in Clement's words, "ministered to Christ's flock faultlessly, humbly, quietly, and unassumingly [and] have offered the sacrifices with innocence and holiness."[21]

St Ignatius of Antioch, a contemporary of St Clement, was martyred in Rome circa AD 110. On his way to Rome, he wrote seven letters describing in vivid and personal terms his understanding of church leadership as embodied in the offices of bishop, presbyter, and deacon. The term "monarchical episcopate" has often been associated with St Ignatius and his authoritarian tone. As one modern commentator puts it, "In Ignatius . . . the single bishop is the leading figure in the Church. Without his

[17] 1 Clement 47.1–7 (Richardson, *Early Christian Fathers*, 65).
[18] 1 Clement 57.1–2 (Ibid.,, 69).
[19] Jn 17.21.
[20] Jn 12.32.
[21] 1 Clement 44.4–5 (Ibid.,, 64).

approval no services are to be held . . . or other action taken."[22] The need for the bishop's approval is certainly spelled out in detail in St Ignatius' letters, particularly Smyrnaeans 8–9.

However, further reading of the epistles reveals the depth of feeling that St Ignatius had for his fellow ministers, namely, his desire for love and harmony among all the people, acted out "decently and in order," so as to preserve and safeguard the faith. St Ignatius' feelings were sharpened and perhaps exposed by knowledge of his impending martyrdom and, as St Paul's epistles conclude so frequently, focus on those dear to him. He views the Church not as institution, nor as a collection of factions, but as people united around the ordained ministers of the Church: the bishops, presbyters, and deacons.[23]

In his letter to the Ephesians, St Ignatius refers personally to the local bishop, Onesimus, and to the relationship that the faithful have with this "man whose love is beyond words. My prayer is that you love him in the spirit of Jesus Christ and all be like him. . . . I congratulate you on having such intimacy with him as the Church enjoys with Jesus Christ, and Jesus Christ with the Father. That is how unity and harmony come to prevail everywhere."[24] Similarly, St Ignatius comments on the presbyters in glowing terms, not only in regard to their personal attributes, but also their communion with the bishop: "Your presbytery, indeed, which deserves its name and is a credit to God, is as closely tied to the bishop as the strings to a harp."[25] Elsewhere, a particular deacon—"my fellow slave, the deacon Zotion"—receives praise both as a servant and for his obedience in love: "I am delighted with him, because he submits to the bishop as to God's grace, and to the presbytery as to the law of Jesus Christ."[26] The connection described here between and among the ministers of the Church and the

---

[22]Richardson, *Early Christian Fathers,* 76.

[23]For a balanced discussion on the mono-episcopacy, see John Behr, *The Way to Nicea: The Formation of Christian Theology 1* (Crestwood, NY: St Vladimir's Seminary Press, 2001), 81–82.

[24]St Ignatius of Antioch, Letter to the Ephesians 1.3; 5.1 (Richardson, *Early Christian Fathers,* 88–89).

[25]St Ignatius of Antioch, Letter to the Ephesians 4.1 (Ibid., 89).

[26]St Ignatius of Antioch, Letter to the Magnesians 2.1 (Ibid., 95).

people is not to be understood in authoritarian categories. It simply fulfills the words of St Paul: "Be subject to one another out of reverence for Christ."[27] St Ignatius clearly identifies the foundation of life in the Church as the body of Christ: "I sing the praises of the churches, even while I am a prisoner. I want them to confess that Jesus Christ, our perpetual Life, united flesh with spirit. I want them, too, to unite their faith with love—there is nothing better than that."[28]

St Ignatius sees the ministers as encapsulating the love of the faithful and ensuring the complete harmony of all with the will of God, provided that they are willing to work together.

> I believed, then, that I saw your whole congregation in these people I have mentioned, and I loved you all. Hence I urge you to aim to do all in godly agreement. Let the bishop preside in God's place, and the presbyters take the place of the apostolic council, and let the deacons (my special favorites) be entrusted with the ministry of Jesus Christ. . . .
>
> Taking, then, the same attitude as God, you should all respect one another. Let no one think of his neighbor in a carnal way; but always love one another in the spirit of Jesus Christ. Do not let there be anything to divide you, but be in accord with the bishop and your leaders. Thus you will be an example and a lesson of incorruptibility.
>
> As then, the Lord did nothing without the Father (either on his own or by the apostles) because he was at one with him, so you must not do anything without the bishop and presbyters. Do not, moreover, try to convince yourselves that anything done on your own is commendable. Only what you do together is right. Hence you must have one prayer, one petition, one mind, one hope, dominated by love and unsullied joy—that means you must have Jesus Christ. You cannot have anything better than that.[29]

[27]Eph 5.21.

[28]St Ignatius of Antioch, Letter to the Magnesians 1.2 (Richardson, *Early Christian Fathers*, 94).

[29]St Ignatius of Antioch, Letter to the Magnesians 6.1–7.1 (Ibid., 95–96).

In the letter to the Trallians, after asking the people to "obey the bishop as if he were Jesus Christ," St Ignatius encourages them to "submit to the presbytery as to the apostles of Jesus Christ." Lastly he insists that "everyone must show the deacons respect. They represent Jesus Christ, just as the bishop has the role of the Father, and the presbyters are like God's council and an apostolic band. You cannot have a church without these."[30] As immediate preface to his oft-quoted statement that nothing should be done in the Church without the approval of the bishop, he declares: "Follow the bishop as Jesus Christ did the Father. Follow too, the presbytery as you would the apostles; and respect the deacons as you would God's law."[31]

St Ignatius thus emphasizes togetherness and mutual responsibility, not a strict mono-authority. The bishop needs help, too, as he declares: "It is right that each one of you and especially the presbyters should encourage the bishop, in honor of the Father, Jesus Christ, and the apostles."[32] The letter that St Ignatius wrote to his fellow-martyr Polycarp, bishop of Smyrna, is filled with advice to bishops, especially concerning his relationship with the people and his fellow ministers.

> Make unity your concern—there is nothing better than that. Lend everybody a hand, as the Lord does you. "Out of love be patient" with everyone, as indeed you are. Devote yourself to continual prayer. Ask for increasing insight . . . [t]ake a personal interest in those you talk to, just as God does. "Bear the diseases" of everyone, like an athlete in perfect form. . . . By your gentleness, subdue those who are annoying. . . . And especially for God's sake must we put up with everything, so that he will put up with us.
>
> I give my life as a sacrifice (poor as it is) for those who are obedient to the bishop, the presbyters, and the deacons. Along with them may I get my share of God's reward! Share your hard training together— wrestle together, run together, go to bed together, get up together,

---

[30]St Ignatius of Antioch, Letter to the Trallians 2.1–2; 3.1–2 (Richardson, *Early Christian Fathers*, 98–99).

[31]St Ignatius of Antioch, Letter to the Smyrnaeans 8.1 (Ibid., 115).

[32]St Ignatius of Antioch, Letter to the Trallians 12:2 (Ibid., 101).

as God's stewards, assessors, and assistants. . . . Be patient, then, and gentle with one another, as God is with you. May I always be happy about you![33]

A century after St Ignatius, St Cyprian, the bishop of Carthage who was later martyred, re-emphasized the central role of the bishop. He had to confront yet another uprising within the Church, this time over the question of what to do with those who had "lapsed" under the pressure of threat of death, i.e., sacrificing to the gods or obtaining a statement that they had done so. The opposing party elected a different bishop to occupy the same episcopal throne as Cyprian. The controversy spread to Rome, with several mutual excommunications among the contending bishops.[34]

Peace finally ensued with the deaths of various persons, including St Cyprian via martyrdom. In the meantime, St Cyprian composed several letters and writings which emphasize the need for unity in the Church around the bishop, as well as the unity of the bishops with one another.

> The Church is a people united with its sacred bishop and a flock which stands behind its own shepherd. The conclusion you should therefore draw is that the bishop is in the Church and the Church is in the bishop: if anyone is not with the bishop, he is not in the Church. It is vain for some to let themselves be seduced by the idea that they can lurk in corners and be in secret communion with certain persons without being reconciled with God's sacred bishops. The Catholic Church is one, and cannot be rent asunder or divided. Rather it is everywhere interconnected and joined by the glue of sacred bishops mutually adhering together with one another.[35]

---

[33]St Ignatius of Antioch, Letter to Polycarp 1.2–3; 2.1; 3.1; 6.1–2 (Richardson, *Early Christian Fathers*, 118–20).

[34]See the "Introduction" in Allen Brent, *St Cyprian of Carthage, On the Church: Select Treatises* (Crestwood, NY: St Vladimir's Seminary Press, 2006) for an extensive discussion of these events.

[35]St Cyprian of Carthage, Epistle to Puppianus 66.8.3 (Brent, *St Cyprian of Carthage*, 33).

We, the bishops who preside over the Church, are under the fore-most obligation to grasp tightly this unity and to assert our title to it, with the object of proving that the episcopate in itself is one and indivisible. . . . The episcopate is one, an individual share in which individual bishops hold as owners of a common property. The Church is a unity, which extends into a plurality by the widespread increase of her fruitfulness.[36]

Later in the life of the Church, many canons were written to deal with violations of this most fundamental commandment of Christ, to love and be one with one another. It is distressing to read some of the canons with their prescribed penalties up to and including deposition and excommu-nication, for the issue would not have occupied the sacred councils of the Church, unless there were significant, and perhaps even blatant, violations of unity.

These disciplinary canons pertain not only to bishops but to presbyters, deacons, and lay people as well. We should bear in mind that these canons may reflect a more Christian society than our own. Certainly, in the past Christianity was not only the predominant religion, but also prescribed by the civil government. However, even under those circumstances the holy fathers of the councils spent considerable effort in ensuring proper rules and penalties for violations.

The pastoral writings of St Gregory Nazianzen and St John Chryso-stom provide ample warnings against certain types of men who might seek admittance to the priesthood or the episcopate. A particularly graphic example is painted by St Gregory.

I was ashamed of all those others, who, without being better than ordi-nary people, nay, it is a great thing if they be not worse, with unwashen hands, as the saying runs, and uninitiated souls, intrude into the most sacred offices; and, before becoming worthy to approach the temples, they lay claim to the sanctuary, and they push and thrust around the holy table, as if they thought this order to be a means of livelihood,

[36]St Cyprian of Carthage, *The Unity of the Catholic Church* 5 (Brent, *St Cyprian of Carthage*, 153–155).

instead of a pattern of virtue, or an absolute authority, instead of a ministry of which we must give account.[37]

Humility and reticence before the responsibility of leadership is essential, according to the saint:

> To undertake the training of others before being sufficiently trained oneself, and to learn, as men say, the potter's art on a wine-jar, that is, to practice ourselves in piety at the expense of others' souls seems to me to be excessive folly or excessive rashness—folly, if we are not even aware of our own ignorance; rashness, if in spite of this knowledge we venture on the task.[38]

St Gregory speaks sarcastically of those who fail to understand humility but instead depend upon superficial appearances to gain attention and approval.

> Most of us, not to say all, almost before we have lost our childish curls and lisp, before we have entered the house of God, before we know even the names of the sacred books, before we have learnt the character and authors of the Old and New Testaments. . . . If, I say, we have furnished ourselves with two or three expressions of pious authors, and that by hearsay, not by study; if we have had a brief experience of David, or clad ourselves properly. . . . or have girt about us some form and appearance of piety—phew! how we take the chair and show our spirit! Samuel was holy even in his swaddling-clothes: we are at once wise teachers, of high estimation in divine things, the first of scribes and lawyers; we ordain ourselves men of heaven and seek to be called Rabbi by men.[39]

These harsh warnings are still applicable today. Candidates for leadership need to be prepared and truly want to serve with humility. Candidates are evaluated and elected by the regional council (or synod) of bishops, according to New Testament qualifications and the guidance of

---

[37]St Gregory Nazianzen, *Oration* 2.8 (NPNF[2] 7:206).

[98]Ibid., *Oration* 2.47 (NPNF[2] 7:214).

[39]Ibid., *Oration* 2.49 (NPNF[2] 7:215).

the apostolic fathers. In some places, the candidates are first nominated by the clergy and faithful of the diocese that they will serve. The finally-elected candidate still remains unworthy to assume the office until the prayers of the people and his fellow bishops are offered to God, and the Holy Spirit descends upon him. This occurs at his consecration as bishop, which clearly specifies his leadership responsibilities and required behavior.

THE CONSECRATION OF THE BISHOP

Following his nomination and election, the candidate for the episcopacy is led before the consecrating bishops for the laying on of hands. The first part of this service takes place at the vigil following the ninth ode of the canon. It is noteworthy that, in the ordination services for deacon and priest, the candidate remains silent throughout the ordination. The bishop-elect, however, is publicly questioned as to his reasons for presenting himself to the bishops and on the content of his faith. The reason is, of course, to receive "the laying on of hands, unto the grace of the bishop's office."[40]

The questions to the bishop-elect are three-fold: the first, inquire generally into the faith which the candidate holds; the second concern the doctrines of the Trinity and the incarnation; and the third focus on the canons, traditions, and regulations of the Church. The first question is answered by a simple recitation of the Nicene creed, the symbol of faith. The second is a more extended exposition on the creed, with emphasis on the two natures and wills of Christ, the veneration of icons, and the person of Mary the Theotokos. The third shifts the tone from doctrine to promises, from what the candidate believes to what he promises to do. We concentrate here on the third set of questions.

There are several general areas of promises. First, the candidate promises to observe the canons, the church traditions, and "decrees, orders and regulations of the Holy Fathers." Second, the candidate promises to "preserve the peace of the Church" and teach "the people entrusted to me" while holding the Orthodox faith. As a corollary to achieving this peace,

[40]Hapgood, *Service Book*, 325. Further references to the words of the service are taken from Hapgood, 323–31.

the candidate pledges to obey the patriarch and holy synod "and to be, in all things, of one mind" with all the bishops and "with all sincerity to cherish towards them spiritual affection: and to regard them as brethren." Specifically, he promises to not exercise any function in any other diocese without the permission of that bishop, nor to receive any clergy from another diocese without a letter of dismissal from that bishop. Third, the candidate promises to govern the flock "committed to me in the fear of God and in devoutness of life; and with all diligent heed to guard it against all heresies of doctrine." Further, he "promises to visit and watch over the flock now confided to me" to see that they follow the faith and exercise good works, "more especially the priests," and to guard against any "schisms, superstitions, and impious veneration" as well as immoral conduct. When people arise who oppose the Church, the candidate promises to deal with them "with reasonableness, uprightness, and gentleness." He also promises that he will do nothing under constraint, even if commanded "under pain of death, to do something contrary to divine and holy laws." Lastly, he promises that these are not merely words: "All those things, my bounden duty, which I have this day promised in word, I also promise to perform in deed unto my uttermost breath, for the sake of the covenanted good things to come."

The new bishop-elect now waits for the moment in the Divine Liturgy just after the singing of the thrice-holy hymn. The gospel book is then placed upon the head of the kneeling bishop-elect while the presiding bishop prays the same prayer as at the ordination of a deacon or priest:

> The grace divine, which always healeth that which is infirm, and completeth that which is wanting, through the laying-on of hands elevateth thee, the most God-loving Archimandrite (or Hiero-Monk) N., duly elected, to be the bishop of the God-saved cities, NN. Wherefore let us pray for him, that the grace of the all-holy Spirit may come upon him.

Two further prayers follow while the bishops continue to lay their hands upon him and the gospel book is on his head. The first prayer is that he may be strengthened by the Holy Spirit, that his episcopate may be blameless, and "that he may be worthy to ask those things which are for the salvation of the people." The second recalls the fundamental attributes of the bishop and asks the Lord God to

> make this man, also, who hath been proclaimed a steward of the episcopal grace, to be an imitator of thee, the true Shepherd, who didst lay down thy life for thy sheep; to be a leader of the blind, a light to those in darkness, a reprover of the unwise, a teacher of the young, a lamp to the world: that, having perfected the souls entrusted unto him in this present life, he may stand unashamed before thy throne, and receive the great reward which thou hast prepared for those who have contended valiantly for the preaching of thy gospel.

The overwhelming responsibility of the bishop is here expressly laid out: the care of the faithful, which involves not only teaching, guiding, and reproving, but also interceding, illuminating, and perfecting. All of this is done in the image of the Shepherd, who gave his life for the sheep.[41]

THE OVERSIGHT OF THE BISHOP

The bishop's oversight role is of critical importance, not only for the proper fulfillment of his own responsibilities as leader of a diocese, but also in the example of oversight leadership he provides to others. These others include the priests and deacons who report to him, but also the people in every parish under his omophorion. They all need to see in him an example of care, concern, and love. In addition, he acts as brother to, and fellow worker with, all the other bishops that sit with him on the holy synod or other bishops' council. He may even play the role of counselor and mentor

---

[41]While the bishop is certainly appointed to guard against doctrinal heresies, guardianship is shared with the entire Church. Alexis Khomiakoff, in his summary of the Eastern patriarchs' 1848 reply to an epistle of Pope Pius IX, said, "The Pope is greatly mistaken in supposing that we consider the ecclesiastical hierarchy to be the guardian of the dogma [of the Church]. The case is quite different. The unvarying constancy and the unerring truth of Christian dogma does not depend upon any hierarchical order; it is guarded by the totality, by the whole people of the Church, which is the body of Christ." In *Russia and the English Church*, W. J. Birkbeck, ed. (London: Rivington, Percival & Co., 1895; republished Westmead, Farnborough, Hants, England: Gregg International Publishers Limited, 1969), 94.

to bishops of lesser experience, as well as to those who encounter problems and issues concerning which they need advice. In every case he must act as a true shepherd, manifesting all of the prayed-for characteristics above.

Similar to the relationship between the priest and the laity, the clergy under the bishop's direct oversight need to focus on, care for, and love him. They need to support him in his responsibilities. They need to be fellow leaders with him, working together as a team, consistent with the above advice of St Ignatius. There will be times when clergy as well as lay leaders will need to speak words of truth regarding situations of which their bishop may not be aware. It is the responsibility of the bishop to create an open, loving, and respectful environment that will also allow others to "speak the truth in love."[42] In turn, it is the responsibility of the clergy and laity to help the bishop and to lift up his arms (as Aaron and Hur did for Moses), especially when he gets tired.[43]

---

[42]Eph 4.15.
[43]Ex 17.12.

PART FOUR

Strategic Planning

The Lord said to the exiles in Babylon: "I know the plans I have for you . . . to give you a future and a hope."[1] Five centuries later, Jesus Christ fulfilled these plans, becoming the future and hope not only of Israel, but of the entire world.

Jesus spoke many times to his disciples about the plans that he had for them. He emphasized three times that they would bear fruit, and even "much fruit," as Israel had not.[2] In addition, Jesus prayed that they would be one, even "perfectly one," in order that all would know that they had been sent by him.[3] These two aspects of Christian ministry, namely, fruitfulness and oneness, are at the core of what it means to be a leader in the Church or anywhere else. They are also at the core of what we call strategic planning.

If our plan, as successors to the disciples of Jesus, is to be fruitful and at one with others, should we expect this to just "happen," or is something more required of us? Solomon advises: "Commit your work to the Lord, and your plans will be established."[4] We might say that we are committed to God, meaning that we have faith in him. But proof of that commitment, that resolution, must be shown in our work, in our fruitfulness. Unfortunately, the temptation to become forgetful, undisciplined, and lazy often frustrates even the best of resolutions. This axiom is especially true when we are making the commitment to work together in community.

[1] Jer 29.11.
[2] Jn 15.5, 8, 16.
[3] Jn 17.22.
[4] Prov 16.3.

We must have a disciplined way of making plans if we are to ensure that our actions are in accordance with God's will and purpose, and to assist us in the commitment of our work to the Lord. There is a direct connection between this planning and our desire to follow the principles laid out earlier on finding God's will for oneself, fearing God, walking in his ways, loving and serving him, and keeping his commandments. Solomon emphasizes the need for congruence between the plans of man and the will of God: "A man's mind plans his way, but the Lord directs his steps."[5]

It is admittedly difficult for us to discover and strive to do the will of God within ourselves. Within a community this task becomes much harder, since many people are involved, and each of them are at different stages of their lives. The temptation for such a group is to set low expectations to avoid disappointment. But if we are servants of the King, nothing less than the best should satisfy us. Attaining the kingdom is not easy, for it requires repentance as Jesus preached after his baptism by John.[6] Further, great effort is required, for as Jesus explains: "The law and the prophets were until John; since then the good news of the kingdom of God is preached, and every one enters it violently."[7] St John Chrysostom states that those who enter it are the ones "who approach it with earnestness of mind."[8]

Nor is "becoming one" an easy task, as Church history shows. In the very early days of the Church, all "were together and had all things in common."[9] In the early days of any venture, the community is in a honeymoon period and all is well. Tensions arose within the Church when difficult issues surfaced, such as the conversion of the Gentiles and whether or not they should be obliged to follow the Mosaic law.[10] In this case a peaceful solution emerged, but not without blunt and personal criticism of St Peter by St Paul.[11] Sometimes there were breaks in relationships. Differences

[5]Prov 16.9. See the prologue to this book for additional background.
[6]Mk 1.15.
[7]Lk 16.16.
[8]St John Chrysostom, Homily 37.4 on Matthew (NPNF[1] 10:240).
[9]Acts 2.44.
[10]Acts 15.
[11]Gal 2.11–14.

between Barnabas and Paul over whether to take John Mark on a missionary journey resulted in "sharp contention, so that they separated from each other."[12] However, reconciliation did finally occur, as evidenced by St Paul's request to the Colossians to receive John Mark.[13] In a community, even one with a common faith, it is never easy to agree on what to do in any particular situation and to be one, as Jesus desired us to be.

St Paul documented other problems afflicting the oneness of the Christian community. His first letter to the Christians in Corinth describes a textbook case of how those who are "called to be saints" can quarrel and, overwhelmed by party spirit, become afflicted with "jealousy and strife."[14] In addition, St Paul addresses problems within the community such as immorality, arrogance, settling internal disputes by appealing to civil courts, disorder in the church arising from the practice of speaking in tongues, and questioning the resurrection of Christ. We recall that St Paul established the church at Corinth over a period of eighteen months, and thus understandably felt a special ownership and kinship with that church.[15] The implication for us is that we, as a community, must care about the community and feel a proprietary interest in it. When we remain on the outside looking in, nothing positive will occur.

What does St Paul do, when he hears about the problems afflicting the church that he founded? He immediately draws their attention to the fact that they are called to be holy—indeed, they are already "sanctified in Christ Jesus," not as mere individuals but "together with all those who in every place call on the name of our Lord."[16] He establishes and confirms the foundation of their community. He emphasizes that they lack nothing, for they were given "the grace of God" and "in every way . . . enriched in [Christ Jesus] with all speech and all knowledge."[17] He calls them back to the initial vision and continuing foundation of their faith and life together.

[12] Acts 15.39.
[13] Col 4.10.
[14] 1 Cor 3.3.
[15] Acts 18.1, 11.
[16] 1 Cor 1.2.
[17] 1 Cor 1.4–5.

St Paul then proceeds to appeal to them to cease their divisions and refuse to be guided by the ways of the world, such as arrogance, toleration of immorality, and lawsuits, but rather by the cross of Christ. He considers the particular ways in which the Corinthians have departed from the "foundation . . . which is laid, which is Jesus Christ."[18] The difficulties that afflict them are those of disunity and disorder, the former brought on by party spirit and the latter by perceived differences in spiritual gifts. Even today we may have differences in party spirit from one church to another, or between ministries within a single church, such as bishops versus priests versus laity.

The healing of these wounds in the body of Christ comes about only through our continual bearing of the cross of Christ in service to one another in love and harmony. St Paul declares, "For just as the body is one and has many members, and all the members of the body, though many, are one body, so it is with Christ. For by one Spirit we were all baptized into one body—Jews or Greeks, slaves or free—and all were made to drink of one Spirit."[19]

Although we are one, we are different by design. St Paul reminds us, as members of the body of Christ, that there are differences in function: "God has appointed in the church first apostles, second prophets, third teachers, then workers of miracles, then healers, helpers, administrators, speakers in various kinds of tongues."[20] He explains in Ephesians that these functions serve "to equip the saints for the work of ministry, for building up the body of Christ . . . from whom the whole body, joined and knit together by every joint with which it is supplied, when each part is working properly, makes bodily growth and upbuilds itself in love."[21] St Paul likens his own work to that of a builder, and compares the flock in Corinth to God's building. He is constantly thinking about the people for whom he is responsible rather than about his own authority.

[18] 1 Cor 3.11.
[19] 1 Cor 12.12–13.
[20] 1 Cor 12.28.
[21] Eph 4.12, 16.

We might expect the words of the great apostle to sting the people of Corinth to such a degree that they would never repeat the same mistakes. However, they were slow learners. St Paul first spent eighteen months establishing the church, and then, hearing about their difficulties, wrote his first and second letters. (In fact, St Paul mentions a letter sent even before the one we know as the first.)[22] In between these letters, St Paul visited Corinth again.[23] Clearly, the Corinthians needed significant guidance—and indeed scolding—on a repeated basis. St Clement of Rome intervened in Corinth once again some forty years later, over "a schism in the Corinthian Church [provoked by] the same factious spirit that Paul had encountered there."[24]

After these letters, we read little if anything about the church in Corinth in the post-apostolic writings.[25] A letter attributed to St Clement has been interpreted as indicating the healing of the Corinthian schism.[26] In any event, "by AD 170, the Christians of Corinth regarded I Clement as Scripture."[27] We hope this footnote indicates a happy ending for the church there.

Are there lessons for us to learn from the difficulty encountered by the church at Corinth, and the obvious frustration and pain experienced by St Paul? In many ways, the environment in Corinth was not dissimilar to that of today: industrial, wealthy, diverse, and influenced by pagan practices and a general lack of morals. One biblical commentator concludes that "the parallels between this first-century Corinth and the great cities of the modern world give St Paul's letters to the Corinthians an exceptional relevance for modern Christians."[28] Given the outside environment, what was the basic cause of the issues troubling the church in Corinth? St Paul

[22]1 Cor 5.9.

[23]2 Cor 2.1; Acts 20.3; cf. Roy Bowen Ward, "Paul and Corinth – His Visits and His Letters," *Restoration Quarterly* 3.4 (1959): 158–68.

[24]Richardson, *Early Fathers*, 34.

[25]I could not find anything in the available English translations, but it would be most useful to follow church development through the second century in Corinth.

[26]Veselin Kesich, *The Birth of the Church AD 33–200*, vol. 1 of *Formation and Struggles: The Church AD 33–450* (Crestwood, NY: St Vladimir's Seminary Press, 2007), 122.

[27]Ibid., 125.

[28]Kugelman, "The First Letter to the Corinthians," *Jerome Biblical Commentary*, 255.

begins his first letter with an emphasis on unity in Jesus Christ, and then proceeds to analyze the various differences in attitudes and behavior.

The fundamental text is: "I appeal to you, brethren, by the name of our Lord Jesus Christ, that all of you agree and that there be no dissensions among you, but that you be united in the same mind and the same judgment."[29] St John Chrysostom, in his homily on this passage, declares that the implications of "united" go beyond our everyday understanding of the word. (As noted earlier, the King James translation uses "perfectly joined together" instead of "united.") St John explains:

> Since there is such a thing as agreement in words, and that hearty, not however on all subjects, therefore he added this, "That ye may be perfected together." For he that is united in one thing, but in another dissents, is no longer "perfected," nor fitted in to complete accordance. There is also such a thing as harmony of opinions, where there is not yet harmony of sentiment; for instance, when having the same faith we are not joined together in love: for thus, in opinions we are one (for we think the same things) but in sentiment not so. And such was the case at that time; this person choosing one [leader], and that, another. For this reason he saith it is necessary to agree both in "mind" and in "judgment." For it was not from any difference in faith that the schisms arose, but from the division of their judgment through human contentiousness.[30]

How, then, do we "perfectly join together"? How can we hope to succeed in doing this when even the great apostle had such difficulty, despite his many exhortations and prayers? We must begin with the foundation of the Church as the body of Christ. According to Fr Georges Florovsky, "The early church was not just a volunteer association for 'religious' purposes. It was rather the New Society, even the New Humanity . . . the true City of God, in the process of construction."[31] The building of any structure needs to be undertaken carefully, with discipline and prudence, and laid upon a

---

[29] 1 Cor 1.10.
[30] St John Chrysostom, Homily 3.2 on 1 Corinthians (NPNF[1] 12:11).
[31] Georges Florovsky, "The Social Problem in the Eastern Orthodox Church," *Christianity and Culture* (Belmont, MA: Nordland Publishing Company, 1974), 132.

strong foundation. The walls must be able to withstand the pressures of wind and rain, and the roof capable of protecting the inhabitants within. In the case of building a community of people, of course, the problems and difficulties are far more intense and extensive, as reflected in St Paul's letters to the early Christian communities.

Some 500 years before St Paul, a young servant ("cup-bearer") to the king of Persia set forth on a project that must have seemed to many to be doomed from the start.[32] His name was Nehemiah. He had heard of the destruction of the walls and gates of Jerusalem by fire.[33] Nehemiah broke down weeping, and with prayer and fasting implored the Lord God that he might be able to rebuild those walls. Following that fervent prayer, he obtained permission from the king to go to Jerusalem with introductory letters to provincial governors to secure safe passage and supplies. Accompanied by a few others, he inspected the gates and walls. He then assembled the "Jews, the priests, the nobles, the officials, and the rest that were to do the work."[34] When he told them of "the trouble we are in" and invited them to "build the wall of Jerusalem," they replied, "Let us rise up and build."[35] And they did.

Nehemiah did not leave the construction up to chance, but organized some forty families and groups of neighbors to undertake various pieces of the project. The construction did not come without external opposition from rivals, who ridiculed the effort and threatened violence. Nehemiah recognized the threat, and organized protection of the workers and the people. However, difficulties still arose internally, with accusations of incipient poverty because of the financial demands of the officials. Nehemiah convened an assembly and convinced the officials to convert the mortgages into outright gifts, thereby averting the crisis.

In our current lexicon, Nehemiah was a strategic planner. He had a vision that was founded upon his love for the people, as shown by his mourning for the depths to which Jerusalem had fallen. His values were

[32]Robert North, "The Chronicler," *Jerome Biblical Commentary*, 434.
[33]Neh 1.3.
[34]Neh 2.16.
[35]Neh 2.17–18.

his fear of and faith in God. He had a well-defined mission to accomplish. He knew what he needed, from beginning to end, to accomplish his objectives. He involved many people, from the king and governors to the nobles, officials, leaders, and families that performed the work. He recognized the threats from outside as well as the issues arising from within. In the end he accomplished his task: "So the wall was finished on the twenty-fifth day of the month of Elul, in fifty-two days."[36]

---

[36]Neh 6.15.

10

"Strategic Planning Is for Business, Not the Church!"

We will first introduce the concepts and processes of strategic planning, and then provide a particular method of planning that has been used to good success in church as well as corporate institutions. We will begin with a real-life example of strategic planning at a theological seminary, starting with the concerns expressed at the beginning of the process and showing how those concerns were resolved.

AN EXAMPLE OF STRATEGIC PLANNING

As a system, strategic planning has been practiced in business and corporate circles for many years. It has also been extended to educational institutions, including theological schools and seminaries.[1] St Vladimir's Orthodox Theological Seminary in Crestwood, New York, began strategic planning in 1989. These efforts did not initially meet with universal enthusiasm. Reluctance and even suspicion were expressed by many sectors within the seminary's governance structure. One bishop spoke for many at the time when he said, "Strategic planning is for corporate business, not for the Church."[2] The seminary administration also had misgivings, since the strategic planning effort was not originally the seminary's idea, i.e., "not

---

[1]Robert S. Landrebe, "Is Strategic Planning a Waste of Time?" *In Trust* 22.4 (Summer 2011): 16–21.

[2]Peter Danilchick, "Strategic Planning at SVS: A Process, Not a Product," *SVS News* 1.2 (Autumn 2003): 6.

invented here." Rather, it was instigated by the Association of Theological Schools (ATS), the accrediting agency for St Vladimir's, which had advised the seminary to develop a long-range plan for the school.

An easy way for the seminary to accomplish this objective would have been to hire a professional planner to develop a written plan, which would then be reviewed by the trustees, administration, faculty, and staff. This would indeed have been easy, but not effective. The administration took a wiser approach by beginning the planning effort at the top, involving the board of trustees and key faculty, staff, and administrators. A two-day intensive kickoff workshop was held in late 1988 for these key personnel, outlining the basics of planning and essentially conducting a "mini-strategic plan" with breakout discussion groups involving mixed constituencies.

The workshop helped overcome some internal and previously unexpressed concerns among some individuals in the leadership and governance structure with regards to how others felt about the seminary. The board of trustees was composed of several bishops from different jurisdictions; the lead administrators, faculty, and staff of the school; and business people ranging from lawyers and doctors to corporate executives. Discussions before the workshop revealed uncertainty among these individuals regarding their colleagues' commitment to the seminary, their perceptions of the seminary's mission and performance, and what the institution might do differently.

The two-day workshop involved sub-teams composed of various combinations of the above personnel categories. These teams discussed the issues in all these areas, then reported their sub-group discussions to the whole group, which reflected as a whole on what everyone said. The result was a new sense of unity and commitment: "As one lay trustee said: 'Even if we don't do anything else, this short experience has shown us all—bishops, laity, faculty, and staff—that we love the seminary, feel strongly about its role, and want to help it better serve the Church.'"[3] Those in attendance, all of whom held the seminary in trust and worked daily to fulfill its mission, had a very strong sense that they had received this institution as a gift. It was their duty to ensure that it bore fruit, whatever that might take.

[3]Danilchick, "Strategic Planning at SVS," 6.

A major breakthrough in attitude was realized at a board of trustees meeting immediately following the kickoff workshop, at which the seminary's dean, Fr John Meyendorff, was asked his opinion of the proposed strategic planning effort. Initially, Fr John had been a bit suspicious of the whole idea of the strategic plan, especially the plan to go out after the workshop and ask the constituency of the school about their ideas for its future. Thus a great sense of relief was felt by those about to embark on the strategic plan when Fr John said, "Well, we do not expect anything revolutionary to come out of it ... but if it is revolutionary, so be it!"[4] This forthright and courageous statement gave the process the imprint of top leadership endorsement, which is required for any strategic planning effort to be successful.

This initial communal experience was continued via the solicitation of input from other faculty and staff, hierarchs, alumni, current students, donors, and benefactors. Face-to-face interviews were conducted, as well as focus groups and written surveys. Teams were commissioned to evaluate different strategic options. Their recommendations were evaluated in 1990 by the board, which then endorsed near- and medium-term goals and objectives for the seminary. This process was again undertaken in late 2001 with the strategic plan "SVS2010," which was performed in much the same way as the first one. The seminary recently completed its third major strategic plan, "SVS2020." For the seminary, the strategic planning process has become an essential and continuing effort to periodically reemphasize its vision, redefine its mission, and reestablish mutual commitment to fulfill that vision and mission.

WHAT STRATEGIC PLANNING IS NOT

Misconceptions arise concerning strategic planning in every institution, whether corporate, nonprofit, or religious. We will first discuss what strategic planning is *not*.

It is not "long-range planning" in the sense of merely extrapolating today's plans to tomorrow, i.e., "keep on keeping on," or perhaps making

[4]Danilchick, "Strategic Planning at SVS," 6.

small adjustments here and there on the assumption that we are doing just fine. Very little deep thought or reflection goes on in such a process. First and foremost, a sense of strategy (as in "how we can be different from today?") is completely missing. The most disturbing absence is that of any comparison between what we are doing and what is demanded of us by God. The Lord may want something quite different of us than what we are doing right now, or what we are comfortable with. If we start with today as our sole basis for going forward, we may never get to where we should be.

On the other hand, neither is a strategic plan a dream which excites people momentarily and is then laid aside. Grandiose ideas may be proclaimed that have little chance of fruition, but which galvanize people with the prospect of something completely new. There may be some short-term increase in organizational energy, but this can rapidly fizzle due to the lack of the disciplined, soul-searching effort that goes into a true strategic plan. The end result is often frustration and skepticism ("we tried strategic planning, but it didn't work").

Sometimes the edict that "planning" must be done comes from an external source such as company headquarters, an accrediting agency, or even potential major donors. People often think of it as the process du jour: since everyone does it, we should do it too. This sort of planning process generally has little in the way of internal roots and motivation. The resulting plan may look good on paper, but it lacks community strength and resilience when issues and problems inevitably arise.

Larger organizations may have professional planning staffs or volunteers with particular expertise. It is a great temptation to turn the planning process over to them without seeking the proper involvement of others who will be impacted by the plan. Smaller organizations may be reluctant to involve "outsiders" and trust only "insiders." This approach, again, leads to a limited perspective that does not reflect the hearts and minds of the community as it seeks to do God's will.

Lastly, the governing body, council, or board may not be involved in the process until the plan, wrapped up with a bow, is presented for a final review. At that time the response may be, "You have presented a very good answer, but to the wrong question, unfortunately." And back to the drawing board we go. Or, the board might disagree with the plan without reject-ing or correcting it, because "so much work has been put into it." Either response is bad, but the latter is deadly.

WHAT STRATEGIC PLANNING IS

Strategic planning is devoted to realizing a vision—not an individual vision, but a shared one. Some people believe that the vision is immutably established by the great forebears, founders, or famous personages of a parish, school, or institution. The current leadership simply preserves this vision. As an example, St Vladimir's Seminary had no shortage of such per-sonages, including former deans such as Metropolitan Leonty and Fathers Florovsky, Schmemann, Meyendorff, and Hopko, and renowned profes-sors such as Verhovskoy, Arseniev, Kesich, etc. These men were highly respected and, in some cases, even revered. Their writings and vision con-tinue to inspire, but they would be the last ones to state that the creation of the vision of the school ended with them.

Metropolitan Leonty questioned the very basis of theological educa-tion in America:

> Should we establish this program of theological education in our American theological seminary on a practical, i.e., missionary, basis? Should the program of study be on the pastoral level? Or should we bear in mind the great importance of the theoretical, i.e., purely schol-arly and intellectual problems and concerns of the future Orthodox Church in America?[5]

Fr Georges Florovsky spoke of the openness of the future: "The future is not something we are looking and waiting for, but rather something we must create. . . . We have not reached the term of our course, the history of the Church is not over yet. . . . The way ahead is still open, even though it is dif-ficult."[6] Fr Alexander Schmemann continued with this specific challenge:

---

[5]Metropolitan Leonty, "Theological Education in America," *Russian Orthodox American Messenger* (1913), translated in *St Vladimir's Seminary Quarterly* 9.2 (1965): 59–67, at 59.

[6]Georges Florovsky, "The Ways of Russian Theology," *Aspects of Church History* (Belmont, MA: Nordland Publishing Company, 1975), 208f.

"The task of theology at any given moment is necessarily determined by the needs of the Church, and the first task of the theologian is always to discern and to accept these needs, to become aware of what the Church expects from him."[7]

To be successful, the people involved in developing the plan, and most especially the leadership, must really believe that the planning effort will have a positive impact on the institution. Strategic planning is oriented towards action, towards creating the future. It does not passively accept what comes to it, nor accept where it may be at this particular point in time and think that no positive change is possible. Nor does it believe that the talents given to the institution by God are to be buried in the ground.[8] It believes that the institution can create the future and fulfill its dreams. It believes that "all things are possible with God."[9] It firmly believes that Christ "by the power at work within us is able to do far more abundantly than all that we ask or think."[10]

The people involved in strategic planning must desire to make the institution better than it is, no matter how good it is today. Strategic planning is motivated by a desire for excellence and profound progress that goes beyond incremental improvements and takes large and bold steps towards the vision. Strategic planning is frankly not for the faint-hearted, nor for those who are prone to remain with the status quo. It is not content with today's level of performance. It does not make excuses for failures or half-hearted efforts. It desires to be what the Lord intends it to be. It hears and responds earnestly to Christ's injunction to "be perfect, as your heavenly Father is perfect."[11]

Those involved in strategic planning must not be internally directed, nor biased towards what is being done right now, i.e., seeking to justify how things are done today. Strategic planning is outward-directed. It is neither inward-directed nor devoted to maintaining a certain lifestyle just "the way

[7]Alexander Schmemann, "The Task of Orthodox Theology Today," *St Vladimir's Theological Quarterly* 10.4 (1966): 180–188, at 180.

[8]Mt 25.14–30.

[9]Mk 10.27.

[10]Eph 3.20.

[11]Mt 5.48.

things are"—an ordinary, comfortable existence for the institution. Nor does it desire self-preservation. It sees what is outside of itself and how it can serve others. It stands with Jesus before his passion when he said, "And I, when I am lifted up from the earth, will draw all men to myself."[12] It is, in short, willing to suffer the cross for others.

Strategic planning is both inclusive and honest, seeking the opinions and judgments of others and welcoming input, even criticism. It asks others who are not directly involved in the administration for their ideas, criticisms, and suggestions. It examines its own performance with integrity and openness. The strategic planning process is from beginning to end the direct responsibility of the governing body, council, or board. Various people may be responsible for carrying out the planning steps, but the buck starts and stops with the governing body.

Throughout these descriptions of the concept and process of strategic planning, one overarching principle becomes evident: the importance of the people who are involved in the process. Nothing happens without people. They initiate, they discuss, they debate, they think, they pray, they decide, and they act. We can craft the most finely constructed plan, the most eloquent expression of mission and values, even the most detailed spreadsheets listing chapter and verse of the desired objectives—but if the people are not there, or not united, nothing will be achieved.

[12]Jn 12.32.

11

The Four Questions

The people involved in strategic planning, and especially the leadership, must ask the right fundamental questions if they are to find the right answers. What does the Lord want us to be? Where does he want us to go? Where are we now in reference to the call of Christ? Where are we going? What lies in our path? What will help us get to where the Lord wants us to go? What will hold us back? What do we do to be what the Lord wants us to be, to get where he wants us to go?

All too often, we have our answers tied up in a neat package before asking these fundamental questions. Jesus asked the lame man at the pool beside the Sheep Gate, "Do you want to be healed?"[1] The man did not answer this question directly, but instead made an excuse for why he did not enter the pool. In the case of a seminary, people ask, "What does your school do?" One possible answer might be a rote repetition of our mission statement: we train priests and perform theological research. However, a better answer, from the standpoint of the gospel, might be: we equip saints for the work of ministry, for building up the body of Christ.[2] The latter answer leads to a deeper, more complex, and ultimately more serious introspection on the subject of what we really "do" and its implications in terms of the Church.

At a fundamental level, strategic planning revolves around the struggle to ask the right questions and find the right answers. If done properly, and if the people involved are serious, this process will indeed be a struggle, not

[1] Jn 5.6.
[2] Eph 4.12.

167

only intellectually, but also from an interpersonal and spiritual perspective. For any organization or institution, the following four categories of questions provide a good starting point.

- Where should we go? What should we be?

- Where are we now? Where are we going?

- What lies in our path to either help or hinder us?

- What must we do to get to "where" and "what" we should be?

Of these, the most fundamental question is the first. It addresses the foundation of the vision that we seek to realize. The answer to this question may appear self-evident to some, but when we compare answers from various people, significant differences can become apparent. In fact, some people may not even know or care where they are going. In this case, any direction is fine.[3]

The second question is also a difficult one and may elicit different answers from different people. Some may think that everything is fine, and we are heading in the right direction. Others may think the opposite. Still others may feel that we are doing reasonably well, but that much more is demanded of us. In any event, to answer this question properly demands the utmost sincerity and openness. Unfortunately, a common result of this exercise may be ruffled feathers and damaged egos.

The third question requires us to identify the opportunities presented to us—and the threats facing us—as we try to accomplish our objective. It is intended to be optimistic, enabling us to grasp positive things that we can use to our advantage. At the same time it is also intended to be realistic so as to ensure that our efforts will not be torpedoed by something that we failed to anticipate, and thus did nothing to avoid.

---

[3]The story told by Lewis Carroll in *Alice in Wonderland* is illustrative. Alice, in her travels, wondered which path she should take. She asked the Cheshire Cat, "Sir, which way should I go from here?" The Cat answered, "That depends a good deal on where you want to get to." Alice responded, "I don't much care where." He then said, "It doesn't much matter then which way you go." Alice said, "So long as I get somewhere." The Cat concluded: "Oh, you're sure to do that, if only you walk long enough."

Once we have come to agreement on our vision, on where we are and are going, and on what is facing us "out there," we can get to work on the fourth question: "What do we do to get there?" This question helps us craft the strategy and action plans that will take us to where we should be.

It must be recognized upfront that planning is never easy. John W. Gardner[4] summarizes the task of the university as "attending to the goals we ought to be thinking about and never do, the facts we do not like to face, the questions we lack the courage to ask"[5]—a statement which can be applied equally well to planning,

THREE QUESTIONS OF JESUS

Jesus asked questions of many different people in vastly different life circumstances. His questions are blunt, and the answers have consequences. We will take here only three examples: questions addressed to his disciples, to a lawyer, and to a blind man.

One day, as the disciples were walking along with Jesus, he began to pose questions. First, Jesus asked the disciples a fairly comfortable question, namely, who others thought he was. After receiving various answers, he asked directly, "But who do you say that I am?"[6] The disciples were merely walking along, perhaps enjoying a pleasant afternoon, when the Lord puts this direct and personal question to them. Peter, having been blessed by the Father's revelation that Jesus was the Christ, the Son of God, answered first. He was then told of the consequence of his answer, namely, that on that rock of faith Jesus would build his everlasting Church.

A lawyer once decided to put Jesus to the test, and asked him the requirements to inherit eternal life. Rather than providing an explicit answer that the lawyer might try to refute, Jesus asked him simply what he, as a lawyer, read in the law. His answer (to love God and his neighbor) was acknowledged by Jesus as correct—and not only correct, but sufficient for life. Not being content with that, the lawyer desired to justify himself by asking,

[4]Leadership writer, founder of *Common Cause* and *Independent Sector*, and a cabinet secretary under Lyndon Johnson.

[5]John W. Gardner, *No Easy Victories* (New York, NY: Harper & Row, 1968), 90.

[6]Mt 16.15.

"And who is my neighbor?" This time, Jesus answered with the tale of the Good Samaritan. At the end he asked the lawyer, "Which of these three, do you think, proved neighbor to the man who fell among the robbers?"[7] The lawyer came up with the right answer again, namely, the one who showed mercy. However, perhaps he did not expect this final charge from the Lord: go and do likewise. His original concern was inward, toward his own salvation. Through the questioning, Jesus turned him around to face outwards toward others.

One day a blind man was begging by the roadside as Jesus passed by. Struck with desperation, he repeatedly cried out for Jesus to have mercy on him, despite the attempts of others to silence him. Jesus asked him this question: "What do you want me to do for you?"[8] The blind man gave the answer, received the granting of his request, and followed Jesus on his way. Prior to this encounter, Jesus had healed extensively. One would assume that a blind man coming up to Jesus obviously wanted to be healed. Yet Jesus needed to hear this from the lips of the man himself.

What is the point of these three examples? Certain critical questions are asked by Jesus not for his own purposes—for he knows the answers already—but rather to force us to look deeply within ourselves and our communities for what forms the true root of our personal and shared lives. Who is this Jesus, and what does he mean to us? Who is our neighbor and what should we be to him? What do we want the Lord to do for us? Here we find the spiritual foundation of the ultimately serious questions we ask ourselves in the strategic planning process.

BENEFITS OF STRATEGIC PLANNING

First of all, the strategic planning process is designed to instill a disciplined approach, to force the community to think about its mission and measure itself accordingly. St Paul offered such a definition of community: "You are fellow citizens with the saints and members of the household of God, built upon the foundation of the apostles and prophets, Christ Jesus himself

[7]Lk 10.36.
[8]Mk 10.51.

being the cornerstone, in whom the whole structure is joined together and grows into a holy temple in the Lord."[9] This sentence alone raises all kinds of questions. What does it mean for us to be considered part of the saintly community of the household of God? What aspects of our lives together are apostolic and prophetic? Are we really founded upon Christ as our cornerstone? Are we joined together in Christ? How do we show it? Are we growing together into the house of God? How would we know that? All of the questions we ask about our mission and how we measure ourselves must be fundamental, personal, direct, and challenging. The strategic planning process offers a way to both ask and to answer those questions.

Second, the process and its outcomes fulfill a stewardship function, helping us allocate resources such as talents, facilities, and funds where they will do the most good. "And his gifts were that some should be apostles, some prophets, some evangelists, some pastors and teachers, to equip the saints for the work of ministry, for building up the body of Christ."[10] Each person in a community is different. We have different backgrounds, different occupations. We have different talents and resources available to us. Often these talents, experience, and expertise are never taken advantage of due to our mutual ignorance. We don't talk with one another to find out what our talents may be. Equally, if not more importantly, we never learn how community members might wish to apply their talents to the mission of the community. The strategic plan process is designed to obtain the input of everyone impacted by the mission. In this way we can discover our mutual God-given gifts, and also how to apply them.

Third, the process demands regular communication among all parties, thus promoting unity, cohesiveness, and conciliarity. Jesus said, "Holy Father, keep them in thy name, which thou hast given me, that they may be one, even as we are one."[11] Every plan will fall short of what it could achieve, unless it is developed in a way that involves the community. The most brilliant person in the community, even if gifted with a clairvoyant insight into

[9]Eph 2.19–21.
[10]Eph 4.11–12.
[11]Jn 17.11.

the minds and hearts of others, cannot replace the simple, direct question of Jesus: "What do you want me to do for you?" People need to be asked that question, and they need to answer it. They must know that their feelings, their heartfelt longings, are not simply desired but absolutely needed. They must be kept informed. The leaders of the strategic planning effort must focus on the people, care for them, and love them. Properly done, such involvement can lead to dramatic results, even if the plan's direction turns out differently from what certain individuals would have wanted. They were asked. They were given respect. They were listened to. They were loved. And love is a powerful force.

12

The Planning Process

The most important part of the process is the people. The main leaders of the organization—the pastor, the clergy, and staff of a parish; the abbot or abbess of a monastery; the administration, faculty, and staff of a seminary; the management and staff of a nonprofit—are on the front line. Their daily lives are devoted to the mission of the parish, monastery, seminary, or nonprofit. They need to participate intimately in the planning process in order to be fully aligned with the final decisions.

The members of the governing council or board also play a vital role in the strategy process. They serve as a link between the administration or leadership and the constituency of the organization. They need to ensure that a personal effort is made to reflect people's needs in the plan, thus empowering them to share in the responsibility of leadership.

The wider community needs to feel a sense of ownership when the plan is finally developed and promulgated. This statement applies to hierarchs and other leaders, including members of the parish and institution as well as its benefactors, donors, and supporters. No one can own the plan, however, unless one feels that one has been a part of its development, and valued enough to have one's needs and desires considered in the process.

STRATEGIC PLANNING CONCEPTS

Several concepts are key to the understanding of strategic planning. Although various sources and references on planning may use slightly different definitions, the ones below are fairly common. We will review these one by one: mission, vision, and values; strengths and weaknesses; threats and opportunities; and goals and objectives.

MISSION, VISION, AND VALUES

Every institution must continuously reflect on its mission, i.e., what it intends to be or, in the case of a church organization, what the Lord intends it to be. A mission statement does not list the current activities of the organization, which answers the question of "what do we do?" rather than "what shall we be?" Such a mission statement can be neither a source of inspiration nor an agent for change. For this reason we will first speak of *vision* and *values*, and then secondarily of a mission statement derived from that vision and those values.

Vision is that which represents our dream for the institution—the source of inspiration that centers us in the midst of difficulties. It expresses the love which fills our minds and hearts when the institution comes into our thoughts. It manifests our personal relationship with it, our hopes for it. We cannot formulate a vision without first retreating into ourselves to contemplate the inner connections between us and what we love.

In his sermon on the day of Pentecost, St Peter quoted the Prophet Joel's saying that when God poured out his Spirit, young men would see visions and old men would dream dreams.[1] I have often wondered what the Lord had in mind with this apparent distinction between young and old, between visions and dreams. Perhaps dreams, in this case, possess a certain wistful quality, a gentler and more introspective hope tempered by disappointments yet encouraged by moments of joy and peace. The dream draws us to itself.

Jesus Christ was full of the Holy Spirit. He was inspired by the Holy Spirit when he told Peter that upon this rock (*petra*) he would found his Church. What did the rest of the disciples think about this statement? Did they think it a foolish dream of their leader to found a church and place a fisherman in charge? Their worries seem to have been substantiated later, for soon afterwards that fisherman was rebuked and called "Satan" by

[1]Acts 2.17.

Jesus. Later, the "rock" denied his master three times. Yet he was indeed faithful in the end, received the gift of the Holy Spirit with the rest, and led the company of the apostles forward to establish the Church foretold by Christ.

No doubt Peter went to sleep each night wondering and perhaps dreaming about what Jesus had said to him: You are Peter, on this rock I will found my Church; you will deny me three times; if you love me, feed my sheep. These dreams and the vision of what Jesus had in mind for him sustained him through every difficulty he endured, the last of which was martyrdom.

In the same way, our own dreams and vision must be inspired, coming from our heart and derived though prayer and contemplation. They act as a beacon shining through the darkest difficulties and sustaining us by their light.

For example, in its strategic plan a monastery stated that its vision was to be:

- A place where those growing in God's love live together and pray for one another, the Church and the world

- A place of prayer and the monastic vocation

- A place where work and stewardship are meaningful and practiced

- A place where quiet and "chaos" are balanced

- A place of striving after internal peace, witness to the truth and out-reach to others

This dream focused on community life, growing together in God's love. The mutual life is to be sustained through prayer, work, and dedication to the monastic vocation. This vision of mutual love and prayer sustains the monastics as they cope with interruptions in prayer ("chaos") and their realization that this life is not only for themselves, but also for outreach to others.

Values are the cherished principles that direct our efforts to realize our vision and guard us from straying from the right path. The best values are ones we would rather die for than violate. They dictate our behavior, how we interact with others, and how we treat them.

The leaders of a youth camp, in developing their strategic plan, gave the following simple yet profound principles as their fundamental values:

- Love of God expressed through liturgical worship and prayer life

- Love of others through fun, fellowship, and forgiveness while
  - emphasizing the value of joy in the Christian life and community and
  - becoming and being a model of Christian nurturing, love, patience, acceptance, and belonging for campers and staff

The values here are centered in the love of God, from which they draw their sustenance. That love is never to be taken for granted, but rather strengthened through mutual worship and individual prayer. It cannot be possessed interiorly, but shows itself through the love of others. This love is to be made manifest in all the camping activities, in fellowship, fun, forgiveness, and joy. The leaders took very seriously the need to be models of virtue for the campers and staff. The complete integration of their relationships with God, each other, and those who looked to them for guidance and love was paramount. Theirs was a 24/7 kind of value.

A short *mission* statement that flows from the vision and values (and which usually takes the form of a short, simple, "compass-heading" statement) can be quite helpful to focus efforts. The mission statement leads the community in the direction of "what shall we do?" It can serve as an excellent monitoring device to help everyone see whether the community is doing what it says it wants to do. The best mission statements are both aspirational and actionable. They need to provide a basis for both near- and longer-term actions and also incorporate a "stretch" that challenges the community to avoid falling into self-satisfaction. One parish, which undertook its first strategic planning effort after being established for about ten years, defined its mission as a parish as follows:

- To be a worshiping and loving community in Christ

- To show hospitality to visitors

- To spiritually develop and grow our life in Christ

- To provide education in the Orthodox Faith

- To reach out to others in witness and charitable service.

This community will now be able to monitor whether it has the structure and openness to welcome and incorporate visitors, to provide education, and to reach out in charitable service. However, to do all of this in love, in Christ, and to spiritually develop and grow in Christ, is certainly aspirational. There is no possibility of self-satisfaction here if the mission statement is regularly reviewed and subjected to rigorous and honest examination.

The vision, values, and mission statements we develop should be constantly reviewed as the planning process proceeds. Everything that follows must refer to these statements if we are to ensure continual focus on what is really necessary. My experience has been that the individual and communal effort required to dig deep within to develop these statements is very much worthwhile. A sense of unity and cohesiveness is gained when we are listened to, contribute, and find kindred spirits who feel, if not exactly the same way, at least similarly. Furthermore, we are often able to learn from one another. However, the hard part of getting down to business ("how are we doing?") comes next.

STRENGTHS AND WEAKNESSES

The exercise to determine an organization's strengths and weaknesses is sometimes given the impressive title of "internal assessment." This term suggests it is somewhat akin to self-examination or the examination of conscience before confession, except that in this case the examination involves a community, be it a parish, institution, seminary, or nonprofit. Additionally, internal assessment does not aim to root out sins, explicitly, but rather to examine, via a rational and in-depth reflection, how well we are accomplishing the mission of our community.

To go forward, we must know where we are. We need to know what we are doing well—not in order to praise ourselves, for we know that we are sinners and can do nothing good by ourselves, but rather so that we may recognize the gifts that the Lord has given us, our talents, our assets, and give thanks. We wish to utilize those talents and assets in the wisest way possible in his service. Similarly, we wish to know our shortcomings and correct them as much as is within our power. If we have been traveling down the wrong path or have disregarded our obligations, it may be an appropriate time for our community to take action to change.

A word of caution is appropriate here. To be open and honest about one's feelings and to listen to others' feelings regarding a critical and passionate part of our lives (namely, the Church) is always a dangerous enterprise. It demands humility and a complete lack of pride. It demands a willingness to really try to understand the other in love, without instinctively defending our own point of view or particular experience. The church fathers emphasize this point time and again. St. Mark the Ascetic warns us: "He who does not understand God's judgments walks on a ridge like a knife-edge and is easily unbalanced by every puff of wind. When praised, he exults; when criticized, he feels bitter. . . . He quarrels with those who reprove him; and those who forgive him, he regards as fools."[2] Proverbs 9:8–9 declares: "Do not reprove a scoffer, or he will hate you; reprove a wise man and he will love you. Give instruction to a wise man, and he will be still wiser."

The category of *strengths* addresses the following questions:

- What resources (human, physical, financial) do we have to help us in achieving the mission?

- What talents and gifts has God already given to us?

- Which resources and talents are we putting to good use, versus those which are lying fallow?

The category of *weaknesses* addresses these questions:

[2]St Mark the Ascetic, *On Those who Think that They are Made Righteous by Works* 193 (*Philokalia*, I, 142).

- What do we need to improve in order to accomplish our mission?

- In which ways have we not been true to our own expressed values?

- What resources and talents are we lacking?

It is extremely helpful for the leaders of the strategic plan to establish various categories of questions to examine strengths and weaknesses. Such questions will be most effectively used in written surveys, but are also very useful when directing personal interviews and focus groups. One seminary utilized the following categories for input, with assessment values to be assigned ranging from 1=outstanding, 2=good, 3=adequate, 4=should be better, to 5=must be improved.

- Academic reputation

- Quality of faculty

- Quality of graduates

- Financial resources

- Library/chapel

- Married students housing

- Placement of graduates

- Campus outreach

- Practical parish training

- Support of alumni

- Public relations

- Press

- Bookstore

- Relations with other seminaries

- Internet/distance education

Another valuable application of this categorized system is in the comparison of evaluations over time. In the case of this seminary, the system was used to gather input twice, ten years apart. The comparative results were very helpful to the governance group and the leaders of the strategic plan.

Following the completion of this exercise, various selected bodies within the community review the findings. It is critical for everyone involved to hear the words of their brothers and sisters with an open and humble heart, suspending judgment for a time and listening for the voice of Christ, who is the Way, the Truth, and the Life, and the Holy Spirit, the Spirit of Truth. People may agree with some comments and not others. What is required of us is to place ourselves in Christ's place—the place of the Crucified One, who loves all and gave himself for all without exception. We are his Church, his body. What does he require of us? What are his standards? How do we measure up? What does he want us to do?

OPPORTUNITIES AND THREATS

Now we turn our attention to the external environment. Whether parish or institution, we know that we do not exist in a vacuum. We interact with many different environments: ecclesiastical, social, economic, political, financial, etc. Some of these environments impact us and our mission positively, others negatively. In all cases, we need to be cognizant of what is happening outside. There are things that will help us, which we term "opportunities." There are things that will hurt or hinder us, which we term "threats." We need to take advantage of opportunities, and defend ourselves against threats. Usually, we can use our previously identified strengths to help us take advantage of opportunities. At the same time, we must be aware that our weaknesses may make us especially vulnerable to threats.

Opportunities. What in the external environment (ecclesiastical, social, political, economic) might help us if we can take advantage of it—especially if we change and overcome our weaknesses? During a strategic planning retreat for a monastery, the participants came up with the following external opportunities to help fulfill their mission:

- Emergence of mid-life vocations or re-orientation
  - People looking for more meaning in their lives
  - Reaction against secular/material society
  - Loneliness/need for community
  - Lack of church attachment

- Increased availability of communication resources
  - Media/Internet
  - Travel/human contact

- Increased possibilities for outreach
  - Elder/disabled care
  - Parishes

The monastery retreat participants realized that St Paul's saying about the early Christians ("we are . . . unknown, and yet well known"[3]) also applies to monasteries. Many individuals may be facing important choices in their lives, but the idea of monastic vocation likely occurs only to a few. These few, however, still deserve to be presented with the alternative of the monastic vocation. Many others are facing significant difficulties and find themselves at a crossroads both with other people and in their interior lives. At all these times, the voice of traditional Orthodox monasticism needs to be heard, not for a monastery's own perpetuation, but for the life-giving nature of a Christ-centered life of discipline, work, and prayer. In addition, people generally come to Christ through a contact with the living Lord, either directly or through the intermediary of another. As Philip said, "Come and see."[4] The monastery realized that it needed to take advantage of the many ways that people can hear about the monastery, such as the internet and media, but most efficaciously by means of human contact.

    Threats. What in the external environment (ecclesiastical, social, political, economic) will hinder the achievement of our mission, especially if we

[3] 2 Cor 6.9.
[4] Jn 1.46.

fail to change and overcome our weaknesses? The participants at the same
monastery retreat came up with the following threats:

- Lack of understanding and support for monastic vocations

- Lack of awareness of Orthodoxy ("Christian" = Catholic or
  Protestant)

- Competing worldly priorities

- Financial pressures

The monastery retreat participants realized that people may jump to
conclusions about monasticism, as in the oft-quoted comment that "the
Orthodox Church doesn't have nuns." Clergy and family may be openly
hostile to monastic vocations for women. Such attitudes are fostered by
a general lack of knowledge concerning true monasticism and monastic
spirituality, which is not only intended for monks and nuns, but for all the
faithful. Furthermore, the world is very busy. People are overworked and
have little time for prayer and reflection, which are at the center of the
monastic life. And lastly, continually rising costs, coupled with a lack of
incoming funds, posed a risk to sustainability for this monastery.

STRATEGIC OPTIONS

After having set forth vision, values, and mission, and having considered
the current strengths and weaknesses, threats, and opportunities, it is time
to begin thinking about what should be done. Suggestions for potential
actions should be sought from a wide variety of people. These suggestions
generally fall into a number of separate categories, which are termed "strategic options." They are strategic, for they point us in a certain direction
aimed at fulfilling our mission, achieving the vision, and remaining true
to our values. They are still options since they have not yet been deeply
considered and discussed, nor evaluated to see which are of highest priority to us.

Sometimes strategic options may be referred to as strategic "initiatives." Organizations concerned about "corporate-speak" may simply use

the phrase "what is to be done?" As long as there are different and open-ended paths to be considered, and these are kept sufficiently well organized to enable fruitful reflection, discussion, and evaluation, then a group is free to invent its own planning language.

One particular parish developed the following strategic options to reflect upon, discuss, evaluate, and then act upon accordingly.

- Intensify emphasis on spiritual and liturgical life

- Promote and encourage development of a fuller Christian life for all in the parish

- Intensify the adult education program in the parish and increase practical resources

- Focus more on charitable outreach

- Increase volunteer assistance for parish administration

- Improve and beautify facilities, especially sanctuary and fellowship hall

- Increase fellowship and social activities, especially for visitors and men

- Develop a plan for handling the membership growth, e.g., stay here, relocate, or form a mission church

Many people, viewing the above initiatives, are likely to say, "Well, let's do them all! They're all good!" However, the question of who should do them, the time frame in which they should be completed, and how they should be accomplished is another matter entirely. The practical aspects of organizing even the most well-intentioned and spiritually motivated people require careful planning and allocation of resources, time, talent, and money. For each option, overall goals and objectives need to be developed and agreed upon.

GOALS AND OBJECTIVES

We will defer the definition of "goals and objectives" until the next chapter, which describes the planning process. That chapter also includes examples that help clarify our preferred definition. Other definitions can certainly be used in the planning process, but it is crucial that the terms are clear and that everyone understands them.

THE PLANNING PROCESS TIMETABLE

The timetable for a strategic planning process can be quite variable, depending on a number of factors. One is the size and complexity of the organization. Another is how experienced the planners are. The process will likely take longer if this is the first time that the organization has gone through strategic planning. The length of time will also directly correlate to the number of people involved and consulted in the planning—the more people, the more time must be budgeted to collect input and feedback. One of the most critical steps in preparing for the plan ("plan for the plan") is to carefully consider who needs to be involved, and to what depth.

There is a high degree of "front-loading" in the plan timetable. Many people will be excited about the prospect of undertaking such a plan. They will want to get moving immediately and work through the recommended steps as quickly as possible. Others may become bored with the discipline involved in the process and try to hurry on to the action steps—particularly if those actions are the ones they want to see the plan endorse! Front-loading requires the careful involvement of the governing body of the organization, the identification of the people who are to be involved, securing outside counsel as necessary, and intensive prayer and mutual consultation during a kickoff workshop. The time and effort spent on this initial phase will pay significant dividends by ensuring that the process is smooth, that no one is left out, and that the end purpose—doing God's will and not our own—is emphasized.

In one case, a parish of approximately 100 families engaged in its first strategic planning process, which from start to finish took about eighteen months. In the case of a seminary engaging in its second and quite complex strategic planning process, the total time elapsed was two years. It is important to set the organization's expectations properly by means of the plan timetable. This goal can be met only by seriously assessing the required tasks and resources, especially people, available to accomplish them.

BEDROCK PRINCIPLES

Before we begin our discussion on how to develop a strategic plan, it is useful to mention some bedrock principles. First, the governing body, whether parish council, parish assembly, or board of directors and trustees, must be involved in the process from beginning to end. Specifically, this means active, fully engaged participation in the initial kickoff workshops, as well as periodic review and endorsement of the process, strategic options, and the final goals and objectives.

Second, we must recognize that the product of the planning process will not be a piece of paper, but rather people—people willing to work and to contribute their time, talents, and money towards the fulfillment of a common mission and unified vision, all the while resolutely adhering to mutually held and precious values. Accordingly, every effort needs to be made to involve in some way throughout the planning process every person who impacts, or is impacted by, the organization, parish, or institution. The details of how and when these people should be involved will be discussed below. At this point it suffices to say that their involvement in the process should be as face-to-face as possible, with the best option being to work together on teams.

Third, the results of the planning process must be widely publicized. Proposed actions versus actual results should be reported periodically and regularly. Did we do what we said we would do, or not? Did we change our minds, and if so why? Have our priorities changed, and why? Many strategic planning processes falter due to lack of proper execution or inadequate communication and stewardship. It is crucial that we do not merely say, "Lord, Lord" and pay lip service while going on our way. Our focus should be to do the true will of the Father, and to be measured accordingly.

13

How to Develop a Strategic Plan

There are a number of available "recipes" for developing a strategic plan, both in print and on the Internet. Some are better than others. Some are best suited for profit-making corporations, others for nonprofit organizations, and a few are geared toward religious groups and churches. There are also consultancies that specialize in developing these plans, and they have their own approaches.

In 1988, I was approached by St Vladimir's Seminary to assist them in developing a strategic plan. I was a senior advisor in strategic planning for Exxon, responsible for several European countries. I developed and managed a planning process for the seminary, based upon corporate best practices, but modified for the special characteristics of a nonprofit organization. Since that time, I have evolved and further adapted that process for successful use in various church organizations ranging from small and medium parishes to a monastery, a youth camp, and a second plan for the theological seminary.

My "recipe," as presented here, should be a good fit for parishes, educational institutions, and other church-related nonprofit organizations. As always, adjustments will need to be made depending on the particular situation. In fact, it could be adapted for use in any nonprofit, commercial, or corporate environment.[1]

We will look at a six-phase approach:

[1]After the second seminary plan, I was told by a fellow trustee, also a corporate executive, that he had successfully applied the principles of our strategic planning process in his division.

1. Plan for the plan

2. Gather input on vision, values, mission, strengths, weaknesses, threats, opportunities, etc.

3. Determine strategic options/initiatives for evaluation

4. Develop detailed goals and objectives

5. Prioritize goals and objectives, and prepare a road map for implementation

6. Communicate, execute, and steward the plan

At the end of each of these phases, the governing body should meet to review the results of the previous phase and the plan for the next. It endorses the direction that the plan is taking, and ensures that sufficient resources are available to complete the plan's development. As well, the general constituency of the parish, school, or organization should be kept informed of the plan's progress.

1) PLAN FOR THE PLAN

The first phase, planning for the plan, is extremely important. The goal of this phase is to assess the readiness of the parish or institution to undertake the planning process. It asks the questions: Do we really want to do this? Are we committed? Are we willing to go where the process will take us? Are we willing to hear what others have to say? Do we have the people and the perseverance to finish?

We need to be brutally honest in our self-evaluation, so that having set our hand to the plough we might finish the race (to mix the metaphors of our Lord and St Paul!). We need to be especially thorough if this is the first time that our organization has conducted a strategic plan. One danger of failing to complete a first-time plan is that the organization is much less likely to want to try one again in the future.[2] Therefore we must

---

[2] This could mean failing to complete the planning process, or failing to actually implement the plan once it has been agreed.

be prepared for phase one's outcome to indicate that the organization is simply not ready for a full-scale strategic planning process. If this turns out to be the case, we need to be willing to step back. Now might be the time to compress our ideal plan in some way, such as a mini-plan, or to extract achievable elements from it. On the other hand, now may be the time for "all systems go," full speed ahead. In any event, honest self-assessment is what this discovery phase requires.

There are four major actions to be taken in this phase, once we have decided to proceed.

a) Select a coordinator. Someone needs to initiate and coordinate the initial planning efforts. It could be the head of the council or board, or someone in the organization who has the desire and the drive to make this process work. The organization's leaders need to have confidence in him or her.

b) Secure internal and external resources. This stage involves the engagement of both institutional leadership and outside volunteers to participate in the strategic plan process. In a parish, the institutional leadership would include the rector and other clergy, council members, and the heads of the church school and auxiliary groups. Volunteers would be others from within the parish, or even outside friends of the parish. The coordinator's job is to work with the institutional leadership to nominate and secure the participation of these potential volunteers.

It is vital that everyone involved has sufficient time, commitment, and trust in one another. Of these, trust is the most important, yet sometimes the most difficult to come by. Often, institutional leaders may be very cautious or even afraid of involving volunteers, let alone trusting them with big decisions. They may be hesitant to open themselves up to outside opinions, or to allow volunteers significant independent thought and action. Because they are used to being in control, they are not used to deferring to others or doing things by committee. But in order for the process to work, they need to get out of their default comfort zone.

For their part, volunteers need to have faith in the institutional leadership to listen to their ideas and respect their opinions. They need to know that the leadership is committed to having open and honest dialogue. They also need to be assured that they can speak openly and honestly, perhaps even saying things that might be considered critical or negative, with no fear of grudges or retaliation.

It can be incredibly useful to have external counsel on call. This role should be filled by someone who has been through the process before, and who can be counted upon as needed for facilitation, advice, and direction on any puzzling or contentious issues that arise. External counsel could be someone from a neighboring parish who has been intimately involved in developing a similar plan, such as a diocesan coordinator or even a professional. Sometimes his or her services can be obtained on a pro-bono, expense-reimbursement basis. Alternately, external counsel may request a donation to the charity of his or her choice. In any event, it is important that counsel's advice and guidance be taken seriously. In some cases, the only way to ensure this is to monetarily compensate for those services.

c) Hold a kickoff workshop. This crucial event should not be skipped or skimped on in terms of time.[3] The workshop ought to be organized by the coordinator mentioned above in cooperation with the leadership group. The list of attendees needs to include the governance body of the parish or institution, key impacted people (e.g., workers, teachers, paid or unpaid volunteers, faculty, staff) and potential plan workers. The required outcomes are enthusiasm, unity, commitment, and understanding. The event must be facilitated by someone who is able to bring people together, encourage them to be open with one another, and reach some form of consensus about what should be done. The facilitator could be the same person as the external counsel, or someone else whom the external counsel recommends. It is helpful if the facilitator has had previous experience with the issues faced by the organization.

The agenda for a typical two-day parish kickoff workshop appears below. The venue should comfortably accommodate the participants in

---

[3]When I was asked by Dean Fr John Meyendorff to lead the first SVS strategic planning effort in late 1988, I mentioned that I needed to meet with the board of trustees. Fr John, wanting to know how much time I would need, asked, "Would an hour and a half be sufficient?" I replied, "I need a day and a half." I received some understandable resistance to that, but after some discussion I did receive my day and a half with the trustees for the kickoff workshop, which was highly successful.

one large group, as well as offering separate spaces for breakout groups as recommended by the facilitator. It can be held at the organization's existing facilities or another venue.

DAY ONE

Time	Topic
12–12:30	Prayers (Sixth Hour)[4]
12:30–1:00	Lunch
1:00–1:15	Opening remarks by the Rector/Dean/Council or Board Chair
1:15–1:45	Presentation: "What is church planning?"
1:45–3:00	First workshop or group discussion *Vision, Values, Mission*: "What does the Lord want us to be?"
3:00–3:30	Prayers (Ninth Hour)
3:30–4:30	Second workshop or group discussion *Strengths and Weaknesses*: "Where are we now?"
4:30–5:00	Wrap-up
5:00–5:45	Prayers (Vespers)
6:00–7:00	Dinner
7:00	Free Time

[4]The prayers referred to here are the normal daily prayers of the Orthodox Church. Third hour is at roughly nine in the morning, sixth hour at noon, ninth hour at three in the afternoon. These respectively remember the judgment of Christ before Pilate and the descent of the Holy Spirit at Pentecost, the crucifixion of Christ, and Christ's death on the cross. See Hapgood, *Service Book*, for texts.

DAY TWO

Time	Topic
9:00–9:30	Prayers (Third Hour)
9:30–9:45	Planning basics, review, and summary so far
9:45–10:30	Third workshop or group discussions *Opportunities and Threats*: "What future do we face?"
10:30–12	Fourth workshop or group discussions *Strategic Options*: "What might we do? What may be possible for us?"
12–12:30	Prayers (Sixth Hour)
12:30–1:15	Lunch
1:30–3:00	Fifth workshop or group discussions *Next Steps*: "What should we do right now? Who should be involved?"
3:00–3:30	Prayers (Ninth Hour)
3:30–4:30	General discussion and wrap-up
4:30–5:00	Closing remarks
5:00	Prayers (Vespers)

The opening comments by the top level of institutional leadership set the tone for the kickoff workshop. It is vitally important that these opening remarks convincingly communicate the leadership's forthright and honest support for the strategic planning effort. If leadership is perceived as not being completely behind the effort, everyone will wonder why they have come, and any momentum will fizzle out. On the contrary, if the leaders are clearly enthusiastic, committed, and ready to work, then others will naturally follow suit.

Following the opening remarks, the designated facilitator gives the opening presentation. This presentation might utilize material gathered from this text to explain the general concepts of church strategic planning. The facilitator should have established the workshop procedures in advance and be prepared to clearly explain them to the participants. Ground rules for discussion and breakout sessions are to be clearly specified—no interruptions of others, ask clarifying questions, don't judge or kill ideas before they have a chance to be developed, etc. The facilitator should reserve time for questions, especially on the strategic planning concepts. Participants should be assured that they will get a better handle on these concepts during the workshop exercises.

Twenty to twenty-five participants is a reasonable number for a workshop, enabling the formation of four workshop groups of five to six people apiece. Participants can be randomly assigned to a work group, or there could be pre-arranged assignments. For example, a seminary workshop should seek to spread bishops, faculty, administrators, and trustees fairly uniformly among the various groups to enable a broad spectrum of ideas and opinions to be expressed. A parish with multiple clergy should distribute these persons evenly among the groups, and so on.

The breakout groups are to select a secretary who will record the findings of the group (flip charts are an effective way to do this), as well as a reporter to present those findings to the entire workshop's participants. An overall workshop secretary should be appointed before the workshop begins to document the proceedings and the major findings in a report to be distributed to all participants as followup. The last two sessions in the sample workshop (general discussion and wrap-up, and closing remarks) are very important to establish and document consensus, especially regarding the path forward. The workshop report should also be distributed to all members of the leadership team.

d) Appoint a steering committee and task force. The steering committee is typically composed of the chief administrators (dean, chancellor and/or rector, parish council president, board chair), selected representatives of the governing body, and other key leaders or persons of influence, whether within or outside the institution. The steering committee should be prepared to hold special meetings monthly or semi-monthly prior to general reviews or endorsements by the governing body.

The task force consists of people with a vital interest in the organization who are willing to work, and work hard. The degree of effort involved in the development of a strategic plan should not be minimized. People need to know what they are signing up for, with no surprises down the road. For people who hold other full-time jobs, participation on the task force, particularly for the leader, becomes the next major activity in their life, paralleling time spent with family. Commitment is thus essential.

2) GATHER CONSTITUENCY INPUT

The second of our six phases is to gather constituency input—in other words, to seek opinions from as many people who will be impacted by the plan as is practical. A critical initial step in this exercise is identifying the organization's constituency, as in the question posed by the lawyer trying to test Jesus: "And who is my neighbor?" For a parish, does the constituency include the existing active membership, the less frequent attendees, neighbors living in the vicinity of the parish who are not members or unchurched, and even the members of neighboring churches? For a seminary, is it students present and future, the bishops, the alumni, the major benefactors, the faculty, staff, trustees, minor donors, and perhaps others? For a nonprofit, is it the employees, the recipients of services, donors both major and minor, or those who should take advantage of the services provided but do not know about them? In all likelihood, for each of these and other similar organizations, it is most or all of these people.

When gathering input, we must be absolutely sure not to leave out people who can make or break the success of the plan. This group includes the existing leadership team, the daily workers in the organization, and its supporters and donors. If possible, input from major supporters and donors needs to be individually requested and obtained. Some key elements of this input-gathering phase are described below.

Obtain people's feelings, ideas, judgments, and wishes. Templates are highly useful to ensure consistent and comparable input from the wide variety of people. Questions about vision, values, mission, strengths, weaknesses, threats, opportunities, and options can be asked, such as "what is to be done?"

It is best to get face-to-face input as much as possible, ideally via individual interviews. The interviewers need guidance and training in how to properly approach the interviewees, obtain the real story, respond to criticism, and leave the interviewee believing that the institution really cares about and values his or her input. Naturally, the interviewers should have participated in the kickoff workshop. These individuals will be those most familiar with the plan so far, and will have experienced the sharing and enthusiasm that we hope was evident during the kickoff event. They will have strong buy-in and should be able to explain the process clearly and convincingly to others—yet another reason why the kickoff workshop is so vital.

If face-to-face interviews are impractical, the next best approach is to use focus groups, ideally involving five to ten individuals. The same template used for the individual interviews can set the scene for group discussion.

The least effective method to collect input involves written surveys. Written surveys cast the widest net, but they do not usually capture the intensity of feeling that can be obtained face to face. In addition, the response rate for surveys is usually fairly low.

Document and summarize input. This activity is best done by a very small group of individuals who can be trusted to operate confidentially and with utmost discretion, protecting all inputs with complete anonymity. To ensure credibility, it is useful for this group to document detailed, but unattributed, quotes for review by the steering committee.

Desired outcomes are conciliarity, communication, and knowledge. Everyone should feel that they were consulted and had a chance to tell their story. Even those who take exception to the outcomes of the plan when eventually finished will then feel part of it, simply because they were heard. The leadership and task force gains a certain increased level of confidence that the work they propose has support from key individuals within the organization's constituencies. Furthermore, the information provided by this input is of inestimable value. No doubt creative ideas and perspectives will be offered which had not been considered previously.

3) DETERMINE STRATEGIC OPTIONS FOR EVALUATION

The third phase is occupied with determining strategic options for evaluation, i.e., what are the critical areas and initiatives that we as an institution should be working on? This phase is critical to the effort since much attention and time is needed to develop goals and objectives for each option. A common organizational effectiveness motto states, "It is more important to do the right thing, than to do the thing right." What is meant here is that choices must be made as to future direction of the institution. The general process for determining strategic options is as follows.

- The task force reviews the constituency input, paying special attention to recurring themes that have been highlighted by a cross-section of people. It develops a set of central issues that require attention and proposes potential strategic options for further evaluation. Some seven to ten strategic options are recommended, both to include a sufficiently wide scope of work and to ensure a comprehensive and continuous perspective. The task force also makes plans for the next phase and recommends the formation and membership of "G&O teams" ("strategic plan: goals and objectives teams") to develop detailed goals and objectives for each of the agreed-upon strategic options.

- The steering committee reviews the findings, recommends revisions, and endorses the options for further review by the governance body of the institution. Special attention must be paid to the makeup of the G&O teams. Individual teams each take one strategic option for further study and the development of proposed actions. These teams need to be composed of "experts" and "questioners." Experts are those who are particularly experienced in the particular issue, such as administrators and key employees of the institution. Questioners are those who have a vital interest in the issue, but hold no institutional position. Their particular role is to question assumptions by asking "why?," to push the envelope by asking "why not?," and to generally ensure unbiased deliberations.

- The governance body reviews the results at an extraordinary meeting involving extensive deliberation that lasts all day, if possible. Major efforts will be dedicated to confirming and finalizing the strategic options. The governance body, following these discussions, endorses the strategic options and the makeup of the G&O teams, and green lights the progression to the next phase.

- At this time, a communication should be issued to the institution's constituency, including those who have been made aware of the strategic planning effort and would be interested in knowing how their own input is reflected in the strategic options.

4) DEVELOP DETAILED GOALS AND OBJECTIVES

The fourth phase is the most detailed. It requires the most extensive interactions and the serious efforts of the largest number of people involved in the plan development. In this phase, the G&O teams turn the finalized strategic options into detailed goals and objectives. Our definition of "goals" is that they represent the target outcomes for the strategic option, while "objectives" provide the interim milestones and desired accomplishments for each goal.

As an example, a strategic option might be to "increase theological competence of clergy without seminary education." Related goals might include actions such as "implement seminars in key regions," "develop specific extension program with Bishop John," or "develop web-based distance education." Objectives tied to the first of these goals might include: "develop trial seminar program on West Coast with Holy Trinity parish by the first quarter of 2013," and "finalize Midwest program with Holy Annunciation monastery by the third quarter of 2014."

The makeup of the G&O teams has already been described above. Each team elects a chairperson to coordinate the effort. The first task of the chair is to emphasize the respective roles of the experts and questioners. In developing objectives, the teams need to keep in mind the people who are likely to be tasked with carrying out the desired activities once the plan is finally approved. These detailed plans need to be close enough to reality to ensure a high degree of alignment and buy-in by those who are expected to implement the plan.

The task force has the responsibility of following up the progress of the various G&O teams to ensure a reasonable consistency of approach. It also compiles the overall plan and the required resources, both financial and human, to accomplish each goal and objective. The task force identifies possible bottlenecks, difficulties, prerequisites, etc. Finally, it takes the first pass at prioritizing the overall plan.

Since the documentation of the individual G&O teams is likely to be extensive, the task force should request executive summaries of two pages or so in length from each G&O team. These summaries are to be shared with the steering committee. Preparing the executive summaries often proves highly useful to the G&O teams as an internal means of focusing and prioritizing their desires.

5) PRIORITIZE GOALS AND OBJECTIVES, AND PREPARE A ROAD MAP FOR IMPLEMENTATION

The steering committee reviews, adjusts, and endorses the plans for further review by the governing body. The greatest contribution of the steering committee in this effort is to review and endorse priorities and resources. Not everything can be expected to be accomplished at the same time, and certain activities may need to wait until human and/or financial resources can be mustered.

As in the previous phase, the governance body must meet to review, deliberate, and endorse the detailed goals and objectives, and then endorse the resource and implementation plan. A major effort needs to be performed to confirm that the goals and objectives are consistent with the mission of the institution. This stage offers the last chance for adjustment before implementation begins. Special attention needs to be given to the near-term (one to two years out) objectives for each goal. It is critical that the near-term objectives be successfully fulfilled to the greatest extent possible so as to ensure confidence on the part of the constituency in the leadership and the institution itself.

6) COMMUNICATE, EXECUTE, AND STEWARD

The sixth and final phase of development is often skimped upon in many strategic planning efforts. A plan must not sit on the shelf or be relegated to the back page of a website, nor should it be met with a sigh, "I'm glad that's over." While this phase is called "final," it is in fact ongoing until the next strategic plan begins. Thus the "final" phase should not be terminated in advance of that event. Every strategic plan is a process, not a product. Major elements of the final (and ongoing) phase are:

- The steering committee, in cooperation with the institutional leadership, will communicate the results of the plan development to all members of the constituency in a fashion similar to the original request for input. Anyone who was personally interviewed or attended a person-to-person focus group should receive a personal visit, the opportunity to participate in a community meeting, or a telephone call conveying the results of the plan in broad outline form, with a follow-up written package giving details. This group will certainly include hierarchs, faculty and staff, present students, key external church leaders, key alumni, every member of the G&O teams, and benefactors, major donors, and supporters. This outreach step is critical in expressing the institution's gratitude to those who helped, as well as for maintaining support for the institution among those people.

- The institutional leadership now proceeds to implement the actions outlined in the goals and objectives. The individuals assigned to achieve the desired objectives ought to receive the complete support and encouragement of the institutional leadership. In many or most cases, these assignments will be in addition to an already heavy and ongoing workload. The leadership needs to be ready to modify priorities, add resources, and make whatever changes to daily operations are required to achieve the best outcome for the organization. Sometimes a careful analysis will result in a scaling back of the timetable to achieve the strategic plan objectives. If this is done after proper study and all involved are in agreement, these adjustments then need to be communicated up the line to top leadership and the governance body according to the stewardship schedule, to be explained next.

- The institutional leadership is in charge of reporting on progress and, with the guidance of the governance body, steering the plan's implementation. A quarterly review of milestones, progress, and plans is recommended. Such a review often takes the form of a matrix which identifies each objective, the milestones to be achieved (usually tracked annually over the next three years), and the status of progress. A stewardship report is prepared for each objective by the person responsible for that objective, endorsed by the leadership, and shared with the institutional governing body. A "traffic light" model might be used with "green" marking good progress, "yellow" reflecting concerns or delays, and "red" indicating a major issue, hindrance, or problem. The leadership uses this reporting system as a way of reallocating resources, shifting priorities, or, in a worst case scenario, delaying some objectives until a later time. The governance body should review the stewardship reports formally on an annual basis to provide guidance on major issues. The results of the annual stewardship are to be publicized on a summarized basis with the constituency, and also more personally with individuals who have an exceptional or strong interest in some aspects of the strategic plan.

POSTSCRIPT

Although the above process has been described from an organizational perspective, it can also be applied to oneself. Consider developing a strategic plan for yourself and your family. The greatest benefit will come in finding out what others think of you, especially family members, neighbors, and friends. The experience can be truly eye-opening. It might even be heart-opening.

PART FIVE

Strategic Management

Our society focuses heavily on the desirability of becoming a "leader." Yet few people talk about how important good managers are. For many, in fact, a manager is perceived as somehow "less than" a leader. Steven Covey, author of *The 7 Habits of Highly Effective People*, once contrasted leaders and managers in a fable about a convoy trekking through a jungle. The managers calculated the weight of the cargo, plotted directions, and determined the best places to rest and spend the night. Meanwhile, the leader climbed the tallest tree and exclaimed, "Wrong jungle."[1] This is a very colorful example. However, were we on a plane flying over said jungle, we indeed might be thankful for the vision of the airline's CEO and the leadership of the ship's captain, yet we would be far more grateful for the maintenance managers and workers (not to mention engineers and air-traffic controllers) who make sure the plane gets up in the air and flies in one piece to its destination.

So yes, we need visionaries, but we also need managers to make plans, and then put those plans into action. Someone may be described as a genius and yet, because he or she lacks common sense and practical skills, it is said that "they can't manage their way out of a paper bag." Managers make things work, and good managers make them work properly.

Who are the managers? We encounter them in every aspect of daily life. In our own lives and homes, we manage our time, resources, and other people. We negotiate with suppliers, car mechanics, teachers, even

---

[1]Stephen R. Covey, *The 7 Habits of Highly Effective People: Powerful Lessons in Personal Change* (New York, NY: Simon and Schuster, 2004), 101.

---

our neighbors. We manage finances to ensure that bills are paid, that our children will be taken care of, and that they will be secure.

Outside the home, managers run various organizations ranging from neighborhood committees and charitable service groups to small and major businesses. These roles may have the added complexity of operating within structures involving superiors and subordinates, as well as peers. Managers can be board or council members, charged with operations oversight of a nonprofit or church organization. Each of these categories of relationships poses its own unique issues, opportunities, and problems.

In Part Five, we will focus more closely on the strategic management aspects of churches and other nonprofit organizations, identifying key areas and offering fundamental principles for guidance. I will also share examples from my own experience in the corporate, nonprofit, and church worlds. Christians who are looking for a Christian foundation underpinning their managerial responsibilities will find this section especially helpful. That said, the numerous parallels between nonprofit and for-profit organizations—especially where people are concerned and how they work together—make the principles outlined here applicable to commercial organizations as well.

Note that there are a number of good books dealing with the subjects raised in the following chapters. The ones I have found especially useful will appear in the footnotes for further reading. I also wish to add a disclaimer that applies to all the chapters on strategic management. I am not an attorney, nor an accountant, nor a tax advisor, nor an HR expert. I have been blessed to know and work with these experts throughout my career, and I have learned a lot from them. However, should one require professional opinions or advice in any of these areas, I recommend seeking it from those who hold the appropriate professional qualifications and credentials.

14

I'm on a Board (or Council): What Do I Do Now?

I asked myself this very question some twenty-five years ago, when I was elected to the governing board of the International School of Hamburg, Germany. The question became even more urgent when that night, at the first board meeting, I was elected as chair. In retrospect, I wonder why I was not immediately concerned by that rapid promotion!

The International School of Hamburg (ISH) is a private school that offered K–12 instruction to some 500 children of over forty nationalities at that time.[1] It was and is a critical part of the international business scene in Hamburg, ensuring high quality education to international children whose parents were posted to that city.

The board was composed of some fifteen elected individuals, with a wide representation of parents and members of the business and diplomatic community, plus the headmaster and certain other school staff serving ex officio. The board chair had a statutory legal role, I discovered later, as the official representative of the institution before the courts if anything went wrong. That discovery definitely raised my level of concern.

Fortunately, I had some previous experience with a nonprofit board thanks to my strategic planning work with St Vladimir's Seminary, and felt comfortable enough accepting this responsibility.[2] I had two immediate

---

[1] ISH presently educates some 700 students of over fifty nationalities. See *International School of Hamburg*. <http://ishamburg.org/welcome/overview/>, Oct. 4, 2016.

[2] I also felt a sense of obligation to "give back" to the school. Our youngest child had spent her last two high school years there and graduated with the International Baccalaureate diploma.

concerns: first, to ensure that my fellow members were united in their duty as a board; and second, to make sure that the school was financially stable, especially since Germany was in an economic recession at the time.

My first action as chair was to hold a one-day retreat/workshop with the board members. This occasion enabled each of us to perform self-evaluations as to our role on the board, to share our individual talents and expertise, and to ascertain the critical issues for the school and begin to address these. The workshop was very successful and received positive feedback. First-time-ever board members were especially appreciative, and became much less apprehensive about what they had gotten themselves into. Committees were formed to address current and potential future issues. In addition, individual members of the board confirmed that they understood their responsibility for the future of the school and their need to work together as a cohesive group. The board continued to meet in person almost every month.

My next action was to ask my vice-chair, the CFO of the German division of a major global conglomerate, to develop a five-year financial outlook for the school. The results of his investigation were shocking. They forecasted a significant and rapidly growing deficit that, if left unchecked, would result in major difficulties within several years. The major cause of the deficit was twofold. First, there was a dramatic increase in overall expenses, due primarily to rapidly escalating faculty costs. These costs were due to annual fixed-step salary increases, which had been contractually agreed to by previous administrations. Second, tuition revenues were significantly declining as international firms cut their expatriate postings in response to the recession.

Once we got over our initial shock and dismay, the board spent the next two years, individually and collectively, addressing and eventually resolving this financial problem in cooperation with the school administration, faculty, and staff. Such a resolution would have been impossible, in my opinion, were it not for the unified and cohesive efforts of the board, especially those members who worked closely with school officials, faculty, and staff.

NOW, HOW ABOUT YOU?

Perhaps you have been asked to serve on the governing board of a church or other nonprofit organization. Maybe the position involves a commercial, profit-making venture such as an industrial corporation. Regardless, the principles remain the same, and build upon the definition of leadership in community already outlined here.

A governing board or council is a team of people with responsibility for an established institution, such as a church or school, or for fulfilling the mission of a charitable, service, or other organization. In all cases boards have what is referred to as a fiduciary (or "trust") responsibility for that organization. Its members are answerable to the people that the institution or organization serves. Boards bear special accountability towards those who support the institution, especially through donations and gifts. The people who support the institution are usually called, collectively, the "constituency" of the institution. The board or council also has specific legal and ethical responsibilities according to the laws and regulations of the country, state, and political subdivision in which it operates.

Board or council members are normally brought together from widely disparate backgrounds, experience, and capabilities to accomplish a task that would be impossible for any one of them to achieve alone. In the case of ISH, our board members were of German, English, French, Swiss, American, Australian, and other nationalities. Some were executives, some teachers, some parents. Typically, they brought different perspectives to the table. Sometimes they did not agree and discussed differences of opinion at length before reaching a resolution. But the benefit of having a wide mix of people is that there is usually no shortage of good and creative ideas.

Later chapters of this book will discuss particular areas of responsibility such as ethics, finances, human relations, project management, and fund raising. The rest of this chapter will focus on the fundamental strategic nature of a board, and what it must do and be to operate most effectively. First, we will address two myths about what boards are—and aren't.

MYTH NUMBER 1: THE "RUBBER-STAMP" BOARD

Let us quickly dispose of the first myth. The board has the critical task of governance of its own institution or organization. It is never simply a rubber stamp for the administration. Similarly, a council or committee has the responsibility to question and perhaps recommend change or, alternatively, to endorse current directions. These responsibilities cannot be shirked; they rest upon the shoulders of everyone on the board, and can be neither hidden nor dispersed to others.

MYTH NUMBER 2: MICROMANAGEMENT

Although the board has governance responsibilities, it knows full well that it must delegate responsibility in certain areas, and within certain constraints, to the administration of the institution. The board asks questions, which sometimes gets uncomfortable for the administration. A defensive response may be the accusation that the board is "micromanaging." This charge normally gets the board to back off, and is thus quite effective from the administration's viewpoint. However, if an administration has to utter this curse, in my opinion it is already guilty of not providing sufficient information to the board about operations, or there is something that a board member "smells" in the operations that he or she has smelled before somewhere else. It is a warning sign, and should not be ignored.

Some experts advise boards to operate "noses in, fingers out." In other words, ask questions but do not meddle. This is not a bad maxim, but I would caution that certain noses are bigger than others. The bottom line is that sufficient trust, respect, and communication should exist between board members and administration to the extent that such concerns do not arise. If and when they do arise, some meeting of the minds needs to be found.

We will now touch on some of the key strategic responsibilities of the board. Boards are sometimes regarded as "top management." While this is certainly true, they are in fact leaders of the organization.

THE THREE JOBS OF THE BOARD:
OVERSIGHT, SERVICE, AND SACRIFICE

My overarching goal is to relate management issues to the Christian foundations of leadership outlined in earlier chapters. Let us now examine how the management tasks of the board relate to the three vocations and ministries of the bishop, deacon and priest: oversight, service, and sacrifice.

1) Oversight. The board exercises oversight, as a bishop exercises oversight. In the New Testament, the bishop looks after, cares for, and visits others to see how they are doing. There is a visceral, intimate relationship between the bishop and his flock. In the same way board members, both individually and collectively, must have this same relationship with their institution. In the parlance of board governance, this is called the duty of loyalty and the duty of care.

The duty of loyalty means, at minimum, that there be no conflict between a board member's own interests and those of the institution. Should such conflict arise in a particular case, the board member must recuse himself or herself from any decision regarding the case. Ideally, the board member should feel that the interests of the institution and his or her own personal interests coincide. That is, one works for the organization as if one is working for oneself.

The duty of care means that a board member is disciplined in undertaking the responsibility of oversight. He or she takes the necessary steps to understand the workings of the institution and whether things are going well, or not. At a fundamental level, it often means making painstaking efforts to understand the physical and financial performance of the institution, and as well the sometimes more difficult to grasp question of whether the institution is fulfilling its mission and responsibility to its constituency.

2) Service. The usual language for board membership is "board service." One is not simply "on" a board; one "serves" on a board. In the Church, the deacon serves, willingly doing whatever is necessary for the flock and caring nothing for himself. He serves without pride, position, or prestige.

Through his example he inspires others to serve as well, and to do what needs to be done even before being asked. His whole life is service.

Individual board members who reflect this diaconal image are those who volunteer for projects, who ask for work, who say "I'll do that" whenever someone needs help. They are not content to be listed on the roster of board members and to include that fact on their CV or résumé. They are not comfortable attending only two or three board meetings a year and remaining silent and uninvolved. They are driven to be involved, to help, to serve.

3) Sacrifice. Nonprofit institutions generally need a consistent supply of funds. Typically, board members with significant financial resources are among those invited to serve. It is also typical and desirable to ask individuals to serve who have expertise in areas of need to the institution, e.g., financial, managerial, legal, etc. This calls for sacrifice on the part of the board members.

We spoke earlier about the vocation of the priest in the Church. He is the one who is willing to suffer and die for his people. The priesthood is not a "job," but a sacrificial vocation. In the same way, board service implies willingness to make sacrifices for the institution. Many times, this means money in the form of major gifts. At other times it means a significant sacrifice of time and effort for the institution. Board members involved in the development of a strategic plan or the initiation of a capital campaign, in particular, should expect to make that effort *the* major personal time commitment after their day job and family.

FIDUCIARY RESPONSIBILITY

Most nonprofits are incorporated in a state, and also enjoy a tax-exempt status granted by the federal government. This status means that there are many laws and regulations that must be followed by the institution. The board bears fiduciary responsibility for the institution before the respective governments, and also its constituency. The word "fiduciary" stems from the Latin *fiduci*, meaning "trust," and thus implies a relationship of trust. That is, the institution and its constituency place their trust in the board. In some institutions, the board members are accordingly termed "trustees."

Some states spell out the fiduciary responsibility in government documents. A duty of obedience can be added to the above-mentioned duties of loyalty and care. This means that board members must ensure that the institution complies with all applicable laws and regulations governing the institution, as well as its own internal governance documents and policies. This is a serious responsibility. Many nonprofits hold so-called directors and officers insurance policies, and indemnify the officers, and directors, within the constraints of their own financial capability. However, board members must still ensure that they, individually, have in good faith and with an expected level of discipline satisfied the duties of loyalty and care described above.

A TEAM OF LEADERS

It is convenient to view the chair of the board as *the* leader. After all, he or she normally convenes and chairs the meeting. However, such an identification of the board chair as the *one and only* leader is a fallacy for a high-performing board. In such a board, every member is a leader. No one follows the chair in a subservient sense, saying to himself, "Well, that person is the chair. We need to do what the chair says." Not surprisingly, there is a great temptation to do just that. Often, board members who view their position as an honor, something to add to their résumé or CV, may think this way. It is always easier to go along with the crowd or, more often than not, to follow the position of the board chair.

Each member of the board needs to take on the responsibility of being a leader on the board. Ideally, statements on institutional mission, vision, goals, and objectives have been established by the board in a strategic planning process, as previously described. However, if such a process has not yet occurred, then each board member is responsible for insisting that such a process take place. Once these objectives have been established, board members must see to it that appropriate actions are undertaken to realize them.

Within a board context, being a leader does not mean having a big mouth and interjecting and objecting every five minutes during a meeting. It means taking a serious responsibility for the work of the board. It means learning about the institution sufficiently to speak knowledgeably about its problems, issues, and opportunities. It means understanding the constraints under which the day-to-day administration and staff labor. It means experiencing deeply within oneself the vision and mission of the institution—to feel in one's gut the institution's yearning to succeed in its appointed mission and achieve its agreed-upon goals and objectives.

Everyone serving on the board is there for a reason. Everyone has expertise and experience which can profitably be brought to bear upon the issues before the board. New members of the board are especially subject to shyness and may not want to ask a foolish question which could expose their ignorance of the institution. Someone early in my career said to me, "The only stupid question is the one you did not ask." They were absolutely correct!

We spoke earlier about humility as a leadership characteristic. Board members must be humble, although this does not imply remaining silent in the background, unnoticed. It means having the courage to ask a question or make a point that others might consider foolish, ignorant, or otherwise uncalled for. In a practical sense, humility is all about being unafraid of others' opinions of oneself, and never being prideful or concerned with protecting one's image in front of others.

THE BOARD CHAIR

In 1994, I was asked by Exxon management to lead a team to develop a plan for a major manufacturing and marketing presence in the Peoples' Republic of China within ten years. Most people I spoke with at the time believed this to be an impossible task, if not a fool's errand. China had no foreign joint ventures in this integrated industry segment—in fact, it was forbidden by law. Nonetheless, this was the task set before me. Fortunately, I was not alone. Exxon management had gathered a number of experienced Exxon executives from the USA, Singapore, and Hong Kong to be members of my team. I could not have asked for anything more. We had experts in planning, marketing, refining, chemicals, engineering, and negotiations along with fluency in Mandarin Chinese, especially the commercial and technical language.

This sounds a bit like the experience I described before, when I joined the school board in Hamburg, right? When we first gathered as the China Study Team, everyone turned to me to see how I wanted to proceed with this grassroots, from-the-beginning exercise. I was greener than any of them concerning China. Fortunately, my ignorance proved beneficial to the team.

I began with an all-day, no-holds-barred session at which we brainstormed various approaches to starting a business in China. We were not talking small potatoes here; we were speaking about a multi-billion dollar project. This project was very important to Exxon, and management was depending on us to deliver. In the end, we decided upon an approach completely different from that of any other oil company in China. We knew we did not know much about China and decided that the only way to learn how to do business was to do business. We fanned out across China and worked with numerous state-owned companies with the intent of understanding their goals and seeking overlaps with what Exxon was looking for. We worked very seriously to reach agreement with each potential partner on commercial and technical terms. At times, we were negotiating several opportunities simultaneously. The team members and the Chinese learned a lot about each other in the process, which served all of us well. More on this aspect will be included in the chapter on negotiations.

The end result was a successful agreement to develop a joint venture in Fujian Province, China. Participating parties were two Chinese state-owned oil companies, plus Saudi Aramco and Exxon. The project has been operating for several years now, with a total estimated investment of five billion dollars. The commercial terms are much the same as the ones negotiated by our team in the mid-1990s.

Why were we successful? Why was this venture the only one of its kind in China? I firmly believe that it was due to the leadership team in place at the time of those first efforts, as well as the ones that followed. We listened to one another. We listened to our colleagues in the USA. We listened to our partners, Saudi Aramco and the Chinese companies. We endeavored to understand where each of us was coming from. We were humble in setting forth proposals that might not be welcomed at first by others, trying to push the envelope. We did not become upset when our best ideas were rejected, sometimes summarily. We welcomed the contributions of others, even when their ideas were different from our own.

Sometimes others' ideas did in fact prove to be better, further adding to our humility. I recall a conversation with a senior Exxon manager, a towering and intellectually powerful figure. I mentioned that the Chinese-proposed design for a particular aspect of the proposed refinery was different from the one recommended by our own expert engineers. He refused to believe that our own thinking was prima facie better than that of their engineers. He asked, very simply, "Why do we presume that their design is inferior to ours?" We took a much harder second look, and agreed that he was right. The Chinese-proposed design was adopted.

In 2000, at a major turning point in the negotiations and technical development of the project, our team held a celebratory luncheon. At this time I was not the leader of the team, but had been called in to assist in the negotiations. In my congratulatory remarks, I quoted Lao Tse in the *Tao Te Ching*: "When the work is done and the objectives fulfilled, the people will all say, 'We did it ourselves.'" This is the true objective of the leader of leaders: empowering others to accomplish more than they think that they are capable of.

The board chair must see himself or herself as the leader of leaders. He or she must strive to ensure that every member has an opportunity to contribute. No one must be left out. If one person is not contributing, the chair must ask, "How do you feel about this? How would you do it differently? What does your experience tell you?" The board chair must be familiar with the background of each member: academic credentials, work experience, interests, family, desires, passions, etc.

Early in my Exxon career, I was fortunate to participate in several leadership seminars and workshops. One workshop leader had us watch a 1973 academy-award winning video of the Los Angeles Philharmonic under the direction of Zubin Mehta, as they prepared to perform Ravel's *Boléro*. The video had me spellbound as I saw the individual musicians come together, each masterful in their own right, to get ready to perform—and performing—under the insightful baton of Maestro Mehta. The short interviews with the musicians and the conductor were priceless, displaying their humanity, their focus, their emphasis on high standards, and their determination to work together in community, in perfect harmony. The Philharmonic truly became more than the sum of its parts. The film marked a turning point for me in my understanding of leadership.

This image of the dedicated symphony conductor must be reflected in the board chair. Otherwise, neither harmony nor true pitch will be present; instead it will be cacophony—or silence.

COMMITTEE CHAIRS

Board work is not carried out solely at semi-annual or even monthly formal board meetings, but typically by committees. Committees get a bad rap sometimes. A common joke is that committees are composed of people who can accomplish nothing by themselves, but come together to say definitively that nothing can be done. However, my experience is that committees, properly constituted and tasked, can perform amazing things.

The key to performance is the committee chair and how he or she works with its members. Again, consistent with the role of the board chair vis-à-vis other board members, the real actors are the members, not just the committee chair. First and foremost, the chair must orchestrate the performances of the individual members. This means facilitating their contributions to the work of the committee. The chair must understand the capabilities and special expertise that each member brings to the common work of the committee. In an ongoing committee, it may be difficult for new members to come up to speed rapidly. This issue can be addressed by assigning an existing committee member to serve as a mentor to the new person.

Furthermore, committee roles and responsibilities need to be carefully spelled out and documented. Such a document should not be static but subject to review and periodic updates. Similarly, the goals and objectives of the committee need to be discussed at committee meetings at an appropriate time of the year, perhaps before and after each board meeting. Plans for the committee over the next several months can then be reviewed with the board and adjusted accordingly following that review. For example, cooperative efforts with other committees may need to be undertaken as a result of the full board discussions.

BOARD EDUCATION

It is critical to conduct board educational programs, and on a continuing basis. These can be one-day retreats, special focused workshops or seminars, provision of reading material, links to outside board governance websites, and so on. Retreats and workshops in particular can help board members periodically reflect on the vision, mission, and values of the institution and their own adherence to them. We all need to be reminded from time to time of why we are serving as board members, and of the trust that has been placed in us by others.

New members especially need access to materials covering the history of the organization and previous activities and decisions of the board. Well before undertaking any board responsibilities each new member should have in his or her possession a minimum of three years' worth of board minutes, financial statements, operational performance reviews, and stewardship reports. The new board member needs to hit the ground running and not be shy about asking questions and offering ideas. Time is of the essence in transitioning a board candidate into a contributing and effective member. New members need to be welcomed enthusiastically by all—especially the board chair—and encouraged to participate.

A well-designed and maintained board member's handbook can be of great value to new and old members alike. Such a handbook provides details about the individual and collective responsibilities of board members, including the statutory, legal, and regulatory requirements. Descriptions of board committees and membership rosters with contact information help keep people informed of board activities and encourage mutual communication. Summaries of past strategic plans and the historical development of the institution are also very useful.

Time must be set aside at every board meeting for calm and reasoned discussion of strategic issues. This is not easy to do, especially for boards that meet only two or three times a year and whose members are geographically dispersed. Nevertheless, such discussions are an essential requirement for an effective board. The responsibility for creating this time rests with the board chair and the executive committee of the board, if one exists. If the board's meeting time can be lengthened by an afternoon or a day, well and good. If not, then other agenda items must be removed, or addressed more efficiently.

Preparation of meeting documents and committee reports should be completed well before a board meeting in order that materials may be disseminated in sufficient time to enable the board to deal efficiently with routine items. Each report should clearly specify the action to be taken by the board on items on the agenda for discussion and/or committee recommendation. Tight control must be exercised on the length of materials presented to the board; for example, a committee report ought to be summarized on one page. Three sections usually suffice to cover the committee's accomplishments and disappointments in the past reporting period; its plans for the next several months; and any actions recommended for full board consideration at this meeting. The committee might also use this last section to obtain a sense of the board's perspective regarding a particular issue on which the committee has been working, rather than a request for a board decision on a final recommendation.

BOARDS AND CONSTITUENCIES

No institution exists for its own sake. Institutions exist to serve others. We call those "others" the institution's constituencies. In the case of a church, the constituencies are the parishioners, employees of the church, the donors and benefactors, those impacted by the church's outreach and educational services, the neighbors of the church, and other nearby parishes. In the case of an educational institution, such as a seminary, constituents include the students, faculty, various church bodies served by the seminary, donors, and the greater society served by retreats and educational offerings such as published books by the faculty.

Boards need to be linked to these constituencies in order to understand their needs. How well does the institution serve its constituencies, and how might it better serve them? In some cases, a link to a particular constituency is obvious, such as the bishop of a certain jurisdiction or the director of the church school. However, the board member needs to represent every constituency equally, keeping the best interests of all of them at heart. In order to do this, the board member must monitor institutional performance versus the needs of various constituencies. This interaction can best be done by careful listening and an openness to how the constituencies respond to what the institution is doing. Mayor Ed Koch of New York City was famous for asking, "How'm I doing?" as he walked the streets of the city. Unfortunately, board members sometimes become defensive in the face of criticism, even if it is justified. This reaction needs to be avoided to the greatest extent possible.

An organized approach to constituency-linking often can be made through the various board committees. For example, a fundraising or advancement committee might have its members frequently call or visit donors to thank them for their gifts, ask for their advice, and solicit comments on how the institution is doing. Buildings and grounds committee members might walk around asking students or parishioners what they think about the facilities. Academic or church school committees might ask faculty, students, or parents what they think about the education being offered. Communications committee members can solicit their friends and networks for opinions of the institution's website. The key is to not remain self-enclosed, but to continuously seek feedback from others.

15

Staying Out of Trouble:
Ethics and Regulatory Compliance

"How can you, a churchman, go to work for a capitalistic oil company?" This question was posed to me by Fr Alexander Schmemann when I became an employee of Exxon in 1970. I had become acquainted several years earlier with Fr Alexander, then dean of St Vladimir's Seminary. We had corresponded and discussed church issues, especially when he visited Syracuse, New York, while I was in graduate school studying engineering. By this time, I was accustomed to Fr Alexander's forthright manner and quickly responded, "Don't worry, Father. Exxon is a very ethical and moral company. If I step out of line one iota, I will be gone." This statement, which I made at the beginning of my Exxon career, I could repeat with full confidence thirty years later.

Exxon had pretty much a zero-tolerance attitude towards violations of its standards of business conduct. These standards regarding ethics, conflicts of interest, harassment, etc., are publicly available today on its website.[1] One quote which always impressed me in early versions of the standards was the very blunt: "We don't want liars for managers." Also the very clear statement: "No one in the organization has the authority to grant exceptions to these foundation policies."

Some people might think that such statements would cause employees to fear higher management, and to worry that they would be severely

---

[1]Exxon Mobil, "Standards of Business Conduct." <http://corporate.exxonmobil.com/en/company/about-us/guiding-principles/standards-of-business-conduct>, Oct. 4, 2016.

punished for small infractions. My attitude was quite the opposite. I felt protected by the forthright emphasis on high ethical standards. They reassured that no one above me would try to pressure me into doing what I considered to be unethical, or would violate the company's standards of conduct themselves. There may be an analogy here to our earlier discussion about the fear of God and following his commandments and statutes.

After I retired from Exxon service, I was asked by the administration of the Orthodox Church in America (OCA) in 2005 to develop best practices for financial accountability for the national church. I am not an accountant, nor an attorney, but I had significant practical experience in Exxon dealing with these issues. The trigger for developing these best practices was the financial crisis at that time in the OCA. Unfortunately, "best practices" seldom get developed before a crisis in order to prevent one, but more often as a result of one. One of the tasks of an effective board or administration is to constantly think ahead as to what might happen, and to keep it from happening.

One of the very first objectives of the resulting document was to place the best practices in terms consistent with the principles of the organization to which they were to be applied. In this case, it was the Orthodox Church. Four foundational concepts were introduced: truthfulness, trustworthiness, openness, and accountability. Fundamental scriptural bases for these concepts were stated:

> As the body of Christ, the Church must be truthful, as Christ is the Truth (John 14.6). We must be trustworthy for "it is required of stewards that they be found trustworthy" (1 Cor 4.1–2). All must be open, as Jesus said: "There is nothing hid, except to be made manifest; nor is anything secret, except to come to light" (Mark 4.22). We must be willing to be measured, as the Lord desired to measure Israel "Behold, I am setting a plumb line in the midst of my people Israel" (Amos 7.8).[2]

Every organization or institution must have core values that are stated, publicized, and emphasized continuously to every employee and person impacted by the institution. Organizational dealings are bound to be

[2]OCA, "Best Practices."

complicated and occasionally ethical issues will be encountered. Some people in the organization may come from different business or ethical cultures. Thus, there needs to be a bedrock belief in the basic ethical standards that govern organizational behavior. No matter the environment in which one operates, these standards are the guiding light by which to make ethical decisions.

An ethics policy must emphasize the need to adhere to the highest ethical standards in all dealings, not just financial activities. To quote from the OCA best practices:

> As a matter of fundamental principle, any nonprofit and philanthropic institution should adhere to the highest ethical standards because it is the right thing to do. . . . Adherence to applicable laws and regulations, including the Charter of the Orthodox Church in America and the Statute of the Orthodox Church in America, is the minimum standard of expected behavior. The Orthodox Church in America administration must do more, however, than simply obey the law. It must ensure that what is done is consistent with the Church's expectations. Transparency, openness, and responsiveness to the Church's concerns must be integral to its behavior.
>
> The Holy Synod, all Metropolitan Council members, administrative management, staff (paid and unpaid), and auditors elected by the All American Council shall act with honesty, integrity and openness in all their dealings as representatives of the OCA.[3]

The bedrock ethical principles need to be echoed in every other institutional policy. As an example, the OCA whistleblower policy reiterates the basic premises of the ethics policy by emphasizing honesty and integrity:

> The OCA Ethics Policy requires the Holy Synod, all Metropolitan Council members, the Pension Board members, administrative management, staff (paid and unpaid), and auditors elected by the All American Council to observe the highest standards of honesty and integrity in the conduct of their duties and responsibilities as well as to comply

[3]OCA, "Best Practices."

with all applicable laws and regulations, the Charter of the Orthodox Church in America, and the Statutes of the Orthodox Church
in America. This Whistleblower Policy is intended to protect those
persons who report a violation of the Ethics Policy.[4]

The Lord does *not* restrict his ethical teachings to financial matters: "Woe
to you, blind guides, who say, 'If any one swears by the temple, it is nothing;
but if any one swears by the gold of the temple, he is bound by his oath.'"[5]
Jesus further proclaims: "Woe to you, scribes and Pharisees, hypocrites!
for you tithe mint and dill and cummin, and have neglected the weightier
matters of the law, justice and mercy and faith; these you ought to have
done, without neglecting the others."[6] The pharisaic emphasis on obeying
every "jot and tittle" of the law obviously gave rise to an extremely limited
concept of ethical behavior that somehow overlooked the proclamations
of prophets like Amos, who said: "Let justice roll down like waters, and
righteousness like an everflowing stream."[7]

    In the same sense, the ethics policy of the OCA enjoined all members
of the governance body, as described above, to the highest ethical standards—not only those dictated by laws, regulations, and procedures, but
also by the gospel and the demands of the Church. These standards are
greater than any of us, no matter how exalted or lowly our position in the
Church, and they apply to everything that is done in the Church, whether
financial, procedural, personal, managerial, etc. The ethics policy further
emphasizes that "no one in the organization, no matter at what level, has
authority to dispense with any of these policy requirements."

    Some readers might raise the following objection: "It is nice that you
are calling others to a strict ethical standard, but what happens when your
boss is doing something that you think might be unethical? What happens
if you can lose your job by complaining or even commenting?" I found
myself in that very situation many years ago while serving in an overseas
position with Exxon. At the time, I did not live up to the principles which

---

[4]OCA, "Best Practices."
[5]Mt 23.16.
[6]Mt 23.23.
[7]Am 5.24.

I espoused then and am espousing now. That experience stays with me always and acts as a goad to ensure that I do the right thing today, regardless of the personal consequences.

I was an expatriate overseas. Expatriates enjoy certain benefits arising from that status since they are away from home, and in a foreign environment. One day, high-ranking members of management were automatically granted certain benefits. However, according to the operations handbook, these benefits needed to be justified individually, not automatically, based upon special circumstances. I was not a high-ranking member of management at the time. To be sure, this was not an earth-shattering ethical issue, but still I wanted to know how a departure from the written policy could be justified. As Jesus said, "He who is faithful in a very little is faithful also in much."[8] I discussed the situation with the expatriate coordinator, who did not have a good answer to my question: why was this done, and is it consistent with policy? My supervisor's manager, who happened to be a beneficiary of the change, heard about this exchange and asked me into his office. When the door was closed, he put his arm around my shoulder and said, "Pete, don't spoil it for the rest of us." To my regret, I remained quiet then and thereafter. That manager was a believer in situation ethics and the principle of "maximizing love." However, maximizing love here meant maximizing love for himself and his colleagues, regardless of what the policy said. Granted, this situation may not seem like a big deal to most people, but it impressed upon me how easily one can be intimidated by high-ranking individuals—particularly when one's career or living depends on them. Since that time, I have been quite reluctant to "let things go" without pursuing them to the end.

Let me take a moment to discuss situation ethics. There are many people who would likely refuse to say that they agree with this particular ethical system, while in fact they act according to it. In its purest form, situation ethics aims at the application of love as its highest principle in making an ethical decision.[9] In situation ethics, there are no absolute ethical rules.

---

[8]Lk 16.10.

[9]See Joseph Fletcher, *Situation Ethics: The New Morality* (Louisville and London: Westminster John Knox Press, 1966).

Everything depends upon the situation. The key criterion is the maximization of love for all concerned. However, there is no actual definition of love, nor any allocation of priority among those upon whom love is visited. Usually, extreme cases are brought up to justify the application of the concept, such as someone who lies in order to protect another from being executed. However, mere mortals who are not in such exigent circumstances will employ the argument to excuse ethically deficient decisions.

A prime example is management behavior in certain churches that overlooks or covers up cases of sexual misconduct on the part of clergy. Bishops and fellow clergy may sometimes seek to "save the priest's vocation" by transferring an acknowledged sexual offender to another parish, or otherwise covering up the transgression—all in the name of love for the offending priest. The bishops will offer this justification: "He has repented." He may have repented, but that does not mean that he can be trusted not to offend again. In this case, the bishop thinks only of the offender when employing situation ethics, not of the people whom this person may offend against in the future. It is much easier to send the offending priest off to some distant suburb than to put everyone through the disturbing process of investigation and judgment. But ethics demands judgment, which is usually uncomfortable for everyone involved. Nevertheless, judgment is absolutely necessary.

I have heard in my career that "enforcement of ethical rules is the best teacher." This normally occurs in the case of someone who has committed an ethical infraction. In another of my overseas postings I experienced a case like this.

A laboratory technician had allegedly decided not to test a certain variable in a product quality examination. The reason given was that almost always this particular variable tested within limits. The technician reportedly decided to simply write in a number which was within limits without doing the test, which of course would have taken additional time. "Why do it when the result is always the same?" we might ask. "It takes time, and just writing in a number is more efficient. Isn't efficiency what we are looking for?" As fate would have it, when the customer received the product and tested it, that variable was off-specification. Internal auditors soon arrived at the laboratory. The end result of the auditors' investigation was that the technician, his supervisor, and their manager were terminated, each for different reasons stemming from the same incident. That very day, every manager in the entire company gathered his or her staff together and explained what had just happened to these three individuals (without names), and why.

The lesson was clear: disobey the rules at your own risk. A person does not have the authority to dispense with the established procedures and rules just because it makes sense to them. There is a higher authority. We may question, but we may not disobey unless we are willing to suffer the consequences.

LEGAL CONSIDERATIONS

Some individuals have questioned whether ethics and whistleblower policies adopted by nonpublic organizations have any "legal teeth." In other words, are violations of these policies enforceable in a court of law, especially in the case of nonprofit and religious corporations? I am not an attorney, but I have been told that in civil litigation courts will look to the nonprofit's own policies and internal regulations as guides for their judgment. In other words, depart from your own policies at your own risk.

Please note that it is certainly possible that some states may have already have some whistleblower statutes in place in labor law or other regulations, particularly as regards health and safety issues. Some state legislatures, including New York, have recently passed or considered enacting various provisions similar to those in the federal Sarbanes-Oxley Act, which apply to nonprofit institutions. Most commentators advise that nonprofits study the Sarbanes-Oxley Act and adopt similar provisions for their own organizations on a voluntary basis. (Indeed, this was what the OCA did several years ago in its best practices policy.) If any case comes into question, it is of course advisable that the organization consult with its legal counsel.

ENFORCEMENT

If enforcement by a court of law is not in the cards, what then? The drafters of the OCA best practices policy recognized that self-regulation and self-enforcement were the best option, in most cases. In other words, as stated several times in the best practices, violations of the various policies are to be investigated and dealt with by "appropriate disciplinary and corrective action." The wording is obviously quite general, and purposely so, in order to enable appropriate judgments to be made regarding particular violations. At the time of adoption of the best practices by the OCA metropolitan council, there was an active discussion regarding a possible table of penalties that could be included in the best practices, similar to some canonical injunctions. Such a table was not included in the final document. However, penalties or penances (*epitimia*) could be imposed, ranging from verbal or written reprimands to termination of one's position, depending upon the severity of the violation.

It is better, of course, to prevent violations before they occur. Attentive listening to one's own conscience in the context of the gospel is the first step in preventing ethics violations. For example, looking at the whistleblower policy from a Christian perspective, the idea that a superior would harass and retaliate against a subordinate who complained to his superiors about unethical behavior is patently opposed to the gospel's message. Jesus says, "If I have spoken wrongly, bear witness to the wrong; but if I have spoken rightly, why do you strike me?"[10] One would expect, regardless of policy, that the one who did the striking would be "cut to the heart,"[11] as would anyone who permitted such striking to occur. If this spiritual recoiling at seeing innocence punished does not occur, we have a fundamental problem not with the whistleblower policy, but with the person who punishes the whistleblower and those who stand by and consent with their silence.[12]

---

[10] Jn 18.23.
[11] Acts 2.37.
[12] Acts 8.1.

HIERARCHY (TOP MANAGEMENT)

The task is further complicated when we consider the possible application of "discipline and corrective action" to the top management of an institution, such as the hierarchy of the Orthodox Church, which is called for in normal ethics and whistleblower policies. Obviously, this is something that no one wants to contemplate as being necessary. In the Orthodox Church, per canonical tradition, the Holy Synod must in all humility listen attentively and reflectively to "the truth spoken in love" by others, recognizing that "we are members one of another,"[13] and then discipline as it sees fit in the eyes of God.

Our Church hierarchy knows better than any of us that we all are subject to a higher authority, whose judgments may be manifested in this life and most certainly in the world to come. The OCA ethics policy sets up a standard for behavior for the governance body of the OCA—a form of self-regulation that requires self-enforcement. It relies upon the internal conscience of all our colleagues and superiors. If that conscience is well-developed, then the policy works. If not, then we have big trouble, and the Church suffers.

A corporation may take a different approach. When I reached a certain executive level in Exxon, my supervisor told me that henceforth every one of my submitted expense reports would be scrutinized by the internal auditors. We all knew that expense reports were subject to random examination, but this was the first time I learned that each and every one would be examined. The reason for this is obvious: if the top people are not compliant with the rules, how can we expect compliance from those below them? Occasionally, we would hear that someone at a high executive level had resigned unexpectedly, "for personal reasons." Further, that individual vacated his or her office in haste, in the company of an internal security official. Although there was never any official announcement, many of us speculated, in such cases, that that individual had in some way violated the standards of business conduct. High-ranking executives had a lot to lose in deferred compensation if they were terminated. It always puzzled

[13]Eph 4.25.

us how people who were quite smart would nevertheless take ethical risks that exposed them to such a loss.

St Gregory the Great, in *The Book of Pastoral Rule*, warns us of the responsibility of high office in the Church. He stresses the importance of reflection and self-examination not only for hierarchs, but for everyone, whether clergy or laity, who exercises leadership in the Church—or anywhere else:[14]

> No one does more harm in the Church than he who has the title or rank of holiness and acts perversely. This is because no layperson presumes to refute the delinquent. . . . And yet everyone who is unworthy would flee from such a great burden of guilt if, with the attentive ear of the heart, he pondered the saying of the Truth: "He that scandalizes one of these little ones who believe in me, it would be better that a millstone was hung around his neck and that he was cast into the depth of the sea" [Mt 18.6].

[14]Gregory the Great, *The Book of Pastoral Rule* 1.2 (*Book of Pastoral Rule*, 32).

16

Meetings, Meetings, Meetings: How to Facilitate Collaboration

My normal work day at Exxon was filled with meetings. Many of them were informational, with one group telling others what they had done: a strategy study, a technical project completion, a financial report, etc. Some meetings, however, were aimed at making decisions. How will we do this? Who should do it? When should it be done by? I always enjoyed the decision-making meetings the most. On the other hand, whenever I received an email stating that an informational meeting had been canceled, I jumped for joy, happy to add one or two more productive hours to my workday. Perhaps most people feel the same way.

Is this attitude fair? Is it right? We constantly hear that we are now in the information society. Knowledge is power, we are told. So why do we feel bored when we are asked to attend an informational meeting intended to fill us in on achievements that some other group has made? The reality is that we are usually passive absorbers of information and not contributors. We ask questions, and the presenters answer them. Everything is very polite.[1] But seldom are we expected to be full participants, contributing whatever we can offer. As a result, there may be no added value from our presence which might accrue to the presenters.

---

[1] Offering challenging questions at such a meeting could result in one's not being invited to the next presentation. Of course, that might not be a bad thing.

A meeting should be a gathering of leaders. It should not be teachers lecturing students. Nor should it be a thesis defense, with a candidate trying to persuade a faculty as to the worthiness of his or her research.

Many high level board reviews are like this, however. At meetings of top-level management or executive committees of corporations, we find two categories of people: those who propose recommendations, and those who decide or dispose. But there is often a third category—those who sit on the sidelines waiting to see which way the management wind blows. While these reviews are a necessary fact of corporate governance, the process can be made much more effective. The key is collaboration.

Many years ago, I performed a major strategy study on Exxon's operations in a certain Asian country, which proposed significant changes to our corporate structure. The time came for me to present my findings and recommendations to the regional executive management for the Asia-Pacific region. I was personally familiar with many individuals in our regional office who had held high-ranking positions in that country in the past. I thought it beneficial to invite them all to the presentation, despite the fact that they had no direct managerial or decision-making responsibilities for that country any longer. Since they had worked there and knew what the business was like, we could not help but benefit in our discussion from their experience and insight. That was the stated basis of my invitation.

The regional CEO was surprised to see so many people at the presentation, but he understood why they were invited. Needless to say, we had a spirited discussion with many different viewpoints expressed and considerable insights shared. The quality of our eventual recommendation was greatly enhanced by the presence of people who were invited not merely for the sake of informing them, but so that we could seek their input. As a side note, many of them came up to me afterward and said that this meeting was the first time in years that they had been asked to contribute to anything regarding their previous managerial and executive experience with that country. They thanked me profusely for, in their words, a very enjoyable afternoon.

This story encapsulates the true objective of a meeting: to be collaborative and enjoyable. If people feel left out and passive, it is a failure. If it is dull and boring, it is a failure. If participants are involved and enjoy the meeting, then it is a success.

HOW TO CONSTRUCT A MEETING

Yes, you heard right—how to *construct* a meeting. One does not just hold or call a meeting; one must construct it. A meeting must be designed and built. It must meet certain specifications and deliver the desired outcomes: a set of decisions, an increased sense of unity, agreement on the path forward, etc. The meeting must be done on time and within budget.

Before going any further, let's talk about time. How many people say, after leaving a meeting room, "Now, that was a waste of time!"

I worked for four years with Exxon in Hamburg, Germany. I arrived a few minutes late to my first meeting with my fellow managers and directors. I was never late thereafter to *any* meeting. Promptness and respect for others' time was a foremost attribute of Exxon management in Germany. Anyone who arrived late entered the meeting room quite abashed, with everyone looking at him or her. A formal apology must be said aloud: "*Entshuldigung fuer die Verspaetung* (apologies for being late)." Naturally, there were very few instances of people coming late to meetings. Everyone arrived early, ready to begin work on time. Furthermore, if the meeting was scheduled to last one hour, it was adjourned within exactly sixty minutes.

Years later, I returned to the United States and observed the opposite behavior. Some twenty senior managers and advisors had gathered together and were waiting for the chair of the meeting to arrive—which he eventually did, ten minutes late. I admit to having been a bit exercised about this, having not yet recovered from my German experience. I did suggest to that individual privately, and in apparent jest, that we ought to have a time clock, which everyone would punch into, stationed at the entry to each meeting room. This clock would be connected to the HR salary database of each person and feature a prominent digital display to show just how much this meeting costs in terms of personnel—especially the cost of keeping people waiting. I did see some improvement in the chair's on-time arrival performance thereafter.

A meeting is a gathering of leaders who respect each other's time and potential contributions. It is apparent to everyone when that respect is absent—when others' time is squandered and their experience and expertise ignored. Such meetings usually fall short of what they could be. On the other hand, when respect is given, major accomplishments can be expected.

Everyone assumes that the chairperson, or the person who convenes the meeting, is the one who designs the meeting. An agenda is normally distributed either shortly before the meeting or at its very start. Most times the agenda is just a list of topics that the chair ticks off as they are discussed. The meeting participants might add one or two items, but control of the meeting is pretty much left up to the chair. The critical question is: who owns the meeting? Who bears responsibility for its success or failure? Most people would say it is the chair, but I submit that responsibility belongs to everyone in the meeting room, without exception.

A CHECKLIST FOR MEETING DESIGN

Let us revisit the six goals of Christian leadership that we discussed in earlier chapters. How might these give us insight or guidance as to how a meeting should be designed?

- Christ and His Kingdom

- Examine and Rediscover Our Values

- Focus on, Care for, and Love Others

- Be Humble

- Desire to Serve, Not to Be Served

- Remain Steadfast in Tough Times

Christ and His Kingdom

Now are we going to run into trouble right off the bat? Let's say that one works for a secular company such as a government agency, factory, or maybe a marketing firm. How is it possible to start with Christ and his kingdom? Isn't there a huge gap between working for a particular organization in our particular job, and believing in Christ? Shouldn't we keep them separate?

The call of Christ and his kingdom compels us to view every moment of our lives and every encounter with others with the utmost seriousness. Christ is present at every moment and in every encounter, regardless of where we are and who we are with. Thus, when we decide to construct a meeting, we must view its purpose as ultimately serious and part of the building up of the kingdom of God—even if said purpose is designing a new website for marketing some product like, say, a new breakfast cereal. The key consideration here is two-fold: first, the impact of the meeting upon the end goal of the meeting (the website), and second, and more importantly, the impact that the meeting will have on the lives of the attendees.

What would be a Christian approach to this seemingly "secular" meeting goal? We could, for example, insist that the website be as good as possible: attractive, appropriate, and easy to use. It should have no broken links that unintentionally frustrate the people who log in to navigate it. It should be honest and not deceptive. As much as possible, it should be done to the glory of God. Depending on the company that one works for, this last desire may not necessarily be expressed aloud. But we should still feel it within and give thanks to God when our labors succeed.[2]

Second, everyone who attends the meeting should feel engaged and valued. They should come away with the sense of having done something

---

[2]Our China team held many negotiating sessions in Guangzhou with our Chinese counterparts regarding a potential joint venture there. One particular time, we had traveled from Hong Kong by train all morning. On that trip I had been reading a book entitled *His Life is Mine* by Archimandrite Sophrony. That little paperback had a large full-color icon of Jesus Christ on the cover. One of the Chinese saw it and exclaimed, "You brought your God with you!" I said, "Yes I bring him everywhere." Christians need to make God present wherever they are by their thoughts, prayers, and actions.

important—of having experienced the joy of working together with others to create something greater than the sum of the parts. They should feel love, each in their own way.[3]

Examine and Rediscover Our Values

There are two major areas to concentrate on here. First, what is our motivation for calling this meeting? And second, are we planning to construct this meeting on our own, or are we subjecting its design to the counsel of others?

First, let's talk about motivation. Is this meeting an opportunity for us to display our own accomplishments? Is it designed to obtain the agreement of others on our recommended plan? Are we hoping for a "rubber stamp"? Will we welcome and invite criticisms, and if so, how extensively are we willing to allow others to criticize? What should we say in the meeting invitation to set the scene for our desired outcome?

There have been occasions when I failed to undertake this kind of self-examination before a meeting I had called. Nevertheless, I still expected to receive appreciation for my efforts and praise for the outstanding work that I had done. When I did not receive those plaudits, I was disappointed. In some cases, I reacted to criticisms in an unfavorable way.

I was taught a lesson many years ago when presenting a certain project proposal to the CEO of our international company. This particular refinery investment proposal had been presented to him several times before, and he always raised questions. After each such occasion I went back to my office, considered the objections (which were usually well-taken), and worked with the refinery people to modify the proposal accordingly. Finally, the time came when I presented the "perfect" proposal—the one I was sure he could not reject, and for which he would therefore be compelled to release the necessary funds. Well, he did not reject it, exactly, but he seemed annoyed that he was unable to come up with any reasonable objection. Whether he simply did not like that refinery, or perhaps the

---

[3] As I write this, I am listening to the words of Coach Mike Krzyzewski of the Duke basketball team, on the day after they won their fifth NCAA title. Coach K said this about his team: "I love those guys." That's motivation.

people managing it, I never knew. At any rate, he threw the presentation papers across the table at me and said, "OK, you got your money."

I thanked him, took the papers, and left the board room accompanied by my immediate manager. I was clearly upset by the CEO's rudeness. My manager, being wiser than me, recognized this and said, "Look, you got what you came for. You got the funds for the project. Be happy with that." However, I had not gotten what I came for. I wanted the project to be approved, yes, but I wanted it on my terms, including the praise and thanks I did not receive.

I was wrong, and short-sighted. Later on in my career, in very difficult and exhausting international negotiations, I learned to carefully analyze upfront what I wanted to obtain from a meeting. I stopped throwing the kitchen sink (especially praise and thanks) into the specifications. I learned I could even suffer antagonism, anger, and arrogance without losing my focus on what was necessary. All of these lessons required me to identify the not-so-positive values of mine which stood in the way of achieving my fundamental objectives.

Now let us turn to the question of how meetings are planned. The best meetings are the ones we plan not in solitude, but in collaboration with others. I am not talking here about sharing the agenda in advance with participants. This worthwhile exercise should certainly be carried out in most cases. However, there is no substitute for the counsel of others when constructing a meeting. Many times we have blind spots when it comes to the attitudes of others, or in how we regard others. A trusted counselor can be very helpful in identifying those blind spots. Often, we can work on this area with a peer.

The construction of a meeting should generally be performed in a low-vulnerability environment, which helps to improve co-worker relations. In many cases a subordinate might fulfill this role. Side benefits such as increasing mutual trust can accrue from enabling subordinates to speak up, especially in situations where one needs help and fails to recognize it. I have been extremely fortunate in having supervisors who allowed me to offer frank and open suggestions not only on proposals, but also about the supervisor's relationship with other managers.

The next example demonstrates what can happen when one does not ask for others' counsel in advance.

Focus On, Care For, and Love Others

My first expatriate assignment was in Tokyo, Japan. I was called in to lead a small team to perform a strategic study on the development of a major import terminal in Japan. I set to work immediately, developing a process for gathering data from other divisions in the company, analyzing the data, and coming up with the best solution for the project. After a few weeks I called a meeting of the various company department and divisional managers to explain my recommendation.

It was a strange meeting. I gave my presentation and, after I finished, asked for comments. No one said a word. I asked if there were any objections. No one said a word. I asked if anyone had anything to add. No one said a word. I said thank you. Everyone got up, bowed politely, and left, all without a word.

What happened? I failed to focus on, let alone care for and love, those managers. I had not bothered to ask in advance how decisions were made in Japan, nor how agreement is reached. I foolishly thought that my way was the best way. Only later did I find out about the Japanese way of *nemawashi*, which was the process that I should have followed well before approaching anyone in management with my ideas.

Nemawashi means literally "going around the roots." The Japanese gardener usually has great success when transplanting a tree. He first cuts around the roots, then trims the foliage. He prepares the hole to receive the transplanted tree far in advance of the actual transplantation, carefully choosing the season and the day. In fact, he may perform cutting and trimming several times over a period of months for the sake of a better transition. The tree usually survives and thrives. Contrast this approach to that of impatient American gardeners like me, who dig up and transplant a tree in one day, and then get disappointed or even angry when it dies.

In Japan, managers expect people to share ideas with them well in advance of making any proposal. They expect to have a hand in trimming the branches, cutting the roots, and preparing the soil. If this is not done (as I was told later), the proposal may likely be rejected out of hand. Fortunately, this outright rejection did not happen in my case. The Japanese managers were far more polite to me than I was to them.

I was abashed after hearing what I should have done but did not do. In fact, I felt quite dumb. So, over the next month or two, I set up person-to-person meetings with each of the department and divisional managers in their offices. I began with small talk about when and how they joined the company, their experiences, and how they viewed current company operations. In short, I expressed my sincere and personal interest in them. I focused on them. I requested their ideas for my project. I asked them for advice. It was an enlightening exercise. It also allowed me to gain their trust and respect. After that, senior managers who brought proposals to the board would insist that their subordinates review any proposal which even remotely touched on my own area with me beforehand, and obtain my signature on the proposal.

The lesson here is simply to know our audience in a way that gives us insight into their customs, backgrounds, needs, and ideas. If that knowledge is coupled with a genuine and sincere caring for them—along with a striving to make any gathering of individuals into an experience in shared accomplishment and community—it will work wonders.

Be Humble

At this point the reader might be wondering, "How in the world will being humble help me to better construct a meeting?" It's a good question. The title of this chapter is "How to Facilitate Collaboration." Attitudes can either foster collaboration, or kill it. The person who approaches the construction of a meeting with humility places himself or herself in an enviable position—that of being completely indifferent to what others think or say with regard to his or her inner personhood.

Our inner person, no matter how exalted our position, title, or status, is fundamentally fragile. From the beginning analyst to the highly experienced CEO, we all have inner egos that can be offended. To prevent this, we create a wall (thicker for some, thinner for others) intended to protect us against any damage to our sensitive egos.

I once knew a manager in Europe whom people described as "prickly." He really was rather like a porcupine. Other employees had to dance around him with kid gloves so that he wouldn't get his back up and let the spines emerge. Meetings with this person were naturally a bit difficult, and it was especially hard to try out new ideas or brainstorm with him. I had another colleague, this time in the Church, who automatically said "no" whenever anyone questioned the way something was done, or suggested a new approach. He was usually on the defensive. A more humble and open attitude would have resulted in more effective collaboration.

In Chapter 4, we discussed how Christ made himself "a person of no reputation" as an example of what being humble means. Of course, all of us have reputations, although they differ depending on the person to whom we are speaking. Our mothers see one side of us, our spouses another; our bosses notice one aspect and our colleagues yet another. But when we assemble as a group in a meeting, we need to have no reputation in order not to distract from the collaborative nature of the work.

In the monastic literature, a story is told of a young monk who asks an elder what it means to be perfect. But in this case the younger monk was perhaps trying to heed the command to "be perfect as your Father in heaven is perfect." How did the elder monk respond to the question? He asked the younger to do something. "Go to the cemetery, and speak to the monks buried there. Praise them. Tell them how wonderful they were, what ascetic exploits they performed, how they were shining examples to others!" The young monk did so and then returned to the elder. The elder asked, "What did they say?" The younger replied, "Nothing." Now the elder said, "Go back and curse them. Tell them what sinners they were, how they disappointed everyone!" The young monk did so and returned to the elder. He asked, "What did they say?" The younger replied, "Nothing." The elder monk smiled and said, "Perfect."

To refuse to be anxious about a meeting or worry about what the outcome will mean for one's reputation, to be unconcerned when one is criticized, never to be puffed up when one is complimented—these are all manifestations of humility. Humility frees us from that inner tension which sets up defensive walls between us and others, and causes creativity to be stifled and collaboration to be thwarted.

Desire to Serve, Not to be Served

We may have a hidden agenda when we call a meeting. Perhaps it is to show off, to publicize our own accomplishments. Perhaps we hope to ramrod agreement on a controversial decision and bury potential dissent from others. Perhaps our goal is simply to get our way on a particular issue, despite the knowledge that others may have different thoughts. These hidden agendas distract and detract from any collaborative possibilities at the meeting.

The constructor of the meeting needs to be the servant of the meeting participants. He or she must serve the overall objective of the gathering. This normally works best in the case of participants who share common values. But what happens when the meeting involves people from two different and competing organizations? Doesn't this necessarily imply an adversarial relationship? How can one side view itself as serving both parties at one time?

International negotiations present particular difficulties in finding common ground. Many things are different between the two sides involved in discussion: culture, language, values, corporate personalities, and, yes, even what is considered ethical behavior. These differences need to be surmounted as much as possible. Unfortunately, often the two sides look out only for themselves. This leads to increased tension and difficult negotiations. Solutions can and often will be reached, but perhaps not without lingering animosities between the participants.

My own experience has been that if we take the radical approach of trying to serve the best interests of both parties, these differences can be reduced and even overcome. It will not be easy, since the other side may be quite suspicious of our intentions. In China, we almost always began a high-level meeting, especially with governmental officials, by emphasizing two presuppositions, namely, mutual respect and mutual benefit. By so doing, we tried to go beyond what is "mine" and "yours" to what is ours, at least potentially.

Remain Steadfast in Tough Times

Even when we apply the principles outlined so far, meeting success is never guaranteed. Meetings can go south in spite of the best intentions and most thoughtful planning. For example, sometimes two participants will ignore the agenda and use the occasion to attack each other or to bring up old grievances. It gets worse if one decides to mediate. This rarely ends well.

The process can be likened to a psychological game called Persecutor-Victim-Rescuer. This cyclic game is usually played to disastrous outcomes for the participants. It works best in families with long-standing grudges and unforgiven offenses. One person starts by criticizing another, the more unfairly the better. The criticizer or attacker is the Persecutor, the attacked is the Victim.

Now you enter the game as the head of the meeting in which two people begin to have at it. You are obviously the most reasonable and emotionally gifted person there, so you decide to intervene, usually on behalf of the Victim. You are the Rescuer. So far, so good. However, the Persecutor interprets your defense of the Victim as an attack on him or her, and you turn into the Persecutor in his or her eyes. The former Persecutor becomes the Victim and, lo and behold, the former Victim becomes the Rescuer. Why? Because they do not like your intervention, probably because they have more history together than they do with you, and for many other reasons. In any event, you are now hopelessly enmeshed. You have lost your position as the most reasonable and emotionally gifted person in the room. The game now goes on and on, and no one can predict where it will end. Your best move is to call the discussion out of order and ask them to resolve their differences outside, preferably with a member of management who has jurisdiction over the both of them.

Once, I was leading a study for a major restructuring of a certain country's operations. I had two representatives of a specialist staff function on my team—one officially assigned to it, and the other an advisor (we will call them John and Mary). At a departmental review of the restructuring plans, the vice-president of that staff function (let's call him Tom) said that he had heard two quite different recommendations from these two individuals as to when the staff work would be completed. I knew that there were issues between the two, but I had not heard of this latest one. Tom said to me, "John and Mary told me two different things," with the unspoken implication, "What are you going to do about it?" I could have tried to resolve the problem then and there, but only at the cost of an unnecessary delay to the meeting. I would also run the risk of appearing to be on the side of one person or the other, especially since I did not have the benefit of knowing what John and Mary said to Tom. However, postponing my questioning, analysis, and decision to a later time would have taken the responsibility away from Tom, the vice-president to whom it rightly belonged. So I replied, "Well, Tom, they both work for you—so I guess it's *your* problem." And that was that. Shortly thereafter I received one recommendation from the team.

Even when meetings go well, others who are not directly involved may criticize the outcome and the decisions made. It is especially troublesome when these critics are at high levels in the organization. In this situation one still needs to remain steadfast and do the right thing.

Many years ago, I managed Exxon's crude and product supply operations for a particular region. We always had choices to make among the various sources of raw materials and dispositions of a product. These decisions were reached according to what was best for the company in an overall economic sense, via consensus among all parties involved. Although what was good for one party or company division might not be good for another, people would tend to agree as long as the general interest was maximized.

Once, we had the opportunity to purchase a large cargo of crude from a third party in the last days of the year at a distressed price. Unfortunately, there was a downside: we could not lift a cargo of our own equity crude from upstream production until the first days of the following year. There were no negative upstream economics for the company, since that crude would be lifted after only a few days' delay. However, it meant that our upstream division would not meet its quantitative stewardship target for that calendar year, but would correspondingly exceed it the following year. I purchased the crude cargo, and the company made considerable bottom-line profit.

After New Year's Day had passed, I was called into the office of the upstream divisional vice-president whose past year stewardship I had impaired. He informed me that he was very disappointed. I explained to him that while his division's stewardship was indeed negatively impacted (if only to a minor extent), the overall economic benefit for the company was very positive. Besides, it was a one-time opportunity, and his people were kept informed along the way. He continued to say with greater emphasis that he was *very* disappointed. It was a frustrating meeting since I could not get him to understand that we worked in the company's general interest, and not just the interest of one division. The company CEO backed us up on that decision, and presumably our careers did not take a hit from that vice-president's disappointment. We could not have done anything differently. We had to make the right decision regardless of what others, even some very important people, thought. That example provides a perfect segue to our next topic: how to deal with disagreeable people.

17

How to Reach Agreement with Disagreeable People (and Others)

Everyone likes agreeable people, and surely we, who are reading this, are all quite agreeable. Unfortunately, however, humans being what they are, even agreeable people can disagree with our position sometimes. Since we are perfect, this disagreement can be chalked up to a temporary mental lapse on their part, of course. No? Is it possible that we are not perfect all the time, and perhaps not even so agreeable at times? Couldn't those disagreeable people out there be right some of the time, and perhaps not be disagreeable all the time?

We conveniently place people into categories to simplify, management or labor, foreigners or Americans, or simply an employee of my company versus theirs. It is an easy jump from there to a more emotional differentiation, namely, agreeable or disagreeable, people we like and people we do not like.

We call the art and science of reaching agreement with these people "negotiation." It is not my intention here to outline principles of negotiation, for those have been laid out already in many excellent volumes.[1] I do, however, want to discuss some fundamental and strategic interpersonal relationships which, in my experience, are critical to begin the process of reaching effective agreement with anyone.

[1] See Gerard I. Nierenberg, *The Art of Negotiating* (New York, NY: Pocket Books, 1981); Roger Fisher and William Ury, *Getting to Yes: Negotiating Agreement without Giving In* (New York, NY: Penguin Books, 1991); and Max H. Bazerman and Margaret A. Neale, *Negotiating Rationally* (New York, NY: The Free Press, 1992).

THE OTHER PERSON IS A CHILD OF GOD

When I was a graduate student at Syracuse University, I took an overload of courses in electrical engineering and applied mathematics. It was tough. It happened to be springtime, and the campus was filled with happy and carefree undergraduates. I was trudging along one beautiful afternoon across the quadrangle between classes, dodging Frisbees and feeling quite curmudgeonly. At this moment, *I* was the disagreeable person. For some reason, I began looking into the face of each person approaching me and saying to myself, "This is a child of God." After saying it a few times, I began to smile. My trudging steps became light. The people who passed me later on must have thought me quite strange since I couldn't stop smiling. I felt quite at peace with the day and very much in tune with all these wonderful people—the same ones whom I thought were anything but wonderful just a few moments before.

I have had similar experiences over and over again in various countries and cultures. Most times my experience was a quiet one, in which I simply pondered the fact that this otherwise disagreeable person sitting across the table from me was really a child of God. He or she was created in the image and likeness of God and therefore possessed enormous potential for love, kindness, generosity, and every other virtue that God grants to his children. This acknowledgment breaks down the artificial barriers of judgment that we so often set up between ourselves and others, allowing the Spirit of God to enter into the relationship.

DISCOVER SOMETHING LOVABLE IN THE OTHER

I once knew a manager, a high-ranking American executive, whom I heard had the reputation of being loud and at times overbearing. He was very smart and experienced. However, some people had difficulty seeing beyond his reputed demeanor. In his later career, he was posted to a senior assignment in a foreign country. One day, while on a business trip to that place, I was introduced to him at lunch in the company of a few others. He announced to us that he had discovered classical music and was beginning to collect certain pieces. He was so enthusiastic that we could not help but smile at his effusive descriptions of the music he was collecting. Granted, for many of us at the table, any such discussion about music was old news, since we had likely listened to and appreciated classical music for years or even decades. But his comments allowed us to see a lovable side of him that we, and certainly I, had not seen before. As a result my personal opinion of him was completely different from his so-called reputation, and we became great working partners.

In the case of this manager, he took the initiative to let us know something about him that was outside the normal course of business affairs. In Japan, it is actually considered highly rude to begin talking about business when first meeting someone else. The parties have a cup of tea and speak about family, hobbies, or the weather until they feel comfortable with one another. This tradition always provided an opportunity to probe a bit and see what one can learn, or even find lovable, about the other person.

One further example: I had a business colleague with whom I dealt infrequently and never got to know well. I should hasten to add that he was not a disagreeable person by any means. The company had decided to send him, me, and several others to an effective presentations course taught by Madison Avenue marketing people. The lead instructor asked us to speak before the class about a hobby or special interest of ours. We had an evening to think about this assignment and to prepare. Our colleague stepped up to the front of the room first. We noticed that he had a fresh beautiful yellow rose in his shirt pocket. He proceeded to speak about breeding roses. It turned out that he had been doing this for years and had won several prestigious competitions. He spoke with such intensity and depth of feeling about roses that we were all transfixed by his words. Needless to say, none of our business interactions with him thereafter were the same. We saw a different person.

DON'T ASSUME THAT WE ARE ALWAYS RIGHT

Fr Alexander Schmemann once said, "There are people who know everything but understand nothing." (Or at least they *think* that they know everything.) In dealing with others, we need to recognize that there is usually something that is true and right about the other's viewpoint, no matter how much it differs from ours. We do not know everything nor, even more importantly, do we understand everything.

Belief in our own "rightness" is a major cause of barriers between ourselves and others. We are right, and they are wrong. We know, and they don't. We are the teachers (or should be), and they are the students (or should be). This attitude can blind us to inherent dangers in our own positions. In addition, the other party may have a good idea that we failed to recognize. In some cultures, national pride may cause the other party to react negatively when they get a sense that we believe we know more than they do.

There is certainly such a thing as absolute truth. But in dealing with people, it is important to ensure that both understand and come to agreement as to what that truth is. In order to enable the other to come to see what the truth is from our viewpoint, it is often necessary to stop pushing our own position and interpretation of truth and instead listen openly to the other.

Earlier, I mentioned a precept from the book *Unseen Warfare* that cautions, "One should never trust oneself in anything." It is quite a jump from this position to assuming that we are always right. A healthy disbelief in what we think can be very useful in ensuring that we do not miss opportunities to explore the thinking of others. However, this cannot be approached as a formal exercise that essentially says: "OK, I'll let you speak all you want and promise to not interrupt you. But then I'll demolish your argument with my unassailable logic!" No, this sort of internal humility, if you will, must come from the heart. It needs to reflect an honest openness to the other.

I was trained at college as an engineer. My education instilled in me a critical attitude towards everything; I always needed to question a design, concept, or calculation. After all, if I were to build a bridge, it was up to me to double-check every calculation and verify every assumption, since I bore responsibility for not allowing that bridge to fail. Over time that critical attitude became so ingrained in me that even when reading a book on philosophy or ethics, I would fill the margin with questions, doubts, and outright criticisms of the author's words. I wonder today how many good and worthy ideas I prematurely discarded with this attitude.

Fortunately, while in graduate school, I read St Maximus the Confessor's "Four Centuries on Love," which states in the foreword: "If a man should read this or some other book not for spiritual profit but in order to find passages with which to reproach the author, that he may vaingloriously show himself to be the more knowledgeable, to such a person nothing useful will ever be revealed in anything."[2] I stood rightly accused and convicted. From that day forth, I tried to read and listen for spiritual profit, at least the first time through. I did allow for some questioning and perhaps criticism later, but never on the first reading.

LOOK TO THE LONG TERM

Most of my expatriate assignments lasted only a few years, and some were as brief as eighteen months. Naturally, it is tempting to try to achieve something extraordinary in that short time, and then to remain insufficiently aware of what transpires after we depart. We may have short-term wins at longer-term expense.

On one of my early overseas postings, I was called in to negotiate a five-year supply arrangement with a third party. It was a fairly complicated situation with some economic impacts that were not, as I discovered later, immediately apparent to the other party. In accordance with the best negotiating practices, I developed an opening position that gave considerable advantage from these economic impacts to my company and much less to the other. This seemed fair to me because I was directly negotiating with a very senior member of the other company, who had a lot more experience than I did. Certainly he would counter with his own advantaged proposal. (This was the first such negotiation I had ever attempted, and I was quite young at the time.)

I gave my proposal to my counterpart, fully expecting that it would be rejected and severely modified. I was very surprised to have it returned with just a few minor modifications. Those "apparent" economic impacts

[2]St Maximus the Confessor, "Forward to Elpidos," in *Four Centuries on Love*. In *Early Fathers from the Philokalia*, 286.

were evidently not so apparent to the other party. We signed the revised contract and all was well—at least until four years later, when it came time for renewal. I was working in a different country at the time while my former boss now worked in the country in which the original contract had been negotiated. He informed me of the trouble that my wonderful contract conditions had caused once the other company had realized that the split of benefits was highly unbalanced in their disfavor. Needless to say, the renewed contract was certainly not in our favor. I imagine that most of the benefits I had secured were probably lost in the renewed deal, and then some.

Economic benefit in the short term does not outweigh the value of a long-term reputation for mutual respect, mutual benefit and equitable dealing. Although *caveat emptor* ("let the buyer beware") is a good maxim for a one-time deal, it is not good for a long-term relationship. Likewise, we can win an argument and score some "points" in a negotiating session, but if that causes the other person to lose face or be embarrassed, we have lost. The relationship will be damaged, sometimes irreparably.

Our China team had a chance to negotiate numerous opportunities in China. In every case but one we encountered conflicting and unresolvable commercial positions. As a result, the discussions were terminated. However, each negotiation and its eventual closure was an opportunity for us to show how we would behave in an ongoing operation if things got difficult. Would we get angry and bang the table? Would we stick to the absolute letter of the law, such as a previous mutual agreement, or would we try to understand the other's position, which might have changed in the interim? There were not very many secrets in China at that time, and we knew that people in other companies were observing our behavior, especially when things turned south. As it happened, we gained a reputation as perhaps not the easiest party with which to negotiate, but we were certainly seen as serious, sincere, and respectful. We normally held a farewell dinner with the other company at which we wished each other well and expressed interest in future opportunities to work together. In some cases, that opportunity arose earlier than expected. Had we banged the table, we might never have met again.

PUT YOURSELF IN THE OTHER PERSON'S SHOES

This maxim is always more difficult than it sounds, but when it works, it is magical. To do this, one needs to focus on that person and try to understand where he or she is coming from. A prerequisite is to suspend judgment, avoiding any reaction to what the other person does or says. This may not be easy in the middle of a negotiation session or meeting with others present, waiting to see how the interchange will go. It is much better to practice it on a proactive basis when the first signs of potential disagreement emerge—especially one with emotional overtones. Occasionally, however, this understanding must come after the fact. In such cases one needs to work hard in order to creatively establish a sense of empathy with the other person without putting him or her off.

I had an occasion to try this during one of our Chinese negotiations. One of my Chinese counterparts was difficult to get to know. He was highly intelligent, articulate, and an excellent negotiator. He was also quite tall. I had asked him about his background, but did not receive much information in return. At one meeting, I announced a change in our desired corporate venture structure, and he took the news quite badly. In fact, he was angry and the rest of the negotiating session did not go particularly well. I was frankly disappointed that he reacted so emotionally. I must admit that previously I did not feel much empathy for this person. That was *my* problem. But I had to renew the relationship now, and to improve it dramatically if possible.

Fortunately, the end of the session did not mean the end of our contacts that day. We had a dinner scheduled for our teams that could not be canceled. My counterpart (let's call him Mr Tan) and I were seated together at the bar before the dinner and had a beer or two. I really do not know what compelled me to say what I said then, but I was determined to get our relationship on the right track.

I said to him, "Mr Tan, I'll bet that I can guess where you were born and where you grew up." He responded, "You can't possibly know that." (As I mentioned, he was a bit of a private person.) I replied, "I'll bet you were born in Shandong Province and raised in Shanghai." He turned somewhat pale and said with a very surprised voice, "That's so. But how did you know that?" I replied, "Well, you are quite tall and everyone knows that the tallest people in China come from Shandong Province." He said, "OK, I get that, but what about Shanghai?" I responded, "It is also well known that the best negotiators in China come from Shanghai, since they are the most intelligent and also quite sneaky." He smiled broadly, ignored the intelligent comment, and said, "Yes, I *am* sneaky." For both of us, "sneaky" was understood to be a compliment between negotiating friends. From that moment, our relationship eased and we were better able to discuss and resolve difficult and sticky issues.

I took a chance on that occasion, and it worked. I doubt it would have worked without a deep desire on my part to know this person better, to relate to him, to put myself in his shoes. I would have most likely crashed and burned. Putting yourself in the other person's shoes out of a fervent wish to better understand and empathize with that person is a powerful tool.

MAKE FRIENDS WITH THE OTHER'S FRIENDS

If it seems difficult to see someone's good side, let alone discover something lovable in that person, try that person's friends. Make friends with those people—not as a ploy to manipulate, but as an honest attempt to understand the other person.

Once, during a certain international negotiation, I was unable to get on the good side of my negotiating counterpart despite my best efforts. We had a few occasions to speak with one another, but although always polite, he remained cool and aloof. I normally sought to establish a friendlier relationship, which I firmly believe leads to a more cooperative and mutually beneficial negotiation. Our negotiation team had two levels: the leaders of the discussions, and the support team who did all the actual work. I asked a member of my support team to ask his friends on the other side about the person with whom I was having difficulty. After doing so, he clued me in to some issues my counterpart had with us (and me), but never expressed openly. I worked on those areas and, after a bit more time, the coolness warmed. We were able to work much more collaboratively together.

INJECT HUMOR INTO THE SITUATION

Humor can work wonders to diffuse ticklish situations. Once, during our China negotiations, I had occasion to accompany a delegation from a Chinese company on a visit to some of our manufacturing facilities in the United States. It was a week-long visit, and I was with them at its beginning and end. The delegation was led by a vice-president with whom I was not especially familiar.

The visit kicked off with a dinner that I hosted at an excellent Chinese restaurant in New York City specializing in Peking cuisine. I then turned the group over to executives of other divisions, who conducted the actual facility visits. I caught up with the tour a few days later at one of our Gulf Coast refineries. I arrived during a morning presentation meeting. Our people came up to me immediately and said, "The vice-president is angry." I asked, "Why?" They answered, "The tours went very well, but he feels insulted since we took them out to very nice French and Italian restaurants, but not any Chinese ones." I said, "Okay, but what are we having for our working lunch today?" The answer was, "Mexican. Fajitas."

I had to think fast. Fajitas are mixtures of grilled chicken or beef, onions, peppers, and salsa wrapped in a tortilla pancake. The Chinese specialty dish of Peking duck is composed of slices of roasted duck with scallions and hoisin sauce, wrapped in a pancake. I knew Marco Polo brought noodles from China back to Italy, where they became the spaghetti of today. Maybe something similar was true in this case. Could fajitas have originated in China?

When the fajitas were served, the entire table of some twenty people fell silent. The vice-president had previously expressed his displeasure, so everyone was waiting to see his reaction. He looked at the dish and exclaimed loudly to everyone, "What is this?" I immediately answered, "Mr Vice-President, these are fajitas. They are the Mexican version of Peking duck." I then made my leap of faith. I said, "The Mexicans learned this from the Chinese." He smiled and laughed. Everyone else around the table laughed. I don't know whether he believed me or not, but it didn't matter. No one was going to do a Google search to find out the truth. The tension was broken. He enjoyed the meal, and the rest of the visit went very well. Needless to say, at each meal after that we dined at a Chinese restaurant, the more like "home" the better. I did greatly enjoy the camaraderie that was gained during that visit, especially when they and we felt at ease in familiar surroundings. We showed, by our hospitality, that we did in fact care about them and were not just trying to impress them.

18

How to Manage HR Issues Such as Performance, Misconduct, etc.

HR, in corporate parlance, stands for "human resources," the division that handles employee issues such as salary, hiring, firing, benefits, evaluations, transfers, retirements, etc. In the old days, this function was sometimes termed "employee relations." That designation seems to me to convey more humanity than the newer one, which simply tacks the adjective "human" onto a noun encompassing steel, concrete, and other inanimate "things" a company needs to carry out its business. But now we have arrived in the world of human resources with capital letters, where HR stands for a seemingly arcane space of procedural manuals and employment guidelines that become increasingly difficult to understand.

I realize that some readers of this book, especially those not employed in a corporation, may think that they, in carrying out their leadership function, never need to deal with HR issues. However, these issues exist almost everywhere outside the home: on parish councils, on school boards or other nonprofit boards, and in any governance group, including the general membership of an organization. HR involves people, and the presence of people gives rise to both problems and opportunities.

Problems. An organization may have people who are not motivated or not performing and thus need corrective guidance. There may be cases of misconduct in various forms, ethical and/or legal. We may encounter people who, despite all reasonable efforts, are just not good fits with the organization, and we need to find a way to terminate their employment without causing more problems, especially legal ones.

Opportunities. We want to motivate people to do their best, whatever their responsibilities may be. We want to ensure that they are performing duties for the benefit of both themselves and the organization. We want them to be integral parts of the organization, not hired servants. We want them to be properly compensated for their work. We want to ensure that those at the top of the organization are properly leading the organization toward the agreed-upon vision, within agreed-upon parameters and constraints.

As in the previous management chapters, I will here offer a few basic principles and concepts, utilizing examples from my own corporate and nonprofit experience. Once again, bear in mind my disclaimer statement that appears at the beginning of Part Five, Strategic Management.

CLEAR MUTUAL EXPECTATIONS

Over the years I developed a practice that I believe served my people and myself well. Whenever I became manager of a new division, I held a meeting of all employees, both those reporting to me directly and those who reported to them down the line. My goal was to hold the meeting within the first few days of taking on my new responsibilities. I told them at this meeting that I wanted us to agree upon our mutual expectations of each other. Further, I wanted to discuss this thoroughly and did not want to leave the meeting room until we were all satisfied. I then showed the group two PowerPoint slides, one listing my expectations of them, and the other giving what I thought should be their expectations of me. The text of these two slides appears below.

My expectations of you

- That you dedicate yourself to your work, doing the absolute best job that you can right now, and continuously striving to learn and to improve

- That you be creative yet disciplined, taking measured risks addressing a range of scenarios

- That you seek and accept increased responsibility

- That you unreservedly contribute your best to the work of the team, assisting (and being assisted by) your co-workers

- That you keep your supervisor closely informed of progress, problems, and issues (no surprises)

- That you scrupulously comply with all company policies

Your expectations of me

- That I will support you in your work, and be your "blocker and tackler" when necessary

- That my door will be open for your questions, requests for guidance, and assistance

- That I will work, as appropriate, to make you visible to higher management

- That I will give you honest and candid feedback on your job performance and future potential

- That I will represent you openly and objectively in management appraisal and salary deliberations

- That if you deserve a raise, promotion, or career-improvement transfer, I will work for you to receive it

- That if you do well in your work, you will take the credit; if you do not do well, I will accept the blame and responsibility and also ensure appropriate corrective actions

From people who did not know me, the response often was a varying degree of incredulity. They were usually quite happy to hear the words (assuming they believed them), but then wanted to know, "What's the catch?" I told them that I had anticipated that question and said, "Yes, there is a catch—the unforgivable sin." I then offered a third and final slide.

The unforgivable sin

- If you see, hear of, or believe that your supervisor (myself included) is making a mistake in business judgment, or reaching an improper conclusion, or in any way are doing—or are about to do—something wrong, and you do not bring this to our attention (especially if you turn out to be right!), this is the unforgivable sin.

- No one is perfect, and we need to rely on and look out for one another. This is a critical mutual expectation. When one does well, all do well.

On the list of their expectations of me, two drew the most attention and seemed to them a bit unbelievable. The first was that I would give credit to them where due, and take the blame otherwise. I had no problem fulfilling this expectation.

My people were great; they did good work, and it was easy to ascribe to them the credit. In fact, several of them received promotions and extra compensation for their consistently good work, and in recognition of their potential. The other part was about blame. Well, I rarely had to call upon that piece of the puzzle. My people knew my expectations of them, and they did not disappoint me. When I went on vacation, I delegated my responsibilities to subordinates. I would tell them that I had faith in them. I told them I did not need to be kept informed each day of how things were going, since I trusted them. I gave them another promise: if, when I returned, they had made a bad decision and caught some criticism for that, I would tell senior management that I would have made exactly the same decision had I been there. In this way I would deflect the blame from them and take it upon me. As it turned out, I never had to act on that promise, because they never made a bad decision. Was it because they were so smart and had such good judgment? Yes, that was certainly true. But I am sure that they thought twice before making a decision, asking themselves, "What would Pete do if he were here?" They knew that I had their backs, and they were not going to disappoint me.

The second item was the "unforgivable sin," namely, failing to tell me when I was wrong. This expectation was a godsend from two perspectives. First, several times I learned things from my people that I had not been aware of previously. That helped me a lot in my decision making. Second, and more frequently, I had the opportunity to spend some really good personal one-on-one time with my people, hashing out difficult issues and learning about them, their families, and their hopes as they took advantage of my open door invitation to discuss.

INCORPORATE EVERYONE INTO THE MISSION

Job descriptions are part of the standard HR mantra in most organizations. And that is a good thing. People should know what they are responsible for and the qualifications necessary for them to do their jobs. However, sometimes these descriptions are too prescriptive and inflexible. In addition, they may be routinely filled out in order to "check the box" and satisfy HR's requirements that everyone have a job description.

Whenever I assumed a new managerial position, one of my first activities would be a review of everyone's job description. I looked for the normally desired characteristics: clarity, completeness, and consistency. So far, so good. I then looked for measures that would help an individual determine whether or not he or she was doing a good job. Even more important, how would the employees know whether or not they were doing *great* jobs? Everyone wants to get promoted, be recognized for their accomplishments, and attain their potential within the organization. Is "good" good enough, or are we looking for "great"? I believe that all of us are looking for "great."

To be "great" means to be in accord with the mission of the organization and to play an active part both in attaining that mission and identifying with the organization's core values and vision. This is a tall order, but one which needs to be fulfilled at all levels of an organization.

So the manager, in looking at the job descriptions, needs to ensure that these values, the vision, and the mission are properly reflected in the document. This may not be an easy task. It will require some soul-searching on the part of the manager, especially if one has just taken on that responsibility. In one such case, I noticed that the job descriptions of my people were very prescriptive, with very specific and detailed responsibilities. A number of those responsibilities were cyclical in nature, such as preparing an annual corporate stewardship report or the forthcoming corporate plans and budget for the next year. Sometimes, there were periods that required less intense time and effort. Still, the expectation was that they would devote themselves to the tasks delineated in the job description. The obvious sense of "no more, no less" was left unsaid.

As a new manager, I took the earliest opportunity to review these job descriptions with the pertinent staff members. As it turned out, almost all the staff were quite interested in broadening their responsibilities. Rather than undertaking a complete review of the entire department's work and delegation of same, I just inserted, with everyone's agreement, one last task: "as assigned by management." This addition allowed me to engage the staff member in a discussion from time to time as to how his or her work fit into the overall mission of the group, division, department, or company. It also enabled me to see how an individual might fit into an area other than the one where they had been working for some time. For a few, this paved the way for a transfer, sometimes with a promotion, to another department.

A further extension of this idea was to hold wider-ranging discussions within the entire group. In one instance, the individual contributors in my division seemed a bit isolated. We had several sections and groups working on quite different functional areas. I arranged for a monthly staff meeting which I opened with a few words about overall company happenings, and then turned the meeting over to an individual staff member who gave a presentation to the group on the work he or she was doing. This turned out best when the work was still in progress, because comments and ideas were welcomed (and forthcoming) from the rest of the group. We then finished with cake and coffee in honor of the staff celebrating birthdays that month.

This exercise served several purposes. First and foremost, it gave recognition to the staff member making the presentation. Then, once questions and ideas began to flow (sometimes from very different perspectives), it increased the sense of everyone working together. In addition, staff members had the opportunity to socialize and chat about themselves and ask questions of others. Lastly, it gave me the opportunity to place the work of the individual staff members into a company perspective, showing how everything fit together into our mission. That also would stir up some comments, which added to the feeling of community.

COMPENSATE AND PROMOTE APPROPRIATELY

This is sometimes not an easy or straightforward task. First of all, several actors are involved: the employee, the manager, the person who can grant the promotion or compensation, and HR. Further, every company and organization has a different process for review and approval of compensation changes and promotions. Most commonly, however, the employee's manager bears responsibility for ensuring that the treatment is appropriate. The manager needs to act as a guardian and shepherd of the employees and make sure they get what they deserve. This requires a thorough knowledge of the HR process, the data underlying the decision that is made, and careful observation as to whether things make sense.

When I became manager of a certain overseas department, I reviewed the list of HR's proposed salary increases for my people. I looked for numbers that did not make sense. In this case, I had two employees who had about the same number of years of experience, the same years with the company, equivalent positions, and the same level of performance, but salaries that differed by some twenty percent. HR did not notice this, but I did. I did more digging into past performance and position data. Nothing had changed between these two employees that could justify the difference. HR shrugged their shoulders. I then requested from HR more data on the timing of past salary increases. I found that the first employee had received increases in good economic years, while raises for the second were calculated in years that were not so good. Over time, this resulted in the discrepancy. HR said, "Well, that's the luck of the draw." I insisted that employee number two get special salary increases over the next two to three years to raise the salary level to where it should rightly be. Employee number one did not receive a salary cut, or anything like that. I had to emphasize my demand to HR fairly strongly, and even threaten to get my superior involved. But in the end all worked out well for both employees, and I had some good news to tell employee number two. The moral is that a manager should always check for aberrations, get the data he or she needs, never take "policy" for the final answer, and push until the right thing is done.[1]

I encountered a similar situation with promotions. Once, when I took over a managerial position, I had my normal handover review with the outgoing manager. As usual, we reviewed the list of employees, positions, and performance. I noticed that three individuals had been at their same position rank for a fairly long period of time. The data indicated that they were ready for promotion. I asked why they had not been promoted. The outgoing manager said, "I didn't propose it to our boss since I felt that he wouldn't approve it." A bit later, after I got to know these individuals well enough to verify their job performance personally, I reviewed the data closely, developed an argument for promotion, and sent an email to my supervisor proposing promotion for the three. I received the approval the following day. The moral is that a manager should do the right thing by his or her people and never be afraid to represent them to the immediate supervisor.

ADDRESSING PERFORMANCE PROBLEMS

Every manager likes to give a positive performance review. Reviews addressing performance problems are far more difficult, and no one looks forward to them. Here, the manager bears a great responsibility for the

---

[1]Similar discipline is required in salary administration and career development to ensure fair and equal treatment of male and female employees. In addition, opportunities for women need to be constantly developed. See United Nations Foundation, "United Nations Foundation and the Exxon Mobil Foundation Release New Report on Most Effective Programs for Women's Economic Empowerment," Sept. 16, 2013. <http://www.unfoundation.org/news-and-media/press-releases/2013/womens-economic-empowerment.html>, Oct. 4, 2016; and Exxon Mobil, "Women's Economic Opportunity." <http://corporate.exxonmobil.com/en/community/womens-economic-opportunity>, Oct. 4, 2016.

welfare and future of the employee who does have problems. I knew a manager many years ago in England who advised me to always be honest with employees, recognizing that we do no favors by remaining silent and keeping poor performers on the job. Problems inevitably escalate to the point that the employee either becomes quite unhappy, or has to be let go. This manager recommended early detection and action.

The roots of performance problems can be basically located in the mismatch between job and person, whether at the very beginning or later on. Employees are sometimes hired with an incorrect understanding of just what their capabilities are relative to the job. For example, an applicant, either at the outside or after an internal transfer, may have good qualifications on paper. However, those qualifications may not work out in practice on the job, due perhaps to an incorrect appraisal by the interviewer or inaccurate qualification descriptions by the applicant. The mismatch could also be between the employee's expectations for the job and the employer's reality. Those mismatches need to be identified and confronted very early on if we are to be fair to the employee.

I once had a case in which an outstanding candidate was offered and accepted a position in my department. I had not interviewed him personally. On his first day at work, I had my normal discussion with new staff members about mutual expectations. As it turned out, he had a completely different idea of what was awaiting him in the company. He chatted with some other people following our meeting to verify these expectations. I received a letter of resignation from him a few days later. While I was naturally disappointed that this had transpired, I took solace in the knowledge that significant future expenditures of both his time and ours were not wasted in trying to patch up obvious gaps in our mutual expectations.

Ongoing performance problems are more difficult to uncover, diagnose, and correct. They are especially uncomfortable when the individuals involved were relatively high performers, perhaps rising stars even, but then slipped in both output and motivation. This situation can become distressing for the employee, especially in cases of mid-career plateauing. In such cases a heart-to-heart continuing dialogue needs to be undertaken between manager and employee. An honest assessment of the employee's work output in terms of both quality and quantity, the vision that the employee has for the remainder of his or her career, and the perception of others in managerial positions is critical.

I have had successes and failures on both counts. I have supervised a number of individuals who were rising stars in their early careers. Then they encountered mid-career plateaus and, according to previous managers, had seen their work performance fall off. In some cases, there was a notable loss of motivation. In others, there were interpersonal issues with their managers.

In both types of cases, I would have a candid and frank conversation with the employees. I would tell them the blunt truth as to how they were being perceived by others, and express my confidence in their inherent abilities which they had amply demonstrated in the past. I stated my desire for them to get back on the right track, to be happy in their work, and to produce outstanding results. I held ongoing and frequent discussions with them about their work, counseled them on their interactions with other company people, and encouraged increased creativity and service to others. I also took advantage of opportunities to facilitate their increased visibility to peers, superiors, and senior management.

What happened? With one exception, performances increased sharply and, very importantly, so did the perception among other managers of that improved performance. The one exception did not think that the extra effort I was requesting would yield sufficient results. Unfortunately, but not unexpectedly, nothing changed for that person.

CLEAR STANDARDS OF CONDUCT

An organization, whether large or small, needs standards of conduct that set boundaries on behavior. These standards must be adequately documented and communicated to every level of the organization, and must be enforced equitably and uniformly throughout the organization.

Much like a bishop, a manager must integrate a close working relationship and the care and concern he or she feels for the staff with the need to ensure observance of the organization's code of conduct. It is sometimes tempting to look the other way, but that is exactly what cannot be done. To do so would be to fail everyone, both those who have committed or might commit an offense and those against whom the offense was or might be committed.

Publicizing the code and ensuring fair and impartial enforcement is the best means of prevention, so that no one thinks he or she might commit an offense with impunity. Such consistency is the desired objective and attitude that should be prevalent throughout an organization. In reality, there can be a wide range of attitudes towards standards of conduct on the part of both employees and managers. Some may think that the standards are just window-dressing designed to protect the organization from legal liability, or believe that there are few enforcement teeth, certainly never to be directed against friends of the insiders. Some may think the standards too rigid and harsh, especially those which threaten violators with discipline up to and including termination.

The job of the manager is to communicate these standards in such a way that staff knows the organization means business. Further, employees need to understand that the standards are there to protect them—for example, from the actions of others who might offend them in some way, such as by harassment; from bringing the company or their own department into disrepute, thereby endangering the health of their employment; or by simply ensuring that they would not be tempted to try something that they should not do.

But the possibility still exists that the staff may be justified in its concerns. At the very least, the manager has a responsibility to give feedback to senior management about his or her own concerns, as well as those of the people. If there is an issue regarding understanding and acceptance of the standards, it is better for it to be aired up front rather than delayed until after a real problem emerges.

In larger organizations, annual business reviews can be held with small groups of employees led by members of the divisions in charge of promulgating and enforcing standards, such as Law or Controllers. Such meetings can be very useful in building understanding and eliciting questions or concerns, especially if the manager of the group is actively involved. In smaller organizations, the manager can take the lead in periodic sessions with the staff. The critical point here is that the manager take a proprietary interest in ensuring that all policies and standards of conduct are understood and followed.

PROPER LEGAL COUNSEL

HR is a complex area fraught with potential problems, including possible legal complications. Development of benefits programs, taxation issues, and compliance with federal, state, and municipal regulations regarding insurance, health, and pension plans all require not only specialist expertise, but also a trained legal eye to review the final documents. Similarly, documentation and treatment of discipline problems, especially suspensions and terminations, require consultation with someone trained in employment law.

19

How to Avoid Program Disappointments and Project Overruns

Most people love new projects and programs. I could be cynical here and add this caveat: especially if someone else is paying for it. In the case of profit-making institutions, the top management has the responsibility of ensuring that funds are available and that proper stewardship of those funds is in place. Likewise, boards and councils of nonprofits have the same responsibility. In that case, however, funds are likely to be in shorter supply, and the requirement for strict stewardship and careful decision making is even more critical.

On the positive side, a new building or outreach program can be very exciting, stirring up enthusiasm and hope. It can help fulfill the institution's mission and drive it towards its vision. A project can bring people together as a team, working towards a common goal. That is a very good thing. But nothing saps the spirit of an organization like a project or program that does not meet expectations, or overruns the budget allocated to it. Unfortunately, in such cases failure can result in financial and morale strains on both staff and constituency.

Perhaps the above statements sound negative and pessimistic, but I have seen too many projects and programs suffer due to inadequate early thinking and lack of hard questioning. So bear with me for the next few pages, and we shall see what can be done to ensure that a project or program is indeed successful and meets expectations.

CHECK AGAINST THE STRATEGY

It is very easy for us, like Martha in Luke 10, to become busy with much doing and distracted with much serving. We value activity and initiative. When that initiative is directed towards a common goal and vision, we even admire it. But what is the first step we should take? The answer is, without exception, to compare any new initiative with the established strategy of the institution or organization.

Normally, a strategic plan includes a number of initiatives. Some require only a small amount of resources, but yield considerable and early benefits. These initiatives are sometimes termed "low-hanging fruit" or "early wins." They are especially attractive because they show that we can be successful and thus inspire confidence in our joint efforts. So far, so good.

However, some initiatives demand considerable resources, both in terms of people and funds. Sometimes commitments may need to be undertaken before we even know the probability of success of the project or program. For example, capital campaigns are usually launched for a building project. However, architectural and engineering consultants often need to be hired before we know whether the fundraising efforts will be successful. In addition, the consultants' findings may show that the project will cost far more than originally estimated.

Before an organization undertakes a project or program which entails even moderate commitment of resources, that initiative should be checked against the strategic plan. That action requires discipline, for we must objectively compare the often-subjective desire to accomplish something worthwhile against other worthwhile initiatives to which the organization has already agreed.

I have been associated with some institutions that jumped onto a project without undergoing this disciplined process. Sometimes so much effort, toil, emotion, and anxiety are required for a particular project that the base mission of the institution can go by the wayside. It is then that I hear the words of Jesus: "Martha, Martha, you are busy about many things, you are distracted with much serving. . . . One thing is needful."[1] It is not

---

[1] Cf. Lk 10.41–42.

easy to slow down the momentum of project initiatives. Very often, one who tries to do so gets tagged with a "conservative" label, or worse. But the discipline of ensuring consistency with the strategic plan is necessary. Further, if any new project is to be undertaken, it needs to have highest priority among all others.

So let's assume that we have checked the project or program against the strategic plan. It is consistent and, if successful, will carry us farther in satisfying our mission than any other initiative. Although in the rest of this chapter I refer only to projects, the principles apply equally well to programs.

NO ROSE-COLORED GLASSES

Things always turn out to be more difficult than we expect. That's just the way it is. Jesus said, "In the world you have tribulation; but be of good cheer, I have overcome the world."[2] What makes us think that every aspect of a program or project will go smoothly? We hope that it will. We may even pray that it will, to the glory of God. But one of our responsibilities, as stewards of God's gifts, is to keep our eyes open, to "be wise as serpents and innocent as doves."[3]

Jesus says that anyone who wishes to build a tower must count the cost before beginning. Otherwise, he will be ridiculed when he is unable to finish it. In our case, the outcome could be even more severe in terms of the loss of community cohesion, morale, and trust.

How do we count the cost in the very first stages of a project? We add up the pros and cons, of course. The pros are why we want such a project. The cons are the possible hindrances and obstacles that prevent the realization of the mission. The normal human bias is to overweight the pros and underweight the cons.

Sometimes faith is brought into the balance. Some people may think that bringing up possible difficulties indicates a lack of faith in God. If God wants it, then it will be done, these people say. On the other hand, God

[2] Jn 16.33.
[3] Mt 10.16.

has given us logical powers and the ability to weigh alternatives. He wants us to count the cost.

Besides the obvious need to be confident that the pros outweigh the cons, a careful analysis of cons can help us to minimize their harmful effects. For example, we should vigorously question an engineering or architectural consultant about how their previous project cost estimates have changed from the first estimate to the final cost. If they dither about this, we should find another consultant. There should be a significant contingency included, perhaps on the order of fifty percent or more, in the initial project cost estimate. Escalation of project costs due to inflation and unforeseen events such as weather, material shortages, environmental issues, permitting, and labor difficulties should also be included in the contingency. It may well happen that after we put the cons under a microscope, they become so large that a different strategic alternative to the project becomes advisable. Sometimes a different and more creative approach to the same project can sufficiently ameliorate its cons. For example, perhaps the organization can purchase a bond that insures against specified unforeseen but possible—and perhaps devastating—events.

On the revenue side, the organization may assume that sufficient funds can be raised and financing obtained. However, economic environments change rapidly. Recessions occur. Interest rates can spike. Otherwise-dependable donors may suddenly become cash-strapped. A contingency plan needs to be developed to handle all these possibilities.

In short, we need to go into a project or program with eyes open and rose-colored glasses off. Let's now assume that, with our clear and flinty-eyed vision, we have decided to proceed with the project. The following principles have proved, in my experience, to be critical for effective project development.

- Adopt a phased approach

- Appoint a gate-keeper for each phase

- Bring in "cold eyes" periodically

- Do not make changes unless absolutely necessary

- Learn from your (and others') mistakes and successes

A PHASED APPROACH

Once the "go" signal has been given, it is tempting to proceed full steam ahead. After all, now that we have decided what to do, let's do it! Right?

No! Let's take it one step at a time. And after each step is completed, let's pause to see if we want to go farther and, if so, how.

There are many ways to manage a project. We give here a simple conceptual outline of what should be done, together with definitions of some special terms used in project management. If you hire a project manager, or have one already on your staff or one who volunteers, that person should have a process fairly similar to this one, or which at least includes the main points. First, we will look at the definitions of project owner, project manager, project scope, project design, and project philosophy. Then we'll look at the recommended phases.

The *project owner* is someone who carries the ultimate responsibility for the project. That individual should have been intimately involved in the run-up to the decision to go forward with this project. The owner knows what the organization is looking for in the project. He or she needs to report to the governance group of the organization, and ensure that the wishes and concerns of the governance group are respected.

The *project manager* supervises the project team and is responsible for successful performance of the specified project actions: definition, design, execution, and closeout. This role is always filled by someone different from the project owner. The manager reports to the owner and keeps the owner closely informed of project progress, hindrances, and, especially, any perceived need to change any aspect of the project scope or design that has been previously approved by the owner. In other words, there are to be no surprises.

How does *project scope* differ from the *project design*? The project scope states "what" the project will do. The project design states "how" it will be done. The "what" of a building defines what facilities it will include, what it will generally look like according to first-pass architectural renderings, the number of people it will accommodate, and what they are expected to do there. The "how" of a building is the detail of the size of the rooms, power, water and sanitation, the restroom facilities, the kitchen layout, the audiovisual equipment, the computer layout, heating and air conditioning, walls, floor covering, exterior material, and so on.

Sometimes the "how" of a project gets ahead of the "what," and that is where trouble begins. For example, monies are spent on engineering design, permitting, environmental analysis, and acquisition of vendor bids to get to "how" before sufficient time and discussion has been spent on "what" the project will do. This common error in project process occurs when the process is not subjected to a disciplined approach. If left to run its course, such emphasis on "how" before "what" can cause significant project overruns in terms of time and expense, and the project may fall short of fulfilling original expectations.

What is a *project philosophy*? It is critical that communication and control responsibilities are well established early in the project process. The responsibilities of the governance group, project owner, and project manager are documented in the project philosophy. Included in the philosophy statement should be the explicit delegation of responsibilities for negotiating and executing project contracts and agreements with permitting authorities. Necessary reviews with counsel and all accounting and internal control functions should also be specified in order to eliminate any misunderstanding. As well, the acceptance of changes to project scope and design needs to be very carefully delineated to prevent excessive costs and delays.

The four phases under the supervision of the project manager are:

1. Define the scope of the project and needed resources: people, time, and money
   – Review with the project owner and obtain approval to proceed

2. Develop the project design and project philosophy
   – Review with the owner and obtain approval to proceed

3. Execute the project under the project design and project philosophy
   - Review project status periodically with the owner and obtain approvals for changes

4. Close out the project and turn over to the owner
   - Reappraise the project and identify lessons learned

GATEKEEPERS

It can be extremely distressing for a project manager and team to be told to "go back and do it over." But that is what sometimes needs to happen in the course of a project. And if it happens, it needs to happen as early as possible in the life of the project.

A project owner can become so close to a project that the idea of changing directions significantly—or worse, scuttling the project—can be unimaginable. In such cases, it is helpful and perhaps necessary to have someone else who makes the decision to go back, reconsider, change, stop, or keep on moving. This person, known as the *gatekeeper*, needs to be someone who serves the organization at a sufficiently senior level, with a certain measure of gravitas. He or she is appointed by the governance group and empowered to act on its behalf. The gatekeeper needs to be taken seriously and viewed as the court of final instance.

A typical process would involve a review at the end of each project phase by the project manager and project owner. Assuming that goes well, a further review would be held with the gatekeeper. The gatekeeper, acting on the authority of the governance group, may allow the project to go forward as defined and/or designed. However, if circumstances so dictate, changes to the definition or design may also be requested by the gatekeeper. The gatekeeper must understand in advance that this will likely cause heartburn for the project manager and owner.

A "COLD-EYES" REVIEW

To prevent heartburn, a "cold-eyes" review can be very helpful. Outside individuals with expertise in the various project areas are invited to meet with the project team at selected points in the project process. These people should not have been previously involved in the project, nor are they part of the population impacted by the project. Thus they have "cold eyes" that can be dedicated to honestly and candidly evaluating whether the project is planned and designed properly. If the review is done well, and their recommendations are appropriately taken into account, the probability of the gatekeeper having to make changes will be greatly reduced.

Sometimes project teams may not welcome an encounter with cold-eyes reviewers. After all, the reviewers appear to have nothing at stake in the project. In addition, they sometimes appear to find fault after fault, with seemingly nothing good to say. However, they do have something at stake: a desire to help the project, even if their comments cause some discomfort to the project manager and team. The humility of the project owner, manager, and team should be encouraged here, as well as the desire of the cold-eyes reviewers to do their best for the project.

I once heard one of our Japanese refinery managers request that the "cold-eyes" team for his project come with "warm hearts." Everyone who heard this desire agreed with it.

NO CHANGES UNLESS ABSOLUTELY NECESSARY

Change is the enemy of good projects. People like to make changes, to improve things, to make the project a bit better. That desire is quite natural, but the problem is that changes during project execution cost money and delay the project's completion. All changes should be proposed and considered at the beginning of the project, not in the middle—and especially not towards the end. Once a project is designed, only very specific and circumscribed changes should be made. In most cases, changes should only be made for safety, health, and environmental reasons.

Projects can be complicated. A change in one element can affect another. Changes cause unnecessary delays and expense. For these reasons one should refer continuously to the documented project philosophy, which specifies firmly and exactly the policy regarding changes.

LEARN FROM MISTAKES AND SUCCESSES

Once the project is completed and up and running for a while, it is time for a reappraisal. Some call this reappraisal a postmortem, but that term can be off-putting. It is never easy to take a hard look at a project, to examine how it was put together and how it turned out. Some people may say that it is water under the bridge, let's get on with life. But there will be other projects in the future, and a disciplined way of reappraising and learning lessons from each project is essential. The reappraisal results should be documented and circulated to the governance group.

If there were mistakes, misunderstandings, miscommunications, overruns, delays, etc., now is the time to learn from them. If everything went smoothly and according to plan, it's time for congratulations all around and a resolve to repeat what worked well the next time. Usually, a reappraisal leads to a mixture of both of these. Some basic questions to ask are:

- Did the project meet expectations as defined for each phase of the work? If not, why not?

- Did the project get completed on time and under budget? If not, why not?

- Did any safety, health, or environmental issues or concerns arise during, and team work?

- Which elements of the project worked particularly well?

- Which elements of the project did not work well?

It can be helpful to take advantage of and learn from others who have completed similar projects and then conducted such reappraisals. This consultation should be done in advance of phase one of your own project. Most people are happy to share their experiences, at least in general terms.

FINAL ADVICE

If you are a member of a governance group, board, or council, never allow yourself to be pressured into agreeing to a project proposal that makes you uncomfortable. Take the time to do your own due diligence. Go back to the strategic plan to see whether this project is really called for, especially if it consumes time, energy, and funds that might be allocated to other endeavors. Keep in touch with the project owner, request periodic updates, and ask questions, questions, questions. Don't let up. Don't give up. You have a fiduciary responsibility that cannot be abdicated.

20

How to Understand
Basic Organizational Finances

People serving in governance positions today are far savvier about finances and financial reporting than ever before, in my experience. However, it is still important to emphasize the need to understand basic organizational finances and, even more important, to ensure that the appropriate processes are carried out effectively. This chapter will not make anyone a financial expert, nor confer expertise in accounting. As stated in my earlier disclaimer, I am not an accountant, nor do I provide any sort of financial or accounting advice that can be relied upon. I do, however, have experience in financial reporting at a high business level as well as experience in various nonprofits from which I draw the conclusions offered here.

THE RUDIMENTS OF ACCOUNTING

Accounting, it is often said, is the language of business.[1] Like any language, learning the first few words is the key to further learning. One concept builds upon another. Also, unless everyone knows the terms and how they fit together, there can be misunderstandings and lots of wasted time as people try to comprehend the financial position of the organization.

---

[1] There is no shortage of introductory texts on accounting. The one that I relied upon many years ago is now out of print, and aptly titled *Accounting: The Language of Business*. Sidney Davidson, *Accounting: The Language of Business* (Thomas Horton and Daughters, 1999 [10th ed.]).

Let's begin with these fundamental terms: entity, assets, liabilities, equity, revenue, cost of goods sold, expenses, operating income, interest, taxes, and cash flow. Then we add three others that tie everything together: balance sheet, income statement, and cash flow statement. (One caveat: a reader already familiar with these terms may find the following paragraphs boring. If the terms are unfamiliar, however, my hope is that they will be helpful in dispelling confusion.)

An *entity* is simply any organization that owns assets, owes liabilities, earns income, and generates cash flow. It may be unincorporated or incorporated, a sole proprietorship, a partnership, or a limited liability company. It could be as big as Exxon Mobil Corporation or as small as a mission parish. The same basic accounting concepts apply more or less equally in most cases.[2]

Assets are those things the entity owns, such as cash, investments in securities, buildings, machinery, office equipment, etc. Assets also can include promises from others to pay money to the entity, such as pledges of future donations or other deferred payments due from others. These deferred or promised payments are known as *receivables*. Assets may also include a portion of prepaid expenses such as an insurance premium paid on an annual basis.

Liabilities are things that the entity owes, like mortgages and loans (usually referred to as *debt*). They also include deferred payments to employees or suppliers (known as *payables*), plus any other obligations which the entity has assumed.

Equity (also known as shareholders' equity, owners' equity, net assets, or net worth) is the monetary difference between the value of the assets and the value of the liabilities. If the entity were liquidated, the equity is what would be left over, but only after any liquidation expenses were taken into account.[3]

---

[2]See Exxon Mobil's 2014 Summary Annual Report pages 41–43 for a summary income statement, balance sheet, and cash flow statement. "2014 Summary Annual Report." <http://cdn.exxonmobil.com/~/media/global/files/summary-annual-report/2014_summary_annual_report.pdf>, Oct. 4, 2016.

[3]The last phrase is inserted for completeness and precision. Sometimes financial reporters are not sufficiently clear and precise. This can cause problems for the managers who make decisions based upon the reporter's words.

The *balance sheet* ties together assets, liabilities, and equity at one particular point in time, such as at year-end. It is a snapshot of the entity's financial picture. The standard reporting form of the balance sheet lists assets first, then liabilities plus equity, to create this equation: assets equals liabilities plus equity. The balance sheet may also be called the *statement of financial position*.

Assets are further organized in the listing from more liquid, i.e., able to be easily converted into cash, to less liquid. They are identified as either "current" or "non-current/long-term." Current assets are available for use (capable of being liquidated) within one year; long-term items are only available beyond one year. For example, cash (in savings or checking accounts) is a current asset that can be drawn upon fairly immediately. Investments in buildings and other fixed items can be liquidated only after a longer period of time (or perhaps never, so long as the entity remains in operation).

Liabilities are similarly described as current or non-current/long-term. Current liabilities are ones which the entity will dispose of within one year, such as a short-term bridge loan or monies payable to a contractor. Long-term liabilities are usually long-term debt, such as a property mortgage loan. It is important to compare current assets with current liabilities to ensure that enough current assets are present when needed to cover the liabilities.

The equity is sometimes divided into various categories depending upon the nature and business of the entity. In the case of many nonprofits, a significant amount of equity or net assets are held in "restricted accounts" designated for a particular purpose. For example, donors may have imposed restrictions on contributed funds, requiring that they be applied to scholarships or future building expenditures. These restrictions may be either temporary or permanent.[4] Governing boards need to be aware of what funds are available to the institution, and for what purpose.

---

[4]See the FY2014 Annual Report of St Vladimir's Seminary, pages 3, 6–7, "June 2014 Financial Statements and Auditor's Report." <http://www.svots.edu/sites/default/files/svots_fs-_fiscal_2014.pdf>, Oct. 4, 2016.

The *income statement* is also sometimes called the *statement of activities*. It shows the revenue earned by the entity over a certain period of time, such as a fiscal year or partial year, e.g., last quarter or year-to-date. It also shows costs such as raw materials and other expenses (e.g., personnel, depreciation on buildings and equipment) incurred in earning that revenue. Of great interest is the bottom-line difference between revenue and costs/expenses, called *operating income* or *income from operations*.

Next, the statement examines interest and investment income and expense. Interest and investment income represents the earnings on cash held in savings accounts and marketable securities. Interest expense represents the costs of carrying debt. These respective amounts are added onto or subtracted from the operating income to obtain *operating profit* before income tax. Income tax[5] is then subtracted to yield *net profit*, sometimes referred to as *net income*.

Cash is king. The *cash flow statement* shows where the entity generated cash, where it consumed it, and whether any cash is left over. The time period is the same as for the income statement. Cash flows originate from operations, investing, and financing activities, and thus need to be separately considered for full understanding.

A positive *operations cash flow* indicates that an entity's normal operations, exclusive of investments and debt impacts, are sufficient to pay employees' salaries, maintain the physical plant, and provide for services. In very simplified terms, it is equal to net profit plus depreciation. (Depreciation is an accounting charge, not a cash charge.) There are other adjustments regarding inventory changes, accounts payable, and accounts receivable.

Investing cash flow comes from other items on the balance sheet, including sales of marketable securities and the purchase of physical assets such as machinery or buildings. Sales of securities are a source of positive cash flow. Purchases of physical plants are a source of negative cash flow.

---

[5] A caution for non-profits who enjoy a 501(c)3 status from the IRS: always be aware of potential tax liability for Unrelated Business Income (UBI). UBI is income derived from a regularly conducted trade or business that is not substantially related to an entity's exempt status. Be sure to keep up to date on IRS regulations, which may change from time to time.

Financing cash flow comes mainly from taking on additional debt or, conversely, paying down debt.

Lastly, an organization's accounting must be performed according to a set of principles that are transparent to the governing group and other key players and constituents, e.g., donors, shareholders, regulators. People need to be confident that they can understand the financial data, and that no misrepresentations have crept in. For profit-making corporations and most nonprofits, this objective is assured by compliance with Generally Accepted Accounting Principles, abbreviated as GAAP.[6] However, in some special situations adjustments to these principles might be made. Those adjustments need to be identified and documented in the financial statements, either directly or in the footnotes. Footnotes are usually the most informative part of the financial statements. They provide insight into potential vulnerabilities and help prevent misunderstandings of the data.

CASH FLOW

Let us step back and think about what we can learn from the three categories of cash flow described above. Assume that our entity has positive cash flow overall. How did it get that way? Was its cash flow from operations positive, meaning that if it did not do anything else, it would survive and do what it is currently doing? If total cash flow was higher than expected while operations were break-even or just slightly positive, how did the total get that high? Did the entity sell off land and buildings, listed in the investing activities section of the cash flow statement? Did it pull back on investing in a new physical plant to save cash? Or did it take on more debt, mortgaging the future?

The job of the financial reporter is to clearly analyze the financial statements and provide a verbal description of the various movements

---

[6]Some small nonprofits such as churches might utilize a cash rather than an accrual form of accounting, or may value properties at market instead of historical depreciated costs as demanded by GAAP. While the former procedure is consistent with Not-for-Profit GAAP, the latter is not. These procedures are called an Other Comprehensive Basis Of Accounting (OCBOA). It is advisable that use of this basis be clearly denoted on the financial statement, and any deviation from GAAP be explained in footnotes.

underneath the overall results. The job of the governing group is to ask questions, understand the financial movements, and use that information to make informed decisions.

THE ANNUAL REPORT

Snapshots are nice, but videos are better. The normal annual report is a snapshot, usually providing only two years of data: the immediately past year and the one preceding it. This timeframe is inadequate for financial reporting to a governance group like a board or council. A minimum of five years of past financial data should be presented at least annually, and certainly when the budget for the next fiscal year is proposed. The new budget year and a minimum of two succeeding years of projected financials also should be presented.

What do we look for in these data? First and foremost, trends: What is happening with revenue? with expenses? with debt? with cash flow? If the trends were unfavorable, what is going to happen in the future to make things right? Is that future realizable, and is the financial prediction believable?

In one institution whose board meeting I attended as an advisor, no historical financial trends were given to the board members before the meeting. However, I had access to past financial reports and had performed my own analysis. When I brought up my findings at the meetings, the controller was not happy. Perhaps he thought I was "causing trouble." The data showed that the institution was generating positive income from operations, and had been doing so for a while. However, the surplus was getting pretty thin and, most alarming to me, expenses were increasing at six percent per year and revenues at only three percent. Clearly, at some point in the future the lines would cross, and the organization would be in danger of running ever-growing deficits.

Another useful trend is to compare the forward predictions based on a proposed budget with actual results over a period of years. It is not unusual for a "hockey stick" phenomenon to occur. In such cases actual results come in continually below the forecasts, with future forecasts tending to be even more optimistic to make up for the shortfall in financial results (hence, the pattern resembles the sharp "V" of a hockey stick—first down, then up). This dangerous situation indicates that the administration is wearing rose-colored glasses and merely hoping that "things will work out."

COLLECTING AND REPORTING FINANCIAL DATA

Sometimes it is easy to miss the forest for the trees. The trees certainly need to be counted, and counted precisely. But reporting on the condition of the forest should not consist of a detailed examination of each tree. Reporting needs to be in a format with an appropriate level of detail to enable the decision makers to understand the forest's condition and take action to ensure its survival, health, and growth.

Questions need to be asked not only about the current year's financial performance, but also historical trends and future projections. Are current assets presently sufficient to cover current liabilities? Do we have enough cash and other assets on hand to cover loan principal payments, plus any other liabilities due within one year? How about loan balloon payments which might fall due two years from now? How do we prepare for that? Are we investing too much and incurring too much debt? Are we drawing down our assets (in the form of endowment funds, for example) more than is reasonable? Will we still be in business five years from now? Will we be able to grow our mission significantly beyond where we are today? What needs to happen to accomplish that goal?

The only way to adequately comprehend an organization's financial past, present, and future financial condition is by means of a Summary Status and Trend Report (SSTR). The SSTR condenses the information, highlights the most critical parameters that a governance group must consider, and then compares these parameters over time. The organization's treasurer or financial reporting officer is responsible for anticipating questions, issues, and concerns that may arise, and drafting a financial summary report that can be used for decision making. Not only that, but the basic collection of data, while being done according to proper accounting principles, should be labeled according to business categories that make sense to the decision makers.

Granted, some financial reporters and treasurers may chafe at the requirement to present historical, current, and forecast data in summary format each year (or as often as required by the governance group). This resistance is understandable, given the complex nature of the basic accounting. However, once the practice of a SSTR is established, it is fairly straightforward to maintain.

RESERVES FOR MAINTENANCE

It is always tempting to put off required maintenance on buildings and facilities. Sometimes, it may be considered necessary due to a tight cash budget. But at some point the piper must be paid. I once had a role in an overseas manufacturing plant where the previous administration had adopted, it seemed to me, a principle of "management by indices." One of the indices was maintenance costs. They had the best maintenance cost index in the company's global operations. Unfortunately, due to the marine environment in that location, corrosion of metal surfaces was prevalent—and the preventive painting and repair budget almost non-existent.

When I took over the management of a certain operations division in that plant, I almost cried when I saw the condition of the facilities on my first day on the job. "How could anyone have allowed this to happen?" I asked myself. The answer, of course, was "out of sight, out of mind." The facilities were located away from the administration building, and no one with any management power went there. I immediately asked for a major increase in the maintenance budget (I believe it was in the neighborhood of 400 percent). Luckily, the plant's top management had recently changed, and the new leaders agreed with my position. However, I received many visits from top executives back home in the US, who were asking themselves, "What is Danilchick doing out there, spending so much money?" But, they too, after seeing the situation, supported my demand for more funds.

What could have been done by my predecessor? He could have estimated the amount of money that would have been required to keep the facilities in good condition, and then requested the grant of those funds. If a request were turned down due to cash budget constraints in any particular year, he might have insisted that those funds be placed in a maintenance reserve. Whether or not this would have made any difference from an accounting viewpoint, it would have placed the issue squarely before the face of the decision makers instead of being swept under the rug. In that case it is no longer an issue of accounting but rather one of responsibility, good stewardship, and courage.[7]

ANNUAL AUDITS

Public companies are required to be audited by a public accounting firm each year. Nonprofits subject to state regulations may also be required to undergo such an audit. Even those not subject to audit by law or governmental regulation should have their financial accounts audited annually. It is simply good practice to have someone outside the organization look into the books.

The governance group, or an appointed committee thereof, meets with the auditor before the process begins to go over the audit plan and discuss any concerns or issues. Following the conclusion of the audit, the audit firm reviews the conclusions with the governance group or committee. If such a committee exists, that committee then presents the findings of the audit to the governance group.

The board has the responsibility for hiring the audit firm each year. The firm's performance should be objectively evaluated each year. The results of that evaluation can then serve as the basis for re-appointing

[7]At that same plant, I was confronted with the urgent need to make a repair to a piece of equipment that I discovered had major safety issues. To repair it, an extensive portion of the total plant would have to be shut down for days, resulting in a significant loss of profits. My manager's manager was the one responsible to give the go-ahead for shutdown, and he was quite reluctant to do so. When I reached the point that I could not wait any longer, I told him that I would document the situation in a report, and send it to him and higher management with my warning of the consequences of no action resulting from indecision. He gave the order that very afternoon to shut down and repair. I did not have to write that report.

the audit firm next year, or seeking a new auditor. Common practice is to consider replacing the audit firm, or at least the lead partner, every five years depending on the results of the evaluation.

21

How to Prepare (or Request) a Stewardship Report

Having to present the results of our work to others can be intimidating for some of us. We may not know what is required. We may worry about what others will think of us. On the other hand, we may be tempted to just push forward with a superficial effort and hope that no one notices or cares.

In the corporate world, the quality of a person's presentation can have a big impact on perceived performance and potential. I recall one example of a young engineer who gave a presentation at a very large conference of managers and executives. He had great difficulty getting his words out at the beginning of his slide presentation, despite the fact that he had a written text. When it became obvious that he could not continue, a colleague took over the oral presentation. The quality of the content and written organization was excellent, as everyone recognized. The oral delivery obviously had problems. After the conclusion of the slide show, the young engineer regained his voice, took the podium again and said, "Well, I shouldn't be surprised. My wife keeps telling me that my road to success is still under construction!" He received a rousing round of applause. I have no doubt that his combination of work quality, humility, and humor have stood him well in his career.

The nonprofit world encounters rather different problems. People in responsible managerial positions may not know what is expected in their reports. People in governance positions may not know what they should expect of others who report on the state of the organization. I hope that this chapter will assist them with both of these concerns.

WE ARE ALL STEWARDS

St Paul says that a bishop, as overseer and guardian, is also God's steward (*Theou oikonomon*).[1] Originally, this term applied to a slave in the service of a master. He did what he was told to do. Not only was he a manager or steward, but he was also a servant. In this same way, Paul called the Christians in Corinth both "servants of Christ and stewards of the mysteries of God."[2]

Whom does the servant serve? Is it the master alone, or someone else as well? St Peter exhorts the one who has received gifts from God: "As each has received a gift, employ it for one another, as good stewards of God's varied grace. . . ."[3] The steward manages on behalf of someone else, and for the benefit of others. The steward is faithful and wise and serves others. Jesus said, "Who then is the faithful and wise steward, whom his master will set over his household, to give them their portion of food at the proper time?" Further, there will be a calling to account: "Blessed is that servant whom his master when he comes will find so doing."[4] St Paul emphasizes that "it is required of stewards that they be found trustworthy."[5]

So we are all in the same boat, prince and pauper alike—all are called to govern, to manage, to serve, and to give account.

EVERYONE NEEDS A SUPERVISOR

Some people think that they are above everyone else, and do not need to answer to anyone. This might apply to the overbearing parent, the oppressive boss, the arrogant CEO, the dismissive bishop, the annoying neighbor, the insolent teenager, and so on.

However, it should not be this way. Everyone needs a supervisor, whether it be a spouse, a bishop, a senior manager, a board of directors, a

[1] Titus 1.7.
[2] 1 Cor 4.1.
[3] 1 Pet 4.10.
[4] Lk 12.42–43.
[5] 1 Cor 4.2.

church council, a neighborhood association, a loving parent, etc. A supervisor helps us by asking questions, which can sometimes be as simple as, "How's it going?" Our responsibility is to understand where that supervisor is coming from, acknowledge the fact that he or she cares about us and our work, and give an answer that will help both of us.

This supervisory relationship begins very early in life and continues at all times and locales. The teenager who comes home from school needs to have an answer other than "nothing" to the parental question, "What did you do today?" Similarly, the haggard employee who is asked that question by a caring spouse needs to say more than, "I don't want to talk about it." The bishop, when questioned by a member of his clergy or laity flock, needs to say something other than, "It's not your business."

A good stewardship report answers the basic questions: "How's it going? What did you do? Did it work out? What do you want to do now? Can we talk about it? How can I help?" The answers to these questions need to be developed and provided in the spirit of at least two of the six goals we explored earlier in this book: to focus on, care for, and love others; and to be humble.

WE'RE ALL IN THIS TOGETHER

Agency theory examines the relationship between a principal and an agent. A "principal" might be the employer, for example, and the "agent" an employee. Or, the principal might be a governing board or council, and the agent the managers of the organization. Normally, the principal is in a superior role and the agent in a subordinate role. The principal delegates or assigns work to the agent and expects that the agent will do as he or she is told. Normally, the best results are obtained when the performance is well defined in terms of expectations, and also measurable and capable of being observed by the principal.

There are a number of issues that arise regarding agency theory, but we will focus here on only two of them. First, each party is considered to have a certain self-interest that may or may not be known by the other, but which can certainly be in conflict with the other's interest. Second, the whole concept of principal-agent can lead to an "us versus them" mentality. I'll give a simple example here.

Many years ago, when I worked in one of Exxon's international corporate offices in the USA, there were conflicts between the field operating management and the head office staff. The head office staff were charged with knowing what was going on in the field, and would often be asked by their own superiors about the current status of programs in a foreign operation. If the staff did not know the answers, off would go a cable asking questions. (I did say it was many years ago!) Unfortunately for some overseas managers, these questions could at times become too frequent and consume too much time to answer, thus negatively impacting the managers' efforts to do their daily jobs. The head office needed to know anyway, however, and kept asking. Frustrations increased and mutual complaints flew across the ocean.

From an agency theory viewpoint, both the principal (the head office) and the agents (the field operations) had certain self-interests. The former needed to have information to answer top management's questions. The latter needed to have time to do their jobs and not be distracted by too many requests. After some time and many difficult discussions, top management established a formal set of communications guidelines that were more or less followed. However, I doubt that anyone, other than top management, was really satisfied by this result.

My own personal approach was far simpler: I assumed that we were all in this together. I refused to believe that I, in the head office, was in conflict with my counterparts overseas. If we look closely, our interests surely overlap; in fact, we share common ground in many areas. We each need to do our respective jobs and, just as obviously, depend on each other to do it.

Following this philosophy, I would pick up the phone on a regular basis and call my counterparts just to catch up on what was happening. I did not send cables unless absolutely necessary. The other managers liked these open and informal chats. I let them in on what was happening in head office, and they let me know what was happening in their operations. If they noticed something happening in their operations that could be viewed as negative, I smoothed the way for them and ensured that there would be no surprises. Hence, knee-jerk reactions were avoided and replaced by calm attempts to solve the problem, whatever it might be. My friends overseas helped me to become highly knowledgeable about the field operations, and as a result I became more valuable to my own management in head office. A win-win situation, as they say, because we're all in this together.

In my previous chapter on board relations, I discussed the myth of "micromanagement." Without repeating here what I said there, I would point out that this myth is a good example of a deficient principal-agent relationship. I can speak from both perspectives, having been on either side of the principal-agent fence.

In general I do not much like the whole idea of principal-agent; I prefer principal-principal. Of course, there are legal and governance distinctions between these two roles. A manager bears ultimate responsibility for the activities and decisions of his or her people. I am not talking about that, however. I am saying that we are all in this together and thus, to the greatest extent possible, we must all act as owners and principals. Our conflicting self-interests will fall away, and we will work for the common cause.

Very early in my corporate career, I participated in a career development and performance appraisal workshop. The facilitator said one thing that really struck me: "Do not be a hired servant. Take a proprietary attitude towards your work." That resonated with me, perhaps because of the parable of the Prodigal Son. Our relationship with one another in any organization has to be a familial one, where all are related and share a common goal of advancing the family. In the corporate world, we do not merely work for a salary. That would be the hired servant mentality. We are working for the common cause as proprietors, as owners. The harder I worked at forgetting myself, my self-interest, and my concern about salary and position, the better things went for me on the job: better work performance, better relationship with the boss, better chances at promotion, better opportunities to do more creative work, better assignments with increased responsibilities.

Why am I spending time talking about agency theory, when I should be speaking about stewardship reports? The answer is this: we find it painfully obvious when someone reports to us with self-interest—with the sole intention of making himself or herself look good without really caring about the greater good of the organization. It is even more obvious when the reporter holds things back, does not give the complete story, and becomes defensive during questioning. Now, let's move on to how to prepare a stewardship report.

JUST THE FACTS, MA'AM

One reference book we should put aside when composing a stewardship report is the thesaurus. The report should center on facts, without a lot of adjectives and adverbs. It should certainly not include a list of excuses. It should clearly and honestly state why one is making the report, what one is looking for from one's listeners, and address the following questions:

- Why am I making this report?
- What do I need from you?
- What were the accomplishments? What was especially good about them?
- What were the disappointments? How could they have been avoided?
- What do I/we plan to do now? What is the path forward?
- What do we all think about what was done, and the path forward?
- What do I need from you to go forward? And do I have it?

We do not want to waste people's time; we want to engage them as fellow workers, even if just for the short time it takes to report. I have made many presentations before very senior and top members of corporate management. Some people may imagine that these managers are ogres, just waiting for the unsuspecting presenter to make a mistake so they can stomp on him or her. I have not had this experience.

What managers do not want, however, is to hear a mystery story. They want to know why we have been spending our time working on something, and why we want to tell them our story today. It may be that our stewardship report asks for the budget to be increased, and they must give approval. It may be that they need to be briefed on a certain country's economic policies or competitive intelligence. We may be telling them what we spent the last week doing, and why we need additional people to help us. Whatever it may be, it is wise for us to spend the first few sentences telling them why we are here, and what we need from them. And heed this warning: if we do not want anything from them, we can expect that they will be bored stiff. They need to feel that they are contributing. Trust me.

A straightforward stewardship report tells them what we (and the people working with us) have accomplished. If we have made certain assumptions in our story, we should clearly set them forth. Be specific. Avoid self-praise. They will know how what we have accomplished compares with the accomplishments and capabilities of our predecessors or current peers on the job. They comprehend the big picture far better than we do. If something worked especially well, and it is worthy of note, describe it—but without passion or pride.

There are invariably disappointments and lessons to be learned about how things could have been done better. These should be volunteered without excuses. If we choose not to mention them, the listeners will ask, and we will be embarrassed to reveal things under questioning that should have been offered up of our own volition. Speaking openly about lessons learned shows that one is a team player concerned about those who will come later. Further, it is a leading indicator that one can be trusted in tough times.

THE "GOOD JOB, CARRY ON" SYNDROME

The hard part is telling listeners what we plan to do—to describe the path forward. This activity requires the greatest degree of humility on our part. Describing our accomplishments and disappointments is nothing. The worst listeners can do is criticize and complain. But our precious plan for the future will be laid out for all to comment on. Since nothing has been done thus far, the field is wide open for our listeners to "help." Often, however, we are not seeking any help; all we want is for them to simply say, "Good job, carry on." Yet if that happens, we (or they) have failed. They have not been engaged by us. They do not feel as if they have a vested interest in what we plan to do. At the end of the day, we will suffer as a result of their quickness to let go and move on.

The "good job, carry on" syndrome happens all too often in nonprofits, and the consequences there are the most severe. Let me suggest a probable scenario.

The presenter (or "agent") has just presented a plan that may involve heavy commitment of time, talent, and resources from the governance group (the "principal"). However, the allotted time for the meeting is running out, the hour is late, and all are anxious to get home. The principal approves the plan without fully discussing, debating, or drawing every member into the discussion about the resource demands to be placed on the principal. The agent, however, has gotten what he or she needs, namely, approval of the plan. The agent thus believes that the full, complete, and unambiguous support of the principal has been obtained. Further, a mandate from the principal has been acquired. Right? Wrong!

The problem is that the principal has not asked this simple question: "What do you need from us"? Nor, having received the agent's honest answer to this question, has the principal replied: "And this is what you will get from us." The agent's self-interest, in this example, is to finish that meeting with the principal's approval in hand. The principal's self-interest is to finish the meeting and get home.

Both self-interests, although satisfied in this outcome, were misguided. Both parties will be disappointed, and begin to trust each other less and less. The agent will say, "Why did they agree to go forward when they really didn't support it wholeheartedly?" The principal (a member of the governance group) will say, "I agreed since everyone else did. I assumed that everyone else was completely behind it. They won't miss me when push comes to shove and they need my time, money, etc." The end result is a bad situation all around.

The rush to approval is the enemy of good decisions. Effective stewardship reporting—and the decisions which will inevitably be made based upon it—depends upon deliberate involvement on both sides of the table. Take your time. Engage others. Be honest. Be together. Avoid self-interest like the plague.

22

How to Raise Funds

I have reserved the topic of fundraising for the last chapter in this book. Why? Because fundraising brings together every other issue covered here, including leadership, planning, and management.

Leadership, planning, and management, taken together, involve working with others towards common goals. We focus on others—loving them, understanding ourselves, being humble and steadfast, and keeping Christ and the will of God at the center. Fundraising draws upon all of these qualities. If one thing is lacking, success will not be achieved. Fundraising is the asking of others to share our goals, listen to our heart's desire, and give of their financial resources. It is intensely personal.

For many people, the idea of asking others for money is very anxiety-producing. Even bringing up the subject of a raise at work fills some people with fear. Yet we must do this sometimes, whether we are asking for ourselves or for others. The Russian philosopher Nikolai Berdyaev once said, "Bread for myself is a material question; bread for my neighbor is a spiritual one."

The act of fundraising to help a worthy cause must be done strategically. We are not merely talking about a fundraising event such as a charity auction, bazaar, or food festival. Those activities and programs have their own special place, especially when designed to raise awareness of a charitable cause in a wider world, and at the same time promote mutual community work among the members. What we are discussing here is the act of asking others for money, whether it be for an annual fund to keep a cause going, a major gift for a new project or program, or a capital campaign for a very significant initiative requiring a large influx of funds.

There are four basic steps to an effective fundraising effort: learn, plan, involve, and ask.

THE BASICS OF STEWARDSHIP AND FUNDRAISING

First and foremost, stewardship is not only about giving money. It goes far deeper than that. It reflects the entire relationship between God and man. Man is the steward of God's creation and thus responsible for it, as we suggested previously when discussing man's kingship role. But this chapter does not concern stewardship in the broadest sense. We are focusing here on stewardship in a very limited and practical scope, namely, raising funds for worthy projects and programs.

A major reason why people are afraid to ask others for money in support of a worthy cause is lack of knowledge about how to go about it. There are many good texts both on stewardship in the broad sense, and fundraising in a more limited sense. I will not attempt here to repeat the lessons they teach, although I recommend that the reader obtain those texts and read them carefully.[1] We can learn a lot from them. However, my basic message is contained in Jesus' clear and straightforward teaching: "Where your treasure is, there will your heart be also."[2] We cannot get away from that message.

Jesus commands his disciples, when they first set out to preach in Israel: "Freely you have received; freely give."[3] Each of us has received and continues to receive gifts from God that we are called upon to give to others, just as the disciples were instructed. Sometimes, the gifts we are called upon to give may be things we do not even comprehend that we have. Did the disciples really believe that they could fulfill Christ's command to "heal the sick, raise the dead, cleanse lepers, cast out demons"?[4] They came from humble stock; they were fishermen, tax collectors, etc. How could they

---

[1]Anthony Scott, ed., *Good and Faithful Servant: Stewardship in the Orthodox Church* (Crestwood, NY: St Vladimir's Seminary Press, 2003); Jerold Panas, *Asking: A 59-Minute Guide to Everything Board Members, Volunteers, and Staff Must Know to Secure the Gift* (Medfield, MA: Emerson and Church Publishers, 2014).

[2]Mt 6.21.

[3]Mt 10.8, based on the KJV.

[4]Mt 10.8.

possibly be expected to perform such miracles? Jesus answers later on that it will not be them that speak, but the Holy Spirit within them. He also says to the disciples that things which they consider to be impossible—and hence impossible for them—will be made possible with God.[5] So the first rule that I encourage all of us to follow is that we *can* do what God expects us to do, and what he calls upon us to do.

THE CASE STATEMENT

Before approaching any potential donor, we must know what we are asking money for, and why we are asking. Both of these points are critically important.

First, we need to have in hand some form of a strategic plan. I say "some form" since it need not be a full-blown plan, only one commensurate with the scope of the program or project for which we are seeking funds. If we are asking for a lot of money, we had better have done our homework. It is also very important to have involved potential donors in the development of the plan, either through individual discussions or via surveys of their opinions. Individual discussions are far superior, and should never be neglected in the case of major donors.

Second, we need to make clear that we are asking this donor, rather than other people, because we believe that he or she shares in the mission and cause that we are asking them to support. This sounds quite simple and unnecessary to say, right? Unfortunately, many solicitors have no clue as to whether the people that they are asking for money do in fact share in the mission. The solicitors may assume that they do, simply because they are previous donors or members of the organization, or perhaps have some other longstanding connection. But whether a potential donor has the fire within to give abundantly to the cause is still an open question. Before we ask, we need to find out the answer. If we have involved them in the development of the plan, it is more likely that they will have a sense of ownership that can form a good start to the asking process.

[5]Mt 19.26.

First, however, we need to develop a simple case statement. This statement will draw upon the strategic plan as well as any information we have about why potential donors might give to the cause. A case statement answers these questions:

- Why is this particular appeal for funds being made? (the cause)

- What will be achieved if this appeal is successful? (the results)

- Who will benefit from it and how? (the people)

The case statement should flow from and remain consistent with an organization's strategic plan and goals. It needs to resonate with the people from whom we will be seeking funds. It must be specific, to the point, compelling, and people-oriented. It should engage the heart and mind and relay a sense of urgency. It must communicate who we are, as an organization, and who we can be.

The expressed vision and mission must be straightforward and energizing. The organization's track record must show results and accomplishments. The organization, and especially its leaders, must be credible and visible. Campaign results must be measurable and trackable. Donors must know our plans and be involved in how and when they are accomplished. A donor should feel that he or she is an investor. No shareholder in a company buys shares and then forgets about them. Shareholders want to see results. Nonprofits need to have exactly the same attitude towards donors.

IDENTIFYING DONORS

Why do donors give? The number one reason, obviously, is because they are asked. I recall a story about one wealthy gentleman whose gift to a university was the largest ever given to that school. His pastor read about it in the newspaper and recognized the donor, an active member of that church. The pastor went to the gentleman's home and said to him, "You've never given anything like this to our church. Why did you give such a gift to them?" The gentleman answered, "You never asked me for a gift. They did."

Donors also give because they are involved in the organization. For example, they may serve on a board or advisory committee, or be otherwise involved in significant volunteer service to the organization. We should expect them to give, for if the people who know the most about the organization and what it does do not give, then why should others? This is an excellent question. More on that question later. However, it does make sense to start at the top.

The major reason why donors give—and give substantially—is because they believe in the organization's mission and goals. If they also have a vital interest in one of the organization's programs or a personal link to one of the organization's leaders, then they are outstanding candidates to approach for a major gift.

The process for identifying donors begins with listing individuals who possess three characteristics relevant to the organization: interest, linkage, and ability. They are interested in the mission, goals, or programs of the organization. They are linked to someone in the organization. They possess the financial ability to give to the campaign.

How do we determine who these people are and whether they have these characteristics? The first step is to get the leadership team of the organization together for an extended period of time, say, a Saturday afternoon. Have everyone list the names of people they think might be potential donors. Put together a table listing the names of these potential donors and label the columns with these four categories: interest, linkage, ability, and next steps. Allow plenty of space for writing inside the boxes.

First, quickly rate each person's interest, linkage, and ability as either high, medium, or low, and note the rating in the appropriate box. Then fill in the boxes with details such as:

- *Interests.* What are the donors' hobbies, activities, talents, etc., that are related to the mission of the organization? What could we do to better involve them in the organization and make it part of their daily life? How might we deepen their interest by communicating, listening for their feedback, and re-communicating?

- *Linkage.* Who knows them? Perhaps someone we know knows them, or knows someone who knows them. How might we bring these "linked persons" into the process?

- *Ability.* What is the donor's financial situation? Is he or she an active donor already, or perhaps a known supporter of other charities and institutions? Ability is the most difficult variable to be assessed. In deciding whether an asking campaign is feasible or not, it is better to be conservative. But remember, when making the final and actual ask, that it never hurts to ask for more than what we think we will get.

- *Next Steps.* What will we do to follow up with these prospective donors? Who is responsible for doing it, and when? This step is usually the most difficult and also the most important part of the table development. Discipline is critical. The person assigned to follow up must be accountable. This part of the table must be completed accurately and realistically.

At the end, the team goes back to reassess the ratings for interest, ability, and linkage. Identify the most favorable candidates to help the organization attain its mission. Ensure that the right action plan is documented for those people, and that the leadership team member who is to implement the action plan is committed to undertaking the assigned action.

What is the purpose of the above steps? We are focusing on those people who are potential donors. We are caring for them, and desiring to involve them in the mission and cause. We are loving them by wanting to know about them, by seeing them as unique individuals whom we will soon ask to love the organization and what it does as much as we do.

Now, assess how much funding is needed for the project or program. Construct a giving pyramid based on the principle that ten to twenty percent of the total goal normally comes from one or two single gifts, while eighty to ninety percent comes from twenty percent of the people who contribute. The fundraising team needs to make more "asks" than the number of gifts needed since there will be people who will be asked but who unfortunately will not contribute for one reason or another. The list of potential donors needs to be sufficiently large, with interest, linkage, and ability ratings high enough to ensure that the campaign will be successful.

Finally, remember this Navy SEAL slogan, which has been attributed variously to Sun-Tzu, an unknown Roman, Rommel, and Patton but remains highly relevant for any fundraising campaign: "More sweat in training, less blood in battle." We want to be strategic, anxious to win the battle, and fully engaged to fulfill the will of God.

THE BOARD IS INTEGRAL

As mentioned earlier, if the board is not completely involved in the plan and its implementation, then chances of the plan's success are greatly diminished. In many nonprofits, individual members of the board are expected to provide a significant part of the funding for the project being proposed. In addition, it is expected that board members will use their influence to convince others to give as well. What is required for the board to be completely involved?

First, the board needs to have closely and continuously participated in reviews of the project or program for which funds are to be raised. This means intensive and inclusive discussions at every stage of the project or program's definition. It cannot have been presented fait accompli as a final proposal to the board, with nothing more requested than a thumbs up or thumbs down vote. Sometimes administrators advocate this type of vote because of an impending deadline: "If the board doesn't act promptly, we will be in trouble." If this scenario occurs, it is a signal that the administration needs to be replaced or, more charitably, that the board needs to be more proactive in questioning what the administrators are doing.

Second, the board needs to know that money will be required to fund the project or program, and that a significant portion will be requested of individual board members. Otherwise, the program or project cannot proceed—and furthermore, if it were to proceed without the monetary support of the board, it would surely fail. The administration needs to be upfront with the board and never sugarcoat this issue. In fact, I have often thought that a board member's ticket to vote "aye" on a project should be purchased beforehand with an advance pledge of a certain percentage of one's net worth. Otherwise, the only honorable thing to do would be to abstain from the vote.

Third, individual members of the board need to be asked by the administration to participate in the fundraising activity. But—and this is a big but—their participation needs to start with the leadership team's effort to identify potential donors, as described above. If board members are not involved at the beginning, then forget about them later on. They will know that they are only being used as figureheads to influence their friends on fundraising visits, and assume that no one really values their input.

Fourth, if we cannot convince the board to give what we think they should give, we should not expect others lower down on the giving pyramid to take up the slack. Something is wrong, and we need to identify what it is. Go back over the above principles. Honestly evaluate what we did and whether it should have been done differently. Do not go forward without resolving the issues with and within the board. This process could be a major teaching and learning opportunity which, even though the present battle may have been lost, can help to increase the probability of winning future battles and the war.

A PROCESS FOR ASKING

There is a process and a seriatim for asking. It involves, as does everything else, communications between one person and another. A general invitation or direct mail request to donate to a particular cause, such as a year-end appeal, will usually generate some gifts. We should always be thankful for people who will give without being explicitly and individually asked. However, major gifts that have a great impact upon the success of an institution's mission only come via person-to-person communication.

First, what about just writing a letter from one person to another? It is true that a letter, especially one which is hand-written, can result in a gift.

However, this method has the lowest probability of success for a major gift. It should only be considered for lower expected gift levels.

How about a phone call? This approach is much better, and shows personal interest: we took the time to call. (But please, if the first call goes to voicemail, be sure to keep calling until you speak directly with the other person. It is better to be thought of as a nuisance than as someone who just gives up after one or two tries.) A phone call is fine for medium gifts. Of course, when planning a fundraising effort, we must first determine the thresholds between low, medium, and high.

However, significant gifts in the higher echelon of giving require an in-person visit. This personal meeting shows a high level of interest. It is a "must do" for large gifts.

A caveat: moving up the seriatim increases difficulty for both solicitor and donor. First, it takes more time and effort on both sides. The solicitor needs to request a personal meeting. Once agreed to in principle, the time and venue for the meeting need to be established. The parties may have to go back and forth a few times. Second, personal involvement can be uncomfortable for the solicitor, who wonders, "What should I say? How should I react? Do I sound like I'm begging? What happens if they say no?" and so on. On the other side, the expectation of "being asked" often raises anxiety for the donors. They do not know what, exactly, is being asked of them and may wonder, "Can we afford it? Do we really want to give? Aren't we too busy for a visit? Why can't they just send us a letter?" The temptation on the donor side will be to delay the visit, or perhaps even to decline it.

The combination of a letter, phone call, and visit will ease the process. A personal letter sent from the solicitor to the potential donor paves the way for a follow-up phone call and visit. First, the letter explains what we would like to discuss with them, by stating the case briefly in just a sentence or two. We tell them what our relationship is to this cause, e.g. a board member, a volunteer, a donor, etc., and whether this is a request for an increase in annual giving, a major gift for a project, or a contribution to a capital campaign. The donor will be able to calibrate in his or her mind what level of support we may be seeking. Finally, we promise to call in a few days to follow up and discuss. For high level gifts, ask for an opportunity to meet in person.

GUIDELINES FOR ASKING

Before we ask someone else to give of their mind and their heart (and pocketbook), we must examine our own mind and heart. Here are five qualities that will serve solicitors well.

First, the solicitor must be *convinced*. We must know in our heart that what we are asking for is worthy. After all, we are neither hired servants nor paid fundraisers. We are doing this because we love the cause. We know that the mission is critical. And if we do not ask, the gift will not be made, which will hurt the cause in which we deeply believe. We are not begging, but representing a great cause that needs help.

The second step after being convinced is to be *committed*. We ourselves must make a contribution before asking others. It makes a difference in the way we speak to others. We do not necessarily have to give at the same level as the donor we are approaching. However, our gift should represent a relative sacrifice of financial resources equivalent to that of the person whom we are asking.

Third, we must be *confident* that we are doing the potential donor a service. It is a privilege and honor to contribute to this cause. Years ago, a successful businessman who was not especially active in church life gave a very large donation to a church program in which I was involved. This gift singlehandedly enabled the church to build a chapel and offices to further its missionary work. At the dedication banquet, the donor was thanked by the bishop. The donor shed tears as he said that giving funds to the mission was the greatest privilege of his life.

Fourthly, we must be *resolute*. We must do our homework on interest, linkage, and the ability of the potential donor. We should come to the meeting with an estimate of what we think the donor could and would give. Then we must ask for this amount. It is a great temptation to get cold feet going into an in-person asking session and think, "I could get thrown out if I ask for too much." But one should not revise downward unless there is good reason. What is good reason? We may pick up vibes to indicate that things may not be going so well for the other person. Perhaps we even learn that he or she has just lost a job or has some personal issue. We should ask for the gift anyway. The prospective donor does not want us to feel sorry for him or her. In such a case we might want to shade the ask downward. On the other hand, if the donor is really living higher than we expected, we might ask for more. Use good judgment.

Lastly, we must *set the scene* carefully and appropriately. Arrange for a time and place to meet that is convenient for the potential donor. Usually, this place would be the donor's home, at a time when disturbances and distractions can be avoided. If the donor is a couple, make sure that both are there if at all possible. This arrangement gives respect to the spouse, who in fact may be the decision maker anyway. Also, if the spouse is absent, the potential donor may want to wait before giving an answer, to allow time to consult with the spouse. That will certainly delay the asking process. More importantly, the opportunity to speak personally and from the heart with the spouse will be lost.

THE MOMENT OF TRUTH

When you ask, be yourself. Be direct and personal. The communication should be in your own words and consistent with the kind of relationship you have with the donor.

Focus on the cause. Talk very briefly about why this organization and this project is meaningful to you—and likely meaningful to the donor as well, based on your knowledge of him or her. Then ask the donor about his or her feelings, using your knowledge of the donor's interests as introduction. Focus intensely on the donor. Invite and listen for any reactions, questions, or comments. Invite the person to speak about his or her own dreams and visions. When they are speaking, put yourself in the other's shoes. Be empathetic.

Now it is your turn to speak. Pray inwardly that, like Jeremiah, the Lord "places his words in your mouth." State your "case for the ask" in no more than five minutes. It is critical that you speak in your own words and from the heart. People will know whether you really believe in this cause or not. If you have memorized the words or they sound canned, you will have damaged your case.

Tell the donor what moved you to make a gift in the first place. Convey to the other the reasons and emotions that brought you to give, and why you think this project is important enough for him or her to give. Have background material brochures, studies, plans, etc., available in case of questions, but do not give them out beforehand. They may distract from the most important source of information—you. You are the plan. You are the case. Take as much time to answer questions as necessary, but don't wear out your welcome by talking too much. Ask if the donor has any questions. Many people will not—they know what's coming.

Now you must make the "ask." Take a deep breath. Most people find this uncomfortable. If you do not, then you've done your "mind and heart" homework. After you have asked for the gift, keep quiet. Do not be the next person to speak. You should expect a silence. It will seem like an eternity sometimes. Let the other person speak. He or she will know what to say. If that person says "Okay," then great. Thank them profusely. If he or she has questions, answer them as best you can. If you cannot answer, say that you'll get back to them soon. If the donor wants more time to think the contribution over, give him or her time—but be sure to follow up. Thank the person warmly for the conversation, and say that you would like to come by again.

Above all, be enthusiastic and thankful. Whatever is contributed (or not), we must believe that this is what the Lord intends, and we should be grateful for that. If it is what we asked for originally, then we are entitled to go wild. If it is not what we asked for, we can be thankful anyway. Be confident that this is God's will. At minimum, we have informed another person about the cause, and perhaps he or she will respond later. Any sign of disappointment may sour them on the cause, and that is not our goal.

After the visit, regardless of whether a gift commitment has been made or not, write a thank you letter to the individual as soon as you get home—do not put it off! Even better, call the person on the phone. Unless the donor has requested to remain anonymous, it is appropriate for the board president and any other "linkages" to send a letter of thanks as well. More thanks is better than less. Let the "thankers" know what is expected of them, and follow up to make sure that they did what they promised to do.

FUNDRAISING AS LEADERSHIP

An effective fundraiser is a person who loves people; otherwise we will not be able to convince anyone to give. We need to be humble if we are to ask people for something that they might refuse to give. We need to work with others to have the best possible plan for a project, or else others may not support it. We need to serve others by enabling them to help the cause, and by helping the cause ourselves through others. We need to be steadfast and take a chance, even if the outcome is not assured. We need to be convinced that we are doing the will of God, and that he will be with us in all we do, even when we are suffering and sacrificing.

I cannot think of a better way to exercise and strengthen your leadership capabilities. Good luck!

Epilogue

Christian leadership must be founded upon Christ.

Leadership begins with oneself and our relationship with God.

Our leadership relationships with others follow
our relationship with God.

We lead together with other leaders to do God's will.

We plan with discipline to determine and fulfill our common mission.

We are responsible managers and stewards
of the resources and people entrusted to us.

All of us are entrusted with ministerial leadership.

We fulfill our leadership ministry in our family,
our vocation, and our community.

We learn from one another, especially the clergy.

Deacons teach us about service—with their lives.

Priests teach us about sacrifice—with their lives.

Bishops teach us about caring and governing—with their lives.

Wherever we are, in whatever we do, we strive to be humble, to serve, to love according to God's will.

We pray continually: "Thy will be done."

Bibliography

A Manual of Eastern Orthodox Prayers. Crestwood, NY: St Vladimir's Seminary Press, 1991.

A Monk of the Eastern Church [Lev Gillet]. *The Year of Grace of the Lord: A Scriptural and Liturgical Commentary on the Calendar of the Orthodox Church.* Crestwood, NY: St Vladimir's Seminary Press, 2001 [1st ed. 1980].

Ancient Christian Commentary on Scripture. Downers Grove, IL: InterVarsity Press, 1999.

Arseniev, Nicholas. *Russian Piety.* Crestwood, NY: St Vladimir's Seminary Press, 1975.

Barrois, Georges A. *The Face of Christ in the Old Testament.* Crestwood, NY: St Vladimir's Seminary Press, 1974.

_____. *Scripture Readings in Orthodox Worship.* Crestwood, NY: St Vladimir's Seminary Press, 1977.

Bazerman, Max H., and Margaret A. Neale. *Negotiating Rationally.* New York, NY: The Free Press, 1992.

Behr, John. *The Way to Nicea: The Formation of Christian Theology: Volume 1.* Crestwood, NY: St Vladimir's Seminary Press, 2001.

Birkbeck, W. J., ed. *Russia and the English Church.* Westmead, Farnborough, Hants, England: Gregg International Publishers Limited, 1969 [1st ed. 1895].

Bloom, Abp Anthony. *God and Man.* Paramus, NJ: Newman Press, 1971.

Bobrinskoy, Boris. *The Mystery of the Church: A Course in Orthodox Dogmatic Theology.* Crestwood, NY: St Vladimir's Seminary Press, 2012.

Bogolepov, Alexander A. *Orthodox Hymns of Christmas, Holy Week and Easter.* New York, NY: Russian Orthodox Theological Fund, Inc., 1965.

St Cyprian of Carthage. *St Cyprian of Carthage, On the Church: Select Treatises.* Allan Brent, trans. Crestwood, NY: St Vladimir's Seminary Press, 2006.

Brianchaninov, Bishop Ignatius. *On the Prayer of Jesus.* Liberty, TN: Saint John of Kronstadt Press, 1995.

_____. *The Arena: An Offering to Contemporary Monasticism*. Jordanville, NY: Holy Trinity Publications, 1997.

Cabasilas, Nicholas. *The Life in Christ*. Crestwood, NY: St Vladimir's Seminary Press, 1974.

Chitty, Derwas J. *The Desert a City: An Introduction to the Study of Egyptian and Palestinian Monasticism under the Christian Empire*. Crestwood, NY: St Vladimir's Seminary Press, 1966.

Chryssavgis, John. *Remembering and Reclaiming Diakonia: The Diaconate Yesterday and Today*. Brookline, MA: Holy Cross Orthodox Press, 2009.

Covey, Stephen R. *The 7 Habits of Highly Effective People: Powerful Lessons in Personal Change*. New York, NY: Simon and Schuster, 2004.

Cronk, George. *The Message of the Bible: An Orthodox Christian Perspective*. Crestwood, NY: St Vladimir's Seminary Press, 1982.

Danilchick, Peter. *Report of Proceedings: The Good Pastor Retreat: What Is to Be Done?* St Vladimir's Seminary internal report, June 2004.

_____. "Strategic Planning at SVS: A Process, Not a Product." *SVS News* 1.2, Autumn 2003.

The Divine Liturgy according to St. John Chrysostom. New York, NY: Russian Orthodox Greek Catholic Church of America, 2nd ed., 1977.

Doolan, Patrick. *Recovering the Icon: The Life and Work of Leonid Ouspensky*. Crestwood, NY: St Vladimir's Seminary Press, 2008.

Dostoevsky, Fyodor. *The Brothers Karamazov*. Richard Pevear and Larissa Volokhonsky, trans. New York, NY: Farrar, Straus and Giroux, 1990.

Drexelius, Jeremias. *Heliotropium: Conformity of the Human Will to the Divine*. Rockford, IL: Tan Books and Publishers, 1984 (first published in Latin, 1627).

Early Christian Fathers. Cyril C. Richardson, ed. New York, NY: Macmillan, 1970.

Early Fathers from the Philokalia: Together with some writings of St. Abba Dorotheus, St. Isaac of Syria and St. Gregory Palamas. Kadloubovsky, E., and G.E.H. Palmer, trans. London and Boston, MA: Faber and Faber Limited, 1981.

Elchaninov, Alexander. *The Diary of a Russian Priest*. Crestwood, NY: St Vladimir's Seminary Press, 1982.

Evdokimov, Paul. *The Sacrament of Love: The Nuptial Mystery in the Light of the Orthodox Tradition*. Crestwood, NY: St Vladimir's Seminary Press, 1985.

_____. *The Struggle with God*. Glen Rock, NJ: Paulist Press, 1966.

Fedotov, George P. *A Treasury of Russian Spirituality.* Belmont, MA: Nordland Publishing Company, 1975.

_____. *The Russian Religious Mind.* New York, NY: Harper Torchbooks, Harper & Brothers, 1960.

Fisher, Roger and William Ury. *Getting to Yes: Negotiating Agreement Without Giving In.* New York, NY: Penguin Books, 1991.

Fletcher, Joseph. *Situation Ethics: The New Morality.* Louisville and London: Westminster John Knox Press, 1966.

Florovsky, Georges. *Aspects of Church History.* Belmont, MA: Nordland Publishing Company, 1975.

_____. *Bible, Church, Tradition: An Eastern Orthodox View.* Belmont, MA: Nordland Publishing Company, 1972.

_____. *Christianity and Culture.* Belmont, MA: Nordland Publishing Company, 1974.

_____. *Creation and Redemption,* Belmont, MA: Nordland Publishing Company, 1976.

Gardner, John W. *No Easy Victories.* New York, NY: Harper & Row, 1968.

Goleman, Daniel. "What Makes a Leader." *Harvard Business Review* (November/December 1998): 93–102.

_____. *Emotional Intelligence.* New York, NY: Bantam Books, 1997.

Gregory of Nyssa. *The Life of Moses.* Abraham Malherbe, trans. New York and Mahwah: Paulist Press, 1978.

Gregory the Great. *The Book of Pastoral Rule.* George E. Demacopoulos, trans. Crestwood, NY: St Vladimir's Seminary Press, 2007.

Grisbrooke, W. Jardine, ed. *Spiritual Counsels of Father John of Kronstadt: Select Passages from My Life in Christ.* London: James Clarke & Co., Ltd., 1967.

Heaton, E. W. *The Old Testament Prophets.* Baltimore, MD: Penguin Books, 1961.

Holy Cross Service Book. Samaras, Kallistos G., ed. Brookline, MA: Holy Cross Orthodox Press, 1978.

Hopko, Thomas. *Speaking the Truth in Love: Education, Mission, and Witness in Contemporary Orthodoxy.* Crestwood, NY: St Vladimir's Seminary Press, 2004.

Houlden, J. L. *The Pastoral Epistles.* Harmondsworth, Middlesex, England: Penguin Books, 1976.

The Jerome Biblical Commentary. Raymond E. Brown, Joseph A. Fitzmyer, and Roland E. Murphy, eds. Englewood Cliffs, NJ: Prentice-Hall, Inc., 1968.

Kesich, Veselin. *Formation and Struggles: The Church AD 33–450; Part One: The Birth of the Church AD 33–200*. Crestwood, NY: St Vladimir's Seminary Press, 2007.

Kimbrough, S. T. Jr., ed. *Orthodox and Wesleyan Ecclesiology*. Crestwood, NY: St Vladimir's Seminary Press, 2007.

Kirov, Dimitar Popmarinov. "The Unity of Revelation and the Unity of Tradition." In *Orthodox and Wesleyan Ecclesiology*. Crestwood, NY: St Vladimir's Seminary Press, 2007. 89–103.

Landrebe, Robert S. "Is Strategic Planning a Waste of Time?" *In Trust* 22.4 (Summer 2011): 16–21.

Leonty, Metropolitan. "Theological Education in America." *Russian Orthodox American Messenger* (1913). translated in *St Vladimir's Seminary Quarterly* 9.2 (1965): 59–67.

McGregor, Douglas. *The Human Side of Enterprise*. New York, NY: McGraw-Hill, 1960.

St Nicodemus the Hagiorite. *Unseen Warfare: Being the Spiritual Combat and Path to Paradise of Lorenzo Scupoli as edited by Nicodemus of the Holy Mountain and revised by Theophan the Recluse*. London: Faber and Faber Limited, 1963.

Nierenberg, Gerard I. *The Art of Negotiating*. New York, NY: Pocket Books, 1981.

Nouwen, Henri J. M. *In the Name of Jesus: Reflections on Christian Leadership*. New York, NY: Crossword Publishing, 1989.

Ouspensky, Leonid. *Theology of the Icon, Volume II*. Crestwood, NY: St Vladimir's Seminary Press, 1992.

Ouspensky, Leonid and Vladimir Lossky. *The Meaning of Icons*. Boston, MA: Boston Book & Art Shop, Inc., 1969.

Panas, Jerold. *Asking: A 59-Minute Guide to Everything Board Members, Volunteers, and Staff Must Know to Secure the Gift*. Medfield, MA: Emerson and Church Publishers, 2014.

The Philokalia: The Complete Text compiled by St Nikodimos of the Holy Mountain and St Makarios of Corinth. G.E.H. Palmer, Philip Sherrard, and Kallistos Ware, trans. Volume I. London & Boston: Faber and Faber, 1979.

The Philokalia: The Complete Text compiled by St Nikodimos of the Holy Mountain and St Makarios of Corinth. Volume II. London & Boston: Faber and Faber, 1981.

The Philokalia: The Complete Text compiled by St Nikodimos of the Holy Mountain and St Makarios of Corinth. Volume III. London & Boston: Faber and Faber, 1984.

The Philokalia: The Complete Text compiled by St Nikodimos of the Holy Mountain and St Makarios of Corinth. Volume IV. London & Boston: Faber and Faber, 1995.

Quenot, Michel. *The Resurrection and the Icon.* Crestwood, NY: St Vladimir's Seminary Press, 1997.

Rodin, R. Scott. "Becoming a Leader of No Reputation." *Journal of Religious Leadership* 1.2 (2002): 105–19

Royster, Abp Dmitri. *St Paul's Epistle to the Romans: A Pastoral Commentary.* Crestwood, NY: St Vladimir's Seminary Press, 2008.

Schmemann, Alexander. *For the Life of the World: Sacraments and Orthodoxy.* Crestwood, NY: St Vladimir's Seminary Press, 1995.

_____. *Of Water and the Spirit.* Crestwood, NY: St Vladimir's Seminary Press, 1974.

_____. *Our Father.* Crestwood, NY: St Vladimir's Seminary Press, 2002.

_____. *The Eucharist: Sacrament of the Kingdom.* Crestwood, NY: St Vladimir's Seminary Press, 1988.

_____. *The Historical Road of Eastern Orthodoxy.* Crestwood, NY: St Vladimir's Seminary Press, 1977.

_____. *The Journals of Father Alexander Schmemann 1973–1983.* Crestwood, NY: St Vladimir's Seminary Press, 2000.

_____. "The Task of Orthodox Theology Today." *St Vladimir's Theological Quarterly* 10.4, (1966): 180–188.

Scott, Anthony L., ed. *Good and Faithful Servant: Stewardship in the Orthodox Church.* Crestwood, NY: St Vladimir's Seminary Press, 2003.

A Select Library of the Nicene and Post Nicene Fathers of the Christian Church. Philip Schaff, ed. Grand Rapids, MI: Wm. B. Eerdmans Publishing Company, 1997.

Service Book of the Holy Orthodox-Catholic Apostolic Church. Isabel Florence Hapgood, trans. Brooklyn, NY: Syrian Antiochian Orthodox Archdiocese, 1965 [reprint of 1922 ed.].

Skobtsova, Mother Maria. *Mother Maria Skobtsova: Essential Writings.* Maryknoll, NY: Orbis Books, 2003.

Stylianopoulos, Theodore G. *The New Testament: An Orthodox Perspective, Volume One: Scripture, Tradition, Hermeneutics.* Brookline, MA: Holy Cross Orthodox Press, 1977.

Tarazi, Paul Nadim. *I Thessalonians: A Commentary.* Crestwood, NY: St Vladimir's Seminary Press, 1982.

Ware, Kallistos. *The Inner Kingdom.* Crestwood, NY: St Vladimir's Seminary Press, 2000.

Zizioulas, John. *Being as Communion: Studies in Personhood and the Church.* Crestwood, NY: St Vladimir's Seminary Press, 2002.

_____. *The One and the Many: Studies on God, Man, the Church, and the World Today.* Alhambra, CA: Sebastian Press, 2010.

Index

Praise for *Thy Will Be Done*

Peter Danilchick's book, *Thy Will Be Done: Strategic Leadership, Planning, and Management for Christians*, is a classic for *all* Orthodox churches and church organizations, hierarchs, other clergy and laity, as well as non-Orthodox Christians and secular organizations. As an initiator and leader of many projects in the law and in the Church (from the first Conference of Bishops, to advising leaders of the Russian parliament on the relationship of Church & state, to International Orthodox Christian Charities, FOCUS North America, Becoming Truly Human, the Orthodox Christian Mission Center and many other projects), my personal experience, too, affirms the validity of Protodeacon Danilchick's wisdom set forth in the book's pages.

He is detailed in his suggestions, providing a clear and wise path to follow for the family, secular work, and work in the Church. This includes advice regarding centering one's work on following Christ with strong faith, asking for God's grace, exercising servant leadership, humility, love and patience in our interrelationships with others. Leadership, he makes clear, also includes having vision, making everyone become an "owner" of the project, building a good team to implement the vision and plan, the need for serious strategic planning and management, as well as the details of how to fundraise, and many other such things. Protodeacon Peter's advice is backed by clear and extensive quotes from Scripture, the divine liturgy, and patristic and monastic writings, as well as specific examples and stories from his tremendous practical experience. It would be a wise organization that makes sure each board member, executive director, and other lay leader has a copy of this book and reads it.

Charles Ajalat, J.D., D.C.L.
Former Chancellor of the Antiochian Archdiocese

* * *

This book brings together scriptural and theological reflections together with a long and rich personal experience to offer pearls of wisdom and insight about the ministry and practice of leadership, in various forms, for Christians today.

Very Rev. Dr John Behr
Dean of St Vladimir's Orthodox Theological Seminary
Author of The Way to Nicaea, The Nicene Faith, Becoming Human, *and* The Case Against Diodore and Theodore

* * *

We are indebted to Protodeacon Peter Danilchick for providing the Church with his own "strategic leadership," most especially via his book *Thy Will Be Done.* Gathering as those responsible for the good governance of the Body of Christ—either by ordination, election, or appointment—leaders and members of diocesan and parish councils (as well as other ecclesial bodies and organizations) are charged to direct the worldly affairs of the Church as good stewards of the "talent" entrusted to them, the goal being the discerning of God's holy will for their every decision and action—in other words, doing the necessary work of Martha while simultaneously following the blessed example of Mary. While it may be presumed that all involved with these groups will do so with good intentions and selfless-ness, the "how" of their accomplishing the "what" can often be problem-atic. Protodeacon Peter, himself an abundantly gifted Christian leader, now shares with us his experience and insight about accomplishing the "how" in accordance with the holy gospel, thus guiding his fellow Christians along the path of strategic leadership, planning, and management.

†BASIL, *Bishop of Wichita and Mid-America*
Antiochian Orthodox Christian Archdiocese of North America

* * *

Living "in the world" while not being "of the world" is the fundamental spiritual challenge for every disciple of Christ. Yet, it is a task that Orthodox Christians are prone to resist, opting instead for "spiritual" or "liturgical" escapes. This book paves the way toward a better understanding and experience of how "the way of the world" should be brought to conform to and coincide with "the will of God."

Rev. Dr John Chryssavgis, editor of *Primacy in the Church*

* * *

The stated purpose of the book is *"to help leaders of churches and other organizations to address leadership issues appropriately in an effective, harmonious, and ultimately Christian way. It will also help individuals working outside the Church in secular occupations to exercise Christian leadership in what may be an agnostic or even anti-Christian environment."*

Based on a lifetime experience of top-level management in a major world corporation as well as a deacon in the Orthodox Church, Protodeacon Danilchick's book endeavors to bring examples from the Bible and the writings and words of saints, to frame and illustrate the key questions that a Christian manager should strive to answer.

Starting from the very basic issues of what makes a leader, he follows with the definition of Christian leadership. He stresses the need for strategic planning and working together with others to define and achieve the common goal of *"seeking the will of God and doing his will in practice".*

The book defines five requirements of what *"God really wants from us"* and frames the answers with examples from the lives of Prophets and Saints.

The author defines the goals of Christian leadership: *"Christians need to have a fundamental understanding of leadership, namely, that the foundation of Christian leadership is the person of Christ".*

He then turns to the practical implications for Christian leaders on how to meet these goals and what they should do.

He moves on to discuss the aims and processes of strategic planning and how to apply them in the context of the Church.

The chapters on strategic management are standard for most lay organizations but provide a comprehensive plan for those in the Church that have not been exposed to industry's standard practices. In addition, as in the other chapters, this is seen and explained from the personal experience and perspective of someone who has served on boards of lay and Church organizations.

Altogether the book provides an interesting perspective on what a Christian leader should do and how he or she should do it. It is a "must read" for those that lack management experience and have to work with others in a leadership sense.

With its many relevant and learned examples from scriptures, I also believe that the book will serve as an inspiration to all Christians who are in leadership positions in lay organizations.

Dr Duccio Macchetto
Emeritus Astronomer and former Associate Director
at the Space Telescope Science Institute
Former researcher with NASA and the European Space Agency

* * *

While there are lots of stories, anecdotes, books, and papers from the business world in this area, a book that can be easily read, understood, followed and used as a reference from a Christian perspective, is sorely lacking. This book will fill that void.

The book is written by a protodeacon with years of experience, study, and learned knowledge in the field, much of it learned on-the-job in the private sector and within the Orthodox Church, supplemented by didactic learning along the way. The thesis of the book is that leadership requires finding out what the will of God is and then using the tools of leadership, planning and management to implement that will, be it in a secular setting or within the Church or one's daily life. The author provides practical approaches to discerning the will of God and then provides approaches to implementing it using the tools of planning and management. The author writes with an interesting and informative mix of personal experiential anecdotes, well annotated knowledge, and practical approaches to accomplishing the goal of implementing the will of God.

While being readable and practical, this is a scholarly book that is well referenced and annotated. Additional reading is recommended in several key areas. The audience of this book has many levels. It should be required reading for all seminary students, priests, parish leaders, board members, church council members and the church hierarchy. This book should also appeal to the Christian laity who are in positions of leadership, as well as those seeking guidance in their daily lives.

Frank B. Cerra M.D.
Member St Vladimir's Board and Chair, Advancement Committee
Emeritus Professor and Dean, former Senior Vice President for
Health Sciences and Services, University of Minnesota

* * *

I have known Protodeacon Peter Danilchick for many years and have repeatedly benefitted from his insights. He is a gifted person who combines extraordinary competence and achievement in the secular world with devoted Christian service on every level of church life, from parishes to patriarchs. This book distills his vast and varied experience in practical and inspiring ways that will be of immediate benefit to anyone interested in how to better lead, plan and manage in churches, church organizations and charitable institutions. But it will also help Christians who have or aspire to leadership roles in the wider business world and who want to figure out how to better work as Christians in those settings. Most importantly, he shows humility to be the root of leadership success anywhere. It is amazing how much good can be accomplished when ego and self-promotion are set aside in favor of noticing, engaging, empowering, and lifting others up. There is no other book like this.

†TIKHON, *Archbishop of Washington*
Metropolitan of All America and Canada
Primate of the Orthodox Church in America

About the Author

Peter Danilchick is a retired ExxonMobil executive with over three decades of international operations, planning, and management experience. He is also an ordained deacon in the Orthodox Church, serving parishes and missions for over forty years, both domestically and overseas. He brings these diverse talents to bear upon current issues of leadership, governance, strategic planning, management systems, organizational development, and negotiations for both profit and nonprofit organizations.

His ExxonMobil career was principally focused in the international arena, working in six different countries. He led and managed many diverse groups in Exxon, ranging from an operations division in its Singapore refinery, to country-wide planning groups in Australia and Germany, to new business development in China. He was particularly called upon by Exxon to lead project, commercial, and joint venture negotiations involving third parties from many different cultural groups, ranging from Western European to Chinese and Saudi Arabian.

At the same time, he worked in the Orthodox Church in these locations, either supporting existing parishes or establishing new missions. He also served on two national church governing boards in the USA and Southeast Asia as well as the board chairman of a major European international school. These experiences gave him a unique perspective on how to develop common ground among individuals from vastly different origins and backgrounds.

He is currently active as a trustee of St Vladimir's Orthodox Theological Seminary and as a member of the secretariat for the Assembly of Canonical Orthodox Bishops of the United States of America—bringing financial, governance, and organizational best practices to bear upon critical issues.

He also offers executive management consultancy services to both profits and nonprofits.